MEMORY AND POWER AT L'HERMITAGE PLANTATION

Cultural Heritage Studies

UNIVERSITY PRESS OF FLORIDA

Florida A&M University, Tallahassee
Florida Atlantic University, Boca Raton
Florida Gulf Coast University, Ft. Myers
Florida International University, Miami
Florida State University, Tallahassee
New College of Florida, Sarasota
University of Central Florida, Orlando
University of Florida, Gainesville
University of North Florida, Jacksonville
University of South Florida, Tampa
University of West Florida, Pensacola

Memory and Power at L'Hermitage Plantation

Heritage of a Nervous Landscape

Megan M. Bailey

Foreword by Paul A. Shackel

UNIVERSITY PRESS OF FLORIDA

Gainesville/Tallahassee/Tampa/Boca Raton
Pensacola/Orlando/Miami/Jacksonville/Ft. Myers/Sarasota

Publication of this work made possible by a Sustaining the Humanities through the American Rescue Plan grant from the National Endowment for the Humanities.

29 28 27 26 25 24   6 5 4 3 2 1

Library of Congress Cataloging-in-Publication Data
Names: Bailey, Megan M., author. | Shackel, Paul A., writer of foreword.
Title: Memory and power at L'Hermitage Plantation : heritage of a nervous
    landscape / Megan M. Bailey ; foreword by Paul A. Shackel.
Other titles: Cultural heritage studies.
Description: Gainesville : University Press of Florida, [2024] | Series:
    Cultural heritage studies | Includes bibliographical references and
    index.
Identifiers: LCCN 2023021909 (print) | LCCN 2023021910 (ebook) | ISBN
    9780813069951 (hardback) | ISBN 9780813080390 (paperback) | ISBN
    9780813070711 (pdf) | ISBN 9780813073187 (ebook)
Subjects: LCSH: Plantations—Maryland—Frederick County—History. |
    Historic sites—Maryland—Frederick County. |
    Slavery—Maryland—Frederick County. | BISAC: SOCIAL SCIENCE /
    Archaeology | SOCIAL SCIENCE / Slavery
Classification: LCC F187.F8 B35 2024 (print) | LCC F187.F8 (ebook) | DDC
    975.2/87—dc23/eng/20230524
LC record available at https://lccn.loc.gov/2023021909
LC ebook record available at https://lccn.loc.gov/2023021910

The University Press of Florida is the scholarly publishing agency for the State University System of Florida, comprising Florida A&M University, Florida Atlantic University, Florida Gulf Coast University, Florida International University, Florida State University, New College of Florida, University of Central Florida, University of Florida, University of North Florida, University of South Florida, and University of West Florida.

University Press of Florida
2046 NE Waldo Road
Suite 2100
Gainesville, FL 32609
http://upress.ufl.edu

Contents

Contents

Illustrations

Foreword

Megan Bailey's book, *Memory and Power at L'Hermitage Plantation: Heritage of a Nervous Landscape*, is an important and necessary scholarship focusing on African American representation on the landscape. This book addresses issues of power and white dominance. Her research focuses on how a plantation owner and family maintained and wielded power over their enslaved workers and their motivations for their cruel and racist behavior.

Nestled in central Maryland, a region settled in the eighteenth century by primarily German and English Protestant immigrants, sits the former 748-acre L'Hermitage plantation. The Vincendière family established the plantation after they fled from Saint Domingue (present-day Haiti) in 1793, in the wake of the slave uprisings in the French colony. The Vincendières brought twelve enslaved workers with them to establish the plantation that eventually included ninety enslaved people.

One of the book's strengths is its focus on a micro-history of this French plantation. The micro-history concentrates on the politics of a slave-owning Catholic family living in a predominantly German Protestant region. Bailey documents the tensions between these two groups. We learn that some of the enslaved workers could go to court and sue for their freedom with the assistance of the surrounding white community, an action that was quite rare.

By the 1820s, the Vincendières no longer owned L'Hermitage, although the property later played a strategic role in the Civil War. In the 1930s, federal legislation memorialized the property not for its role during the antebellum history, but rather for its role in the battle that saved Washington, DC. L'Hermitage sits in the middle of what is now known as Monocacy National Battlefield, operated by the National Park Service.

Bailey's book is instrumental in retelling an unknown story about the will and power of a forgotten people, the enslaved community of L'Hermitage.

For several field seasons, the National Park Service supported an archaeological survey of the national battlefield to identify battlefield lines. They
did not expect to find the remains of the plantation's slave village. These archaeological discoveries introduce a more complicated narrative of Monocacy National Battlefield. While it is common to learn about the history
of the battle at national battlefield parks, the National Park Service is now
confronted with the question of how to interpret issues related to enslavement, domination, and resistance.

What is groundbreaking in this book is that Bailey introduces the issue of nervous landscapes—which is novel to the discipline, yet central to
her study of L'Hermitage. The tensions of the history of L'Hermitage echo
throughout the landscape, past, and present. Fear, anxiety, and nervousness
about one's precarious position motivated the inhabitants of L'Hermitage,
both enslaved and free, to try to assert control over the environment and
the movements within it.

Denis Byrne used the phrase "nervous landscape" to explore colonial
Australia through a spatial lens, focusing on the ways that colonizers limited and controlled the movement of Indigenous people and also how the
colonized subverted spatial control. Byrne notes that "what makes the landscape 'nervous' was not the containment of Aboriginal people so much as
the failure of containment" (Byrne 2003:188).

During her discussion of nervous landscapes, Bailey also brings in other
points about how archaeologists can explore issues related to emotions and
the anxiety felt by plantation owners who were always under the threat of
slave rebellion. Emotion is not often addressed in archaeology; however, it
helps bring a fuller human experience into focus. While the Vincendières'
inhumane treatment of their enslaved workers is an outcome of racist co-
lonialist norms, their behavior was motivated by their nervousness and
anxiety about their precarious situation of being outnumbered by ninety
enslaved workers.

The archaeology and the history of L'Hermitage allow us to think more
broadly about race and racism across time and space. While the exploration of the history of the plantation is important scholarship, what makes
Memory and Power at L'Hermitage Plantation even more significant (and
a bit more complicated) is how Bailey grounds this research in the present and describes the contemporary landscape—the national park—as a
nervous landscape. She discusses some current, meaningful, and relevant
issues—like how to interpret African American history and issues related
to enslavement at a national park battlefield. While the slave quarters from

the plantation have disappeared from the battlefield landscape, the problem and debate focus on how to make these histories part of the national public memory and interpret these issues to the general public. Monocacy National Battlefield is more than a battlefield. It can be more broadly understood as a nervous landscape of memory.

Paul A. Shackel
Series Editor

References

Byrne, Denis. 2003. "Nervous Landscapes: Race and Space in Australia." *Journal of Social Archaeology* 3(2): 169–193.

Acknowledgments

This project has been a collaborative effort from the beginning. I am extremely grateful to everyone who played a part in helping me through this long and oftentimes arduous process.

First and foremost, I must thank Joy Beasley, without whom this book literally would not exist. In 2010 Joy hired me to work as a seasonal intern at Monocacy National Battlefield, and this project grew out of the two summers I spent excavating there. I had an incredible experience at Monocacy, and that was in part thanks to the fact that Joy was an excellent boss and mentor.

I would also like to express my appreciation to the past and current staff at Monocacy National Battlefield, including Kate Birmingham, Tom Gwaltney, Andrew Banasik, and Susan Trail. The opportunities, resources, and support they provided made this project possible.

The staff at the NPS Museum Resource Center, particularly Marian Creveling and Karen Orrence, provided support throughout the process of artifact analysis and processing.

While at Monocacy, I got to work with an incredibly smart and funny team: Megan Berry, Shayla Monroe, Alex Brueggeman, Janie Inglis Monier, Jordan Riccio, and Kelly Johnson. They always made fieldwork fun, even when the temperature was 90° and we were excavating in full NPS uniforms.

We were also lucky to have local residents George Evans and Maxine Grabill volunteer with us, and I loved having them on site and in the lab.

Most of this book was written while I was at the University of Maryland, where there are many people who supported my work. I would especially like to thank Paul Shackel, Barbara Little, Augusta Lynn Bolles, Don Linebaugh, and Stephen Brighton. They formed my graduate committee and were generous with their resources, knowledge, wisdom, and feedback.

A special thanks goes to Paul Shackel, who has provided me with advice, guidance, and encouragement for more than fifteen years. He patiently worked with me through many starts and stops to ensure that I saw this project through to the end, and he gave me about a thousand pep talks over the years. I truly couldn't ask for a better advocate and mentor.

In addition, Barbara Little gave me a great deal of support and mentorship during my time at University of Maryland and beyond. I'm grateful for her ideas and scholarship around archaeology and social justice, which first inspired me when I read *Public Benefits of Archaeology* as an undergrad, and it continues to shape the things I write (including this book) and the way I think about the potential of archaeology.

I would like to thank my first editor, Meredith Morris-Babb, for taking on this project, and my second editor, Mary Puckett, who kept the wheels turning on the project while having the utmost patience with me.

I'm so grateful to Caitlin Shanley: my prince, my rock, the best person I know. She provided the meals, pep talks, and tough love that got me through the most difficult months of this project; this book never would have been published without her.

A very special thanks goes to family—Dan and Becky Bailey, Emily and Ray—who have cheered me on since the very beginning. Having them in my corner has made all the difference.

1

Introducing the Nervous Landscape

On June 15, 1798, Polish writer and nobleman Julian Ursyn Niemcewicz was traveling by coach in western Maryland. He was midway through a three-year tour of the New England and mid-Atlantic states, during which he recorded detailed observations and vignettes of American life in his diary. On that day, Niemcewicz wrote:

> After dozing till four in the morning, I set out the next day for Friderik Town. . . . I took up my favorite place, that is, on the driver's seat next to the citizen driver. The reasons for my predilection to this place are, coolness, the fresh and open air, a view on all sides, and finally a pleasant, interesting and intimate conversation with the citizen coachman. . . . My friend, the coachman was a third-generation German settled in America. . . . The driver not only told me about everything I asked, but even things I did not ask; and we were yet 40 miles from Frideriks Town when I already knew the whole history of the town and its environs. (1965:111)

As he traveled east on Georgetown Pike toward the town of Frederick, Niemcewicz spotted a plantation on his left, noting,

> Four miles from the town we forded the [Monocacy] river. On its banks one can see a row of wooden houses and one stone house with the upper storeys painted white. This is the residence of a Frenchman called Payant, who left San Domingo with a substantial sum and with it bought a two or three thousand acres of land and a few hundred negroes whom he treats with the greatest tyranny. . . . This man is 60 years old, without children or relatives; he keeps an old French woman with two daughters; she, in sweetness of humour, even surpasses him. (1965:111–112)

The unsavory characters he described were the matriarch of the Vincendière family, Magnan, and her husband's relative, Jean Payen de Boisneuf. The family was of French origin but prior to their arrival in Maryland had been living in colonial Saint Domingue (present-day Haiti). There, the Vincendières had owned several plantations until 1793, when they traveled nearly 600 miles in the wake of widespread slave uprisings in the French colonies of the Caribbean. The Vincendières and Payen de Boisneuf brought twelve enslaved people with them from Saint Domingue and went on to establish a 748-acre plantation that they called L'Hermitage. According to census records, an enormous enslaved population lived at L'Hermitage. Niemcewicz was decidedly antislavery, commenting that the institution was an "insult to human dignity," so perhaps this is why he took special notice of the Vincendières' treatment of their enslaved workers, saying,

> One can see on the home farm instruments of torture, stocks, wooden horses, whips, etc. Two or three negroes crippled with torture have brought legal action against him, but the matter has not yet been settled. . . . This charming group has caused about 50 legal actions to be brought. They foam with rage, beat the negroes, complain and fight with each other. In these ways does this man use his wealth, and comforts his life in its descent toward the grave. (1965:112)

The sight of "instruments of torture" and the cruelty, violence, and brutality they represented clearly made an impression on Niemcewicz.

More than three centuries after Niemcewicz wrote those words, his journal entry would become the key to a richer understanding of the plantation. After the Vincendières sold L'Hermitage, the land was occupied by a series of tenant farmers, including the Best family, who lived on the property during the Civil War and witnessed the 1864 Battle of Monocacy that partially took place on their farm. In 1993, the National Park Service (NPS) acquired the Best Farm, which is composed of the southern 274 acres of L'Hermitage. The farm became one of six properties that together make up the 1,647-acre Monocacy National Battlefield. Three structures dating to the L'Hermitage plantation era remained on the Best Farm landscape, including the main house, a secondary dwelling, and a stone barn; however, there is no aboveground evidence of the slave quarters and yard area observed by Niemcewicz. His journal entry describes a "row of wooden houses" on the land between the historic building cluster and Georgetown Pike, now Maryland Route 355. Based on this information, the NPS employed systematic metal detecting, magnetic gradiometer surveys, and limited excava-

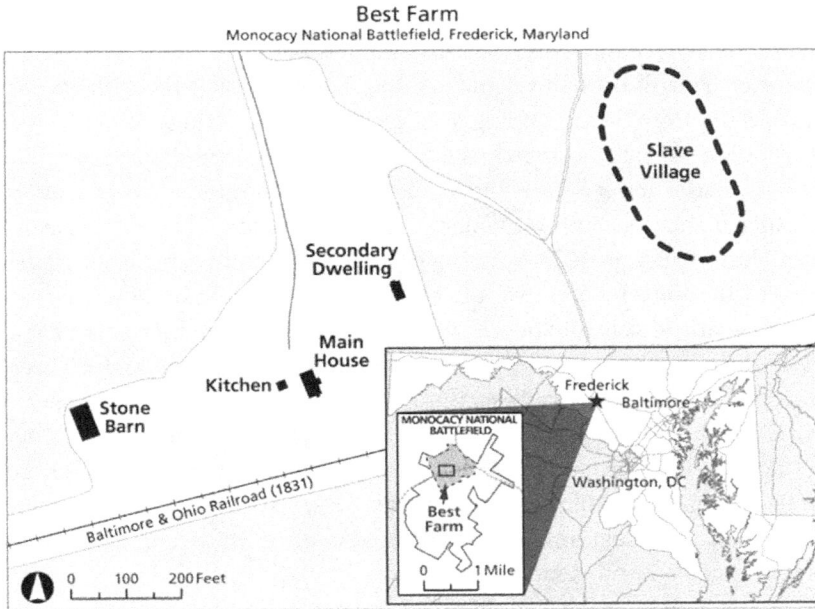

Figure 1.1. Site of L'Hermitage plantation within the present-day Best Farm at Monocacy National Battlefield. Image courtesy of the National Park Service.

tions to explore the area described by Niemcewicz and identify the location and boundaries of the so-called slave village (Beasley et al. 2005) (Figure 1.1). Additional excavations took place in 2010, 2011, and 2012 and revealed several substantial features, including a row of stone-and-mortar chimney foundations (corresponding to the "row of wooden houses") as well as a midden, an outdoor activity area, and the footprint of a fence (Birmingham and Beasley 2014). Though most of the findings were domestic in nature, an industrial feature—a lime kiln—was discovered northeast of the slave village. Collectively, these findings provide a sense of what L'Hermitage had looked like and how the enslaved population may have lived.

I worked with the team of archaeologists—consisting of NPS staff, university students, and volunteers—to uncover material evidence of the slave village, and I vividly recall when we knelt in an open field and scraped back soil until we exposed the first of six chimney bases. The revelation of this feature was both astonishing and sobering. On the one hand, archaeology had helped reveal a material link to the past that had been hidden for centuries and was largely unknown to Monocacy National Battlefield visitors and local residents. However, the intrigue of this discovery was tempered by the reality that the existence of enslaved workers' quarters was evidence of the racism, oppression, and violence that has persisted throughout American history and on this very landscape. Despite losing their plantations and fleeing from Saint Domingue to escape the beginnings of the Haitian Revolution—which occurred as a rebellion against the inhumane practice of chattel slavery—the Vincendière family committed to re-creating another plantation built on violence and subjugation. Historical research on L'Hermitage exposed horrifying evidence of brutality and strict control used by the Vincendières over their enslaved workers. To be sure, slavery is an inherently violent and oppressive system, and no plantation was a happy place for enslaved individuals. However, historical records and archaeological excavations revealed that the Vincendières' practices were unusually cruel and tyrannical, particularly compared with their neighbors in Frederick County. Evidence of torture and abuse was found in eighteenth-century court documents, while the archaeology of the slave village revealed a layout designed to maximize surveillance and control while suppressing individuality and free movement.

Throughout my participation in this project, I was often overcome by the painful, unsettling history borne by this landscape. Standing in the footprint of a slave cabin, looking across the grassy field to take in the main house, barn, and other parts of the former plantation site, I couldn't help but think about the controlling, inhumane, and cruel actions of the Vincendières, and the pain and resilience of the many enslaved individuals who once occupied the landscape. Following the excavations of the slave village, it became clear that the L'Hermitage landscape was characterized by careful planning and intentional design concerned with order and symmetry. This was unique for western Maryland, which consisted primarily of family farms with less formal layouts, but not unusual for plantations in the American South or Caribbean; strictly ordered plantation designs were well documented across these regions and were intentionally selected to maximize productivity and surveillance of enslaved workers. However, I wondered about the significance of the design of L'Hermitage in the context of the Vincendières' experiences and choices in running a plantation. As cited in Niemcewicz's journal entry and later documented in court records, there were multiple reports of the Vincendières and Jean Payen de Boisneuf abusing their enslaved workers, providing inadequate food and clothing, and restricting their movement and relationships. Given this combined evidence, a picture was forming of a slaveholding family that exerted enormous control over the day-to-day lives of enslaved people.

The archaeological excavations of L'Hermitage's slave quarters contributed to our understanding of the plantation and inspired many of the questions I explore throughout this work. The results of the archaeological investigations are recounted in detail in technical reports (Beasley et al. 2005, Birmingham and Beasley 2014), and these should be referred to for a more in-depth examination and analysis of the artifacts and features recovered. For this study, I will not reproduce the information in the reports except where needed, and I have been selective in the features and artifacts I have chosen to highlight. I do not view this book as a straightforward archaeological study, but rather an examination of dynamics on a landscape that has been in part explored archaeologically. Because archaeology alone cannot tell the whole story of L'Hermitage, I drew upon landscape studies for a spatial framework, early American history for social and economic context, psychology to understand the motivations behind behavior, and literature for a richer understanding of human experience. I regard the plantation history and archaeology of L'Hermitage as a jumping-off point from which to think more broadly about connections across time and space. Archaeology is one tool among many that I use to tell a story about the past and link it to the present, exploring the threads that connect a plantation in 1800, with all the power dynamics and tensions it contained, to our modern world.

On a fundamental level, the history of L'Hermitage is a history of people in power working to maintain that power, and of oppressed people working to find spaces in which to assert their own power or personhood. This tension is inscribed in and reinforced by the landscape in the past and present. No single slave quarter, barn, or grove of trees holds all the contested dynamics enacted by people and objects; rather, the dynamics exist in all these places, and more. Consequently, my study takes a landscape approach which considers all aspects of the environment. These include "the buildings, yards, streets, fields, trails, fences, tree lines, and all other elements of our surroundings that are products of human intervention" (Ellis and Ginsburg 2010:2), which form "the arena for all of a community's activities" (Anschuetz et al. 2001:157). A landscape approach considers visibility, mobility, and the layout and arrangement of space and structures (see Singleton 2015, Tilley 1994) in order to examine "how people in the past conceptualized, organized, and manipulated their environments and the ways that those places have shaped their occupants' behaviors and identities" (Branton 2009:51). The landscape itself is regarded as a constructed space, both in a physical sense, as a built environment, and in a cultural sense, as an environment where people "have used everyday space—buildings, rooms, streets, fields, or yards—to establish their identity, articulate their social relations, and derive social meaning" (Groth 1997:1). A cultural reading of the landscape is a reading of the relationships between people, places, and things in the past, present, and future.

Assertions of dominance and control on the part of the Vincendières, and personhood and agency on the part of the enslaved workers, likely contributed to a constant tension that composed the shifting power dynamics of the plantation landscape. Archaeologist Suzanne Spencer-Wood (2010:464) coined the phrase "powered cultural landscapes" to describe "power relations that are expressed through human alterations to land." Spencer-Wood makes a distinction between the forms of power available to groups versus individuals, arguing that dominant groups exert "power over" subordinate groups through the design, construction, and manipulation of the built environment, while subordinate groups exercise the "power to" alter the aspects of the landscape that are within their control (2010:515–516). Applied to a plantation landscape like L'Hermitage, these forms of alteration could take the form of slaveowners dictating the placement and appearance of slave quarters, while enslaved workers influence the arrangement and appearance of their yardspace, gardens, and animal pens.

The interplay between "power to" and "power over" within a powered cultural landscape is illustrated by archaeologist Denis Byrne's (2003) study of colonial Australia, which Byrne calls a "nervous landscape." This phrase describes a space where power is not always effective and where resistance is possible. According to Byrne, white settlers in Australia imposed a system of land divisions and uses on Aboriginal territory; the grids and fences trained Aboriginal people to remain within certain boundaries and outside of others. However, these colonizing efforts were not completely effective. By jumping fences, raiding orchards, and creating unmapped paths through mapped territories, Aboriginal people found gaps in the grid in which to exercise independence and autonomy (Byrne 2003:177–180). As with Spencer-Wood's powered cultural landscape, Byrne's nervous landscape is a place in which "a dominant culture spatially controls a population's presence in and movement through a landscape" while incorporating "the full range of methods a minority group may use to subvert that system of spatial control. That contestation makes the built environment tense, nervous" (Sies 2005:3). While a dominant group may exert a strong influence over the environment, there are almost always "spaces in between" where the rules do not apply, and subordinate groups can exercise autonomy (Bates et al. 2016:5).

The transformative properties of space allow for it to be a potentially oppressive or liberatory force. Lefebvre points out that "The dominant form of space, that of the centres of wealth and power, endeavours to mould the spaces it dominates (i.e., peripheral spaces), and it seeks, often by violent means, to reduce the obstacles and resistance it encounters there" (1974:49). McKittrick (2006:xv) characterizes these "geographies of domination" as spaces where hierarchies are formed. But while the process of space production has the potential to oppress, it also has the potential for radical and disruptive political action when one has an understanding of space that can be used to "subvert or challenge the authority of the hegemonic concepts and practices in space" (Zieleniec 2007:72).

One reason I am especially drawn to Byrne's characterization of a contested landscape is that it is particularly apt for a plantation context like L'Hermitage. As Robert Chidester (2009) argues, "the mechanisms of social control . . . were embedded in the local landscape" of plantations, which served as the slaveholder's "power domain" (Orser 1990:115). Manifestations of this power included "making important decisions regarding plantation operation, empowering agents to act on his or her behalf, and controlling the acquisition, use, maintenance of material objects on the plantation . . . [and] assignment of work to slaves." Slaveowners were particular about the ways they arranged their properties, putting great care into the placement of the main house, slave quarters, out buildings, and other features. The efforts on the part of slaveowners to control the landscape and bodies of enslaved workers were fundamental to maintenance of order and control and display of absolute power. Slaveowners required these social controls "to ensure and facilitate the quintessential activity of the slave plantation: the production of cash-generating crops produced by the labor of African slaves" (Yates 1999:35). At the same time, these controls could be subverted or circumvented, demonstrating that in spite of slaveholders' efforts, enslaved workers "had a will of their own, that they were sentient, articulate human beings, that they were members of society as well as capital assets. . . . The slave could never become the thing he or she was supposed to be" (Morgan 1998:261). Therefore, slaveowners' power was not, in fact, absolute; enslaved people carried out acts of resilience, resistance, and rebellion.

Furthermore, while enslaved people were generally the constructors of the landscape, rather than the designers of it, they did sometimes have influence over how it functioned, how they moved through it, and how slaveholders perceived it (Battle-Baptiste 2011:96). As Theresa Singleton

(2015:90) describes it, "The power dynamic between enslavers and the enslaved was always unequal, but enslaved people seized control of plantation spaces occasionally in plantation uprisings and on a more frequent basis through negotiations with their enslavers." These instances of defiance indicate spaces in which enslaved workers could exercise some agency among the constraints imposed by slaveowners—what Byrne would call "gaps in the grid" (2003:177). In my analysis of the archaeological, archival, and landscape records of L'Hermitage, I kept returning to the question of how the Vincendières exercised *power over* their enslaved workers through manipulation of the landscape and the structures upon it to maximize surveillance and control, and how the enslaved workers exercised *power to* create something of their own, reclaim some modicum of agency, autonomy, and personhood, and take advantage of "gaps in the grid" where they could be found (or made).

While Byrne's concept of the nervous landscape gave me a framework with which to analyze the built environment and material culture, it also inspired me to think about the ways in which the emotional experience of nervousness can be read in the archaeological and historical record. Until the 1990s, archaeological investigations rarely incorporated emotionality or, more broadly, experiential aspects of the human experience, so it is a relatively recent (though growing) area of inquiry, one that arose with the introduction of postmodern and critical theories to archaeology. Cultural anthropologists have long engaged with the subject of emotion, for instance in ethnographies and in the development of psychological and cognitive anthropology. But unlike cultural anthropologists, archaeologists usually cannot consult with the subjects of their research about their emotions. Consequently, emotional studies within the field of archaeology have been "stubbornly underinvestigated," according to Harris and Sørensen (2010:145), as such studies are regarded as inherently "subjective" or "speculative," with emotions being unrecoverable from the archaeological record. Postmodernism encouraged some archaeologists to move away from the strictly scientific, materialist, or quantifiable pursuits of processual archaeology to explore other dimensions of human experience, such as identity, spirituality, and memory. Even so, past feelings and sensations are considered inaccessible and unknowable, and asking questions about anything so intangible would be both difficult and imprudent. After all, what can a projectile point or ceramic sherd tell us about what people were thinking or feeling? These concerns are legitimate given the types of evidence available to archaeologists. We must be critical about attributing emotional states, motivations, or concerns to people of the past, and imposing a present-day or Western understandings of emotion on another era.

Still, in the late 1990s, a number of scholars recognized that experience, emotion, and meaning might be worth looking for in the archaeological past, and some archaeological research, primarily mortuary studies, has begun to incorporate considerations of affect theory and explorations of emotion. For example, burial contexts inspired archaeologists to think about empathy, fear, and guilt (Hill 2013, Spikins et al. 2010, Stutz and Tarlow 2015:8–9), as well as grief and bereavement (Farrell 2003, Metcalf and Huntington 1991, Cannon and Cook 2015). Archaeologists have also begun to explore the sensory experience of people in the past (see Hamilakis 2014, Sørensen 2015). While this is exciting new territory that has produced fascinating work, the focus on intangible aspects of experience is challenging and requires the development of a new set of tools, theories, and methodologies. To study emotion, affect, and the senses within the archaeological record requires "the imaginative interpretation of archaeological evidence," and attention to "the way that emotion works through material things and places" (Tarlow 2012:179). However, I believe the results are well worth the effort. Sarah Tarlow, who has done extensive work in this area, provides a compelling argument for incorporating emotionality into archaeological interpretations:

> The actions and motivation of human beings are shaped by their emotional experiences—their desires, fears, and values. . . . Emotional ideologies play key roles in the reproduction and transformation of relationships of power, and therefore to neglect consideration of the emotional is to impoverish our social archaeologies generally. The meaning of architecture, artifacts, or landscapes in the past is animated by the emotional understandings which inform their apprehension. A landscape may be a place of dread or of joy; an artifact may be a token of love or a mnemonic of oppression. Emotion, in short, is everywhere. Emotion is part of what makes human experience meaningful. Emotionless archaeologies are limited, partial, and sometimes hardly human at all. (Tarlow 2000:719–720)

I don't believe it is necessary or appropriate for all archaeologies to include a consideration of emotions, but I do think Tarlow makes a powerful point. Emotion is central to the human experience and social, political, and economic interactions, and our understanding of volition and motivation requires the incorporation of emotion. For the purposes of my research I think this is worth exploring, and I particularly want to engage with the ways in which human interactions with their environment and the material world are fundamentally connected to emotionality and affect.

I am inspired by Byrne's concept of the nervous landscape, and the emotion I am most interested in exploring in this context is nervousness, as well as related emotions such as anxiety, fear, and paranoia. Unfortunately, the primary sources related to L'Hermitage rarely reveal the feelings of the Vincendières or their enslaved workers about their experiences in Saint Domingue and Frederick, Maryland (Rivers Cofield 2002:8). However, an interpretation of archaeological and historical sources can shed light on the experiences of the Vincendières and their enslaved workers, and how these experiences shaped them psychologically and behaviorally.

The occupants of L'Hermitage had many reasons to be nervous and seek ways of minimizing nervousness. Enslaved people were most at risk, as their lack of autonomy meant that every day had the potential for harm, mistreatment, sale and separation from family, and death. Enslavers made it clear that their workers' bodies, labor, and time were not their own; they were property no different from an animal, furniture, or farm equipment. While enslaved people did manage to find ways to foster joy, pleasure, and community, they lived within a system of chattel slavery that ensured a constant threat of violence and loss hung over them. The documented evidence of the Vincendières' cruelty and lack of care toward their enslaved workers indicate that precarity was a dominating feature of enslaved life.

For their part, the Vincendières had far more resources and privileges at their disposal, yet they still may have been plagued by insecurity. The family's experience with the slave uprisings in Saint Domingue led to the loss of their wealth and colonial property and demonstrated to them that the power and control of the white and wealthy were not absolute; thus they had reason to feel nervous and uneasy when they reestablished a plantation with an enormous enslaved workforce that far outnumbered them. The violence and instability they witnessed in Saint Domingue surely affected them on some level; the Vincendières' experiences in Saint Domingue and Maryland may have instilled a sense of fear, nervousness, and distrust in them, and subsequently affected their behavior by prompting the controlling and brutal measures they took against their enslaved workers.

I am interested in the mechanisms used by dominant or elite powers to control a landscape, and how those in authority use the landscape to express and maintain power and reinforce the social order. Furthermore, I am interested in how challenges to this authority result in discomfort, fear, and anxiety on the part of the dominant power, and increased efforts to secure their status, power, and resources. In this regard, I am particularly influenced by the words of Roy D'Andrade, one of the early developers of cognitive anthropology, who states, "It is to be hoped . . . that at some point anthropologists and other social scientists will come to see that a reasonable theory of power . . . needs *some* psychological theory. A theory of power has to have some explication of the kinds of events that 'make' people do things, and this *always* involves postulating a psychological theory" (1995:242). The concept of the nervous landscape strikes me as the ideal framework through which to examine the relationship between emotion and power.

The dominant powers at the center of my study are, of course, the Vincendière family during their occupation of L'Hermitage, where they used a variety of methods to assert their control over their enslaved workers. My focus on the Vincendières specifically, and elites or people in power in general, is not motivated by a disregard or devaluation of the lives and experiences of the enslaved individuals who lived at L'Hermitage; rather, it is an intentional response to Laura Nader's call for anthropologists to "study up." Published in 1969, Nader's article, titled "Up the Anthropologist," proposes that anthropologists could make significant contributions to an "understanding of the processes whereby power and responsibility are exercised in the United States," and argues that citizens need to understand power dynamics, including who has control in our society and institutions, and the processes of domination (289). Nader points out that within the discipline, comparatively little research has been done on upper-class populations. Nader characterizes "studying up" in a way that is particularly apt for my study of the Vincendières, proposing, "What if . . . anthropologists were to study the colonizers rather than the colonized, the culture of power rather than the culture of the powerless, the culture of affluence rather than the culture of poverty?" (289). An anthropology of elites does not preclude the study of other groups and classes, however; Nader (1969:292) insists that "we aren't dealing with an either/or proposition; we need simply to realize when it is useful or crucial in terms of the problem to extend the domain of study up, down, or sideways." In doing so, we can study the cultures of both the powerful and the powerless (Gusterson 1997).

Anthropologists are uniquely positioned to produce insightful studies of elites, because we try to understand the group from within, studying the behavior, social routines, self-representation, and ideals that are internalized and enacted over and over (Abbink and Salverda 2013:2–3), or *habitus,* as Pierre Bourdieu termed it (1984). Anthropologists can wield their empirical and qualitative methods to study the way that elites construct, employ, and perpetuate their power and influence, and they can document the reactions and strategies of non-elites (Abbink and Salverda 2013). Questions explored by anthropologists that are relevant to my study include, "What makes an elite? How do elites in different societies maintain their position of dominance over subaltern groups? What legitimates the power and leadership of elites and how do they reproduce themselves over time?. . . . How do elites maintain their authority and elite status?" (Nugent and Shore 2003:1–2).

I apply these tools and concepts to my study, as they are deeply relevant to my analysis of L'Hermitage. Archaeological research has historically not focused on critically examining and exposing those with power, though this has changed within the last thirty years (e.g., see Blakey 2020, Croucher and Weiss 2011, Franklin 1997, Roller 2018, Spencer-Wood 2016). Early plantation archaeology took a planter-focused approach but, crucially, did not problematize or complicate the planters' privilege or social position. Similarly, public interpretation at historic sites has traditionally focused on and celebrated the lives of wealthy white men, even if they were slaveholders. As time went on, some archaeologists and heritage interpreters expanded from a planter-focused approach to slave-centered and dialectical approaches (e.g., Orser 1990). One way to frame the issue of power and oppression is to view plantations as sites of dynamic social relations fraught with contradictions, inequalities, and tensions caused by the planter's desire to control and the enslaved individual's attempt to resist that control (for example, see Thomas 1998, Odewale 2019, Orser and Funari 2001, Singleton 1995, Weik 2012, Wilkie 2000).

I believe there are multiple valid strategies for an ethical and socially just archaeology and public interpretation. One is to promote marginalized stories and historically oppressed peoples, and another is to critique, deconstruct, and expose the oppressor. I view both tactics as essential and not mutually exclusive. Writer Toni Morrison (1992:11–12) argues,

> there is a pattern of thinking about racialism in terms of its consequences on the victim—of always defining it asymmetrically from the perspective of its impact on the object of racist policy and attitude. A good deal of time and intelligence has been invested in the exposure of racism and the horrific results on its objects. . . . The scholarship that looks into the mind, imagination, and behavior of slaves is valuable. But equally valuable is a serious intellectual effort

to see what racial ideology does to the mind, imagination, and behavior of masters.

Psychologist Aida Hurtado (1996:124) echoes this thought, saying, "We have explored and meticulously documented the effects of oppression on its victims. The victims of racism and sexism have borne powerful testimony to their injuries and their resilience, but we have yet to chronicle how those who oppress make sense of their power in relationship to those they have injured." Hurtado goes on to explain that a nuanced discussion of oppression is hampered by the fact that "we do not even have the language to speak about those who oppress—how they feel about, think about, react to, make sense of, come to terms with, maintain privilege over, and ultimately renounce the power to oppress" (124). But teasing out these points is part of the necessary work to "avert the critical gaze from the racial object to the racial subject; from the described and imagined to the describers and imaginers; from the serving to the served" (Morrison 1992:90). Following this line of thought, I wish to reveal the mechanisms of power and how they persist or evolve over time. I take my cues from historian Trevor Burnard and his study (2004) of Thomas Thistlewood, a plantation owner in eighteenth-century Jamaica who was notorious for his brutal treatment of his enslaved workers. Burnard explains his choice of subject matter, stating: "I make no apologies for the book's focus on Thistlewood. We need to know more about the foot soldiers of imperialism, especially the men involved at the most intimate level with slaves and slavery in the eighteenth-century British Empire" (2004:7). Burnard explains how Thistlewood was a cruel slaveowner, rapist, and racist, and goes on to ask the same question of Thistlewood that I have for the Vincendières—and all slaveowners: "We do, however, need to explain why ordinary people such as Thistlewood acted in the ways they did—ways that dismayed contemporaries as much as they horrify us today. How could Thistlewood behave as he did toward his slaves and develop strategies of control that were designed to demean, demoralize and traumatize them when in other situations and in relations with fellow whites, he adopted patterns of behavior that we associate with a man of intelligence and integrity?" (Burnard 2004:32).

It is important to consider how "ordinary people" exercise power over others, because as Hurtado (1996:124) says, "We are all potentially in the oppressor category, because whether we have power over others varies from context to context and is primarily determined by race, class, and gender."

An understanding of these dynamics can help disrupt them in the present: by engaging this conversation, we can link past events to oppressive practices, events, and policies in the present. Paul Farmer (2004:309) points out that "Those who look only to powerful present-day actors to explain misery will fail to see how inequality is structured and legitimated over time. Which construction materials were used, and when, and why, and how?" Making connections between the past and the present demonstrates that the former isn't "over," and the latter doesn't exist in a vacuum.

The following chapters will explore these power dynamics on the former L'Hermitage, now Best Farm landscape. Chapter 2 focuses on the journey of the Vincendières and some of their enslaved workers from Saint Domingue to Frederick, Maryland. This will provide important background and context for the experiences of the Vincendières and their enslaved workers, illustrating what their lifestyle was like in colonial Saint Domingue and how the culture and environment may have influenced their behavior. Though we have limited information about the specific plantations belonging to the Vincendières and the details of their daily life in Saint Domingue, extensive research has been conducted on Haiti's history during the French colonial era, which provides valuable information. We then follow the family and their enslaved workers to Frederick, Maryland, and I describe what they would have encountered upon arrival at this region. The chapter ends with a description of how the Vincendières began their new life in the United States, with the establishment of L'Hermitage and a significant enslaved workforce.

In chapter 3, I examine how the Vincendières imposed their colonial vision on L'Hermitage via the organization of the plantation landscape and the spatial arrangement of the structures therein, as well as their control of the movement and behavior of their enslaved workers in other ways. This chapter also considers how the Vincendières tried to hold onto what power, status, resources, and sense of control they had.

A spatial analysis is key to my understanding of the Vincendières. The spatial arrangement of a plantation landscape can indicate the plantation owner's intentions and desire for control over their environment and enslaved individuals. Manipulation of the landscape can reflect a desire to "assert domination over and difference from slaves," for example, by keeping the enslaved workers separate from the main house but close enough to facilitate surveillance (Epperson 1999:171). By keeping the main buildings and slave quarters within a relatively small distance from each other, the slaveholder could monitor his workers and suppress any sign of rebellion.

The spatial organization ensured that enslaved workers were less likely to gain power and participate in any kind of insurrection (Joyner 2003:15). The arrangement of structures at L'Hermitage can be interpreted as a conscious effort to maintain order and hierarchy on the plantation: there is evidence that the enslaved individuals' quarters and relationships between plantation buildings were carefully and precisely designed. These characteristics could reflect the Vincendières' insistence on forced control and order with regard to their landscape, as well as their desire to closely monitor their enslaved workers. The methods used to manipulate the landscape were tools to exert dominance and further oppress the enslaved population. This desire could have stemmed from a fear that the resistance efforts of enslaved Africans that occurred in Saint Domingue would be repeated at L'Hermitage. By controlling the architecture and landscape, the Vincendières could actively attempt to suppress any challenges to their authority by their enslaved workers. Still, while the Vincendières employed several techniques designed to maintain control over their enslaved workers, the enslaved individuals found "gaps in the grid" where they could exercise agency. Through use of yard space, forming relationships with local residents, and running away, among other practices, the enslaved population at L'Hermitage challenged the Vincendières' power over their bodies and landscape.

In chapter 4, I explore how the Vincendières' behavior can be interpreted as a manifestation of their fear of loss (of status, resources, power), fear of vulnerability and precarity, and fear of the Other. While their controlling and brutal treatment of enslaved workers doubtless was motivated by racist colonial norms, I argue that their behavior was also motivated by their nervousness and anxiety around their (real or perceived) precarious situation: having a sizable enslaved workforce controlled by just a few slaveholders, and having just witnessed what these lopsided ratios could produce—that is, the uprisings in Saint Domingue that were precursors to the Haitian Revolution—and their motivation for leaving for Maryland. It was well documented that colonists in plantation societies were deeply paranoid and fearful of slave uprisings, and consequently behaved with greater violence and aggression toward their enslaved workers.

In chapter 5, I examine what L'Hermitage has become in the present day: the Best Farm, a component of Monocacy National Battlefield and a site of tourism, education, and preservation. This chapter is primarily an ideological analysis of the ways in which the excavation of the L'Hermitage slave village highlighted a more complicated narrative for Monocacy National Battlefield's public interpretation of its history, one that dealt with slavery and oppression. Now interpreted primarily as a site of Civil War conflict, the plantation past is mostly erased from the national battlefield landscape. The focus on the Civil War historically supported consistent narratives and ideologies promoting patriotic devotion, heroism, and sacrifice. However, the ongoing research on the L'Hermitage slave village introduced another aspect of history that had been previously unaddressed. As I will describe in chapter 5, some visitors were upset that Monocacy National Battlefield would put time, energy, and resources toward a project that, in their eyes, was not explicitly related to the Civil War. Others were uncomfortable with the newly emerging discussions about plantations, slavery, oppression, and other, darker aspects of American history. The additional interpretation of the Best Farm landscape as a site of slavery threatened the park's primary narrative about the battlefield, as well as deeply ingrained national narratives that honor war and military sacrifice. My hope is that, at some point in the near future, visitors to the park will come away with knowledge of not only battle strategies, victories, and losses, but also knowledge of the people who once occupied this land and the cultural context in which they lived.

In the final chapter after the past and present of the Best Farm landscape, I look to its future. What might it become? What can it teach us? The land has a rich and complex past; its representations in the future must be equally so. The investigation of Monocacy National Battlefield's plantation history provides an opportunity to explore dynamic and ever-changing power relations in the past and present as they played out over the landscape. The history of L'Hermitage links multiple countries, people, and stories to create a complex narrative of precarity and control in the past and present.

2

From Saint Domingue to Maryland

The history of L'Hermitage is a fascinating one that has been extensively researched through studies commissioned by the National Park Service. In this chapter I will provide a rough sketch of the lives of this study's subjects, but interested readers should consult previous reports for a more in-depth exploration of the economic, social, personal, and political activities of the Vincendières and the enslaved population at L'Hermitage (see Rivers Cofield 2002, 2006, 2011, Reed 2002, 2005, Reed and Associates 2004, Reed and Wallace 2004, Beasley 2003, 2005, Beasley et al. 2001, Birmingham and Beasley 2014, Hait 2011, 2016).

While this study focuses primarily on L'Hermitage plantation in the early nineteenth century, it is necessary to begin this study further back and farther away, in Saint Domingue in the mid-to-late 1700s. This French colony was home to the Vincendière family for several decades before their arrival in the United States in 1793. A discussion of the Vincendières' environment and circumstances in Saint Domingue will provide necessary background and context for much of what happened at L'Hermitage. We have limited information about the Vincendière family and their enslaved workers when they were living in Saint Domingue, but primary sources and historical studies about the colony provide some idea of what their lives looked like.

At the time when the Vincendières lived in Saint Domingue, the colony was flourishing economically due to the plantation system established by French colonists. Attracted by the potential for wealth, thousands of French nationals migrated to Saint Domingue, particularly between the 1760s and 1790s. While many sought to participate in the plantation economy, as either a plantation owner, manager, or overseer, others settled in urban areas and became merchants.

In the eighteenth century, the phrase *riche comme un creole* had caught on in France, referring to the famous wealth of the white, European, native-born population of Saint Domingue. Saint Dominguan society was shaped by its unprecedented prosperity and rapid growth, which had made it the richest Caribbean colony after less than a century of existence. An account from the 1780s notes that "The flourishing state of trade and the prosperity of its inhabitants were without parallel perhaps in the world; for here there were no poor, I may say, either white or black. . . . There were no beggars in the streets and no poorhouses in the cities" (A Merchant, quoted in Babb 1954:11). This dramatic growth was fueled by enslaved labor and a brutal plantation system that produced the goods that composed a large part of France's overseas trade in the late eighteenth century. Those in adjacent industries, such as the slave trade and manufacturing, also prospered by serving the needs of the colony. By 1791, Saint Domingue had more than 7,000 plantations, including 793 sugar plantations, 3,150 indigo plantations, 789 cotton plantations, and 3,117 coffee plantations, the sum of which made up at least two-thirds of France's overseas trade (Gillikin 2014:5). These numbers are all the more notable when one considers that 100 years earlier, not a single sugar plantation had existed on the island, and more than 100 of the plantations had been established in the short period between 1700 and 1704 (Fick 1990:22). Most of the sugar was grown in the fertile Plaine du Nord, described by Jamaican colonist Bryan Edwards as the place that yielded "greater returns than perhaps any other spot . . . in the habitable globe" (quoted in Geggus 1999:31). By the 1780s, exports from the relatively small island of Saint Domingue were equal to the total exports from the United States and "supplied half of Europe with its sugar, coffee, and cotton" (Babb 1954:7). In addition, Saint Domingue produced 60% of the coffee sold in the Western world in 1789 (Trouillot 1990:36). Plantation owners exported approximately 163 million pounds of sugar to France in 1791 (Stein 2000:225). This trade activity made Saint Domingue enormously prosperous, and it quickly became France's most valuable colony.

While I have not found records that provide detailed information about the Vincendières' wealth, slaveholdings, or landholdings in Saint Domingue, it is clear that, as white European planters, they had opportunities to build large fortunes via their participation in the types of activities described above. Members of the Vincendière family inhabited the western section of Saint Domingue, in the Petite Rivière district of Saint Marc, a region that French statesman and writer Moreau de Saint-Méry described in glowing terms: "No place is an honest stranger welcomed with as much enthusiasm and affability as in Saint-Marc" (1985:885). More specifically, they lived in Saint Jérôme parish in the Artibonite River valley, a region that primarily produced coffee, sugar, indigo, cotton, and rum (885) (Figure 2.1).

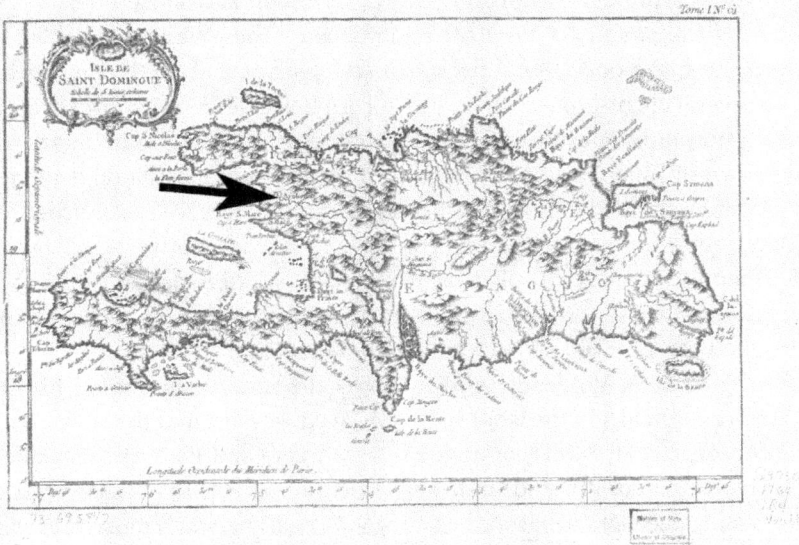

Figure 2.1. Map of Saint Domingue created by Jacques Nicolas Bellin, 1764; black arrow indicates the region where the Vincendière family lived. Library of Congress, Geography and Map Division.

The land was extremely fertile and productive, thanks to the construction of irrigation canals in the 1740s and 1750s (Rivers Cofield 2002:14). Moreau de Saint-Méry observed in 1798 that "The establishments of the parish of la Petite-Rivière all in all add up to ten plantations producing white sugar, ten other making brown sugar, 410 indigo plantations, 126 cotton, 140 coffee, three rum distilleries, seven brick pottery works, over fifty lime kilns, and a very small number of stock or stud farms" (1985:163).

Étienne Bellumeau de la Vincendière, the patriarch of the family, was a merchant and planter in this region, where he had lived since arriving in Saint Domingue in 1747, at the age of twelve (Hait 2016:23). He owned a coffee plantation in Saint Marc and co-owned the firm of de la Vincendière and Berard, which managed several plantations for absentee owners who were living in France. Many French colonists viewed their time in Saint Domingue as temporary, planning only to stay long enough to establish plantations before returning to France to live off the profits of their colonial endeavor. Moreau de Saint-Méry (1985:22) reported that "the general craze is to talk of returning to, or at least a trip to, France. Each man tells that he will leave *next year*. . . . This adds sparkle to life. A resident thinks of himself as camping—on an estate worth several millions." Absentee owners hired *procureurs* to act as agents and managers, bestowing upon them the power to make operational decisions and oversee daily activities. Étienne had several clients, one of them being Paul Belin des Marais, who owned a plantation in the parish of Cordes-à-Violon on the Artibonite Plain, near the town of Saint-Marc, where enslaved workers produced indigo and cotton that he shipped to France. Once his plantation was well established, des Marais returned to France and hired Étienne and his relative, Jean Payen de Boisneuf, to manage his plantation. A series of letters dating to the 1760s reveal that they sent regular reports to their employer about his plantation's productivity, profits, and personnel (Palmer 2016).

Étienne de la Vincendière likely enjoyed financial success on his own plantation, thanks to the labor of his enslaved workers and the coffee boom that took place in Saint Domingue between 1750 and 1780. Perhaps due to this increase in profits and land value, Étienne was able to purchase two additional coffee plantations in the late 1760s or early 1770s, a move that effectively ended his duties as a *procureur,* as the management of his own properties was a time-consuming endeavor (Birmingham and Beasley 2014:10).

Étienne married Marguerite Elizabeth Pauline de Magnan (referred to as Magnan in historical documents) on February 12, 1769, in the Petite Rivière district, around the time that he purchased his coffee plantations. His wife's family, through her mother Marie-Francoise Sterlin De Magnan, had a successful indigo plantation on the Plaine de l'Artibonite and enjoyed wealth and influence in the colony (Reed and Wallace 2004:95). Étienne and Magnan had ten children between 1769 and 1794: Étienne Paul Marie, Marie Francoise Pauline, Elizabeth Louise Marie Michel, Jean Victoire Marie Eugene, Victoire Pauline Marie Gabrielle, Jean Baptiste Marie Benjamin, Prosper Henry, Jean Pauline Émerentiénne, Adelaide, and Hélène Victoire.

Étienne's relative Jean Payen de Boisneuf owned three large sugar plantations on the island—located in the Montrouis, Les Verettes, and des Roseau districts—as well as additional land and a house in Saint-Marc, on the Rue de Bourbon (Rivers Cofield 2002:13). Boisneuf was born and raised in Saint Domingue, though his wealth also allowed him to purchase land in France. Thanks to his status, Boisneuf was able to wield influence and political power as a member of the military, the Estates General of France in 1789, and the Colonial Assembly of Saint Domingue; he also represented Saint Domingue within local and international politics (Birmingham and Beasley 2014:10). A Frederick newspaper later noted that Boisneuf was reported to be "quite a fashion plate, wearing a queue. gold-buckled slippers. silk knee breeches. ruffled shirts. and carrying a gold-headed cane. His horses and carriage were the finest in the community" (Russell 2001:226).

The key features of Saint Domingue—its wealth, productivity, and hierarchical society—were founded on and supported by a plantation economy that relied on a system of enslaved labor. As John Garrigus (2006:32–3) notes, "By this time every aspect of life in Saint-Domingue involved slavery, on and off the plantation. Bound workers turned the wheels of the colony's economy so that masters with little more than a livestock pen, banana grove, or carpentry shop considered slaves vital to their livelihood. In plantation houses and in city residences slaves served as cooks, housekeepers, valets and grooms; they cut wood in thickly grown hollows, dug irrigation channels, and shouldered roof beams in urban construction projects." The pronounced wealth of the Vincendières and other European residents of Saint Domingue was generated via the exploitation of enslaved labor to reach enormously productive outputs on the island's plantations (Figure 2.2). An active transatlantic slave trade supported this economy by bringing huge numbers of captive Africans to the French colonies. Between 1784 and 1790, 40% of the slave trade disembarked in Saint Domingue (Burnard and Garrigus 2016:253), and during the 1700s the colony received at least 80% of Africans from French vessels (Burnard and Garrigus 2016:253, Geggus 2001:125). During the eighteenth century, more than 800,000 African slaves were imported into Saint Domingue, and between 1780 and 1788 alone, Saint Domingue's enslaved population saw a 60% increase (Burnard and Garrigus 2016:250). The high mortality rate of enslaved Africans resulted in a constant demand for labor. French colonial author Hilliard d'Auberteuil observed that of the 800,000 enslaved Africans brought to Saint Domingue between 1680 and 1776, only 290,000 remained by the end of that period (Fick 1990:26). An estimated 50% of enslaved Africans died within their first three to eight years in Saint Domingue.

There are no known records of how many enslaved workers the Vincendières owned in Saint Domingue, and for the most part their names and other identifying details are unknown. However, David Geggus's research on the Caribbean slave trade indicates that sugar plantations in the western portion of Saint Domingue, where the Vincendières were located, tended to import Africans from the Bight of Benin and the Congo during the years between 1773 and 1791 (1989:39). Furthermore, French Jesuit missionary Jean Mongin observed that the minimum number of enslaved workers needed to run a sugar plantation is 100, with some plantations having up to 600 or 700 enslaved workers (Harrigan 2021:229). In addition, Étienne Vin-

Figure 2.2. Engraving of an indigo plantation in Saint Domingue by Elie Monnereau, 1765. Image courtesy of the John Carter Brown Library, CC BY-SA 4.0.

cendière's enslaved workers were reportedly known for their woodworking skills, having made "some of the finest known armoires known to have survived the colony before the slave revolt" (Birmingham and Beasley 2014:10).

What we can presume, however, is that enslaved workers suffered at the hands of plantation owners like the Vincendières. Slaveowners and overseers in Saint Domingue overworked and abused enslaved workers and relegated them to miserable, subpar living conditions. Planters were primarily concerned with productivity and profits, and they viewed enslaved Africans as a necessary yet disposable aspect of the plantation machine, one that was not self-sustaining but could be continually replenished (Burnard and Garrigus 2016). Therefore, it did not matter to slaveowners that the high mortality rate meant that the enslaved population could never reproduce itself; it was less expensive to replace enslaved workers than to provide them a high quality of life. As C.L.R. James (1963:14) succinctly put it, "planters deliberately worked them to death rather than wait for their children to grow up."

Ideologically, what allowed colonies built on slave labor to justify exploitation was racism and dehumanization. All participants in slave societies— traders, owners, etc.—collapsed the various ethnic identities of Africans into a single category, that of the Black slave. In doing so, the enslaved African became a person without a history or a place. Furthermore, white Europeans viewed the enslaved as not individuals or even human beings, but as a mass of animals. Jean Mongin, a Jesuit missionary living in the French Caribbean, observed of the enslaved workers that "They are bought and sold, in truth, like horses or oxen; most of them carry out the same duties, and half of them . . . have barely anything human about them but the voice and the body" (Harrigan 2021:218)

Saint Dominguan slavery and plantation systems were regulated by the Code Noir, signed into law by King Louis XIV in 1685. The Code Noir, along with later edicts, was ostensibly intended to protect enslaved workers by establishing a basic level of care, but this system was borne out of practicality rather than a true concern for the well-being of enslaved individuals (Midlo Hall 1971:86–87, 112). The slave code and other racist policies were in place to maintain social order, so that nothing would threaten the property, money, or power of the white colonists. It was in the interests of the colonial elite to create discriminatory policies because through the degradation and dispossession of non-whites, whites could protect their social status. For the most part, slaveowners viewed enslaved individuals as objects that were valuable only for the labor they provided.

While slaveowners in Saint Domingue developed brutal and inhumane strategies to increase the productivity and efficiency of their resources and workforce, enslaved individuals countered these efforts with their own strategies of resistance. Resistance took many forms, including *marronnage* (running away) and establishing communities of escaped enslaved people, plotting and carrying out insurrections, committing suicide, performing abortion, infanticide, and poisonings, practicing Vodou (rather than Catholicism), and selling crops for personal income (Forster 1990, Fick 1990, Midlo Hall 1971, Gaspar and Hine 1996, Shepherd and Beckles 2000). The latter was especially common; to establish a bit of distance between themselves and their enslavers, enslaved laborers could, at times, own property, goods, or money. For example, provision grounds, found in Martinique, among other places, provided enslaved workers with plots of land to use for cultivation as they pleased (Tomich 1993). By growing their own food, enslaved workers allowed planters to save money, but this activity also "gave slaves a distinct time and space dictated by the plantation yet detached from it" where they could raise their own crops and livestock (often to sell at urban markets), bury their dead, and worship their ancestors (Trouillot 1998:25).

By 1789, the population demographics and political climate in Saint Domingue enabled an environment in which enslaved workers and free people of color (known as *gens de couleur*) could organize a major revolt against French colonists. While these oppressed classes lacked the structural, societal, and economic power of the planter class, they did have one significant tool of resistance on their side: numbers. The importation of enslaved Africans during the seventeenth and eighteenth centuries led to a unique demographic profile in the colony. White residents held the majority of wealth, property, and power, but they formed the smallest population in Saint Domingue, owing to the fact that as many as 30,0000 captive Africans were brought to the island per year in the 1780s (Kelly 2009:82). Colonial records are reportedly unreliable and have varying population figures (in part because slaveowners underreported the number of enslaved workers to avoid a head tax), but the 1789 census records a total population of 523,800, which included 30,831 whites, 24,848 free people of color, and 434,429 enslaved people of African descent (Babb 1954:9). In other words, 90% of Saint Domingue's residents were enslaved in 1789, a larger percentage than anywhere else in the West Indies or North America (Dessens 2007:8).

In that same year, the French Revolution was reaching its climax with the creation of the National Assembly. Several members of the assembly belonged to the *Societé des Amis des Noirs* (Society of the Friends of Blacks), which was founded in 1788 and proposed the abolition of slavery. Their proposals were not initially accepted, and some members of the National Assembly took up the cause of *gens de couleur*, arguing that they should receive the same rights as white colonists. Free people of color in Paris were successfully able to secure more civil and political rights, a move that inspired their counterparts in the colonies to send delegates to France to agitate for the same rights. Sensing a possible threat to their wealth and prospects, white planters sent their own representatives to argue on behalf of their interests. Vincendière relative Jean Payen de Boisneuf was one of these colonial representatives; he belonged to a group of politicians who supported the French Revolution—believing that it would bring them new freedoms—but wanted to maintain the plantation economy and the practice of enslavement in Saint Domingue, even though to do so would be in contradiction to the Revolution's promotion of *Liberté, Equalité, et Fraternité* (Rivers Cofield 2005:5.4). As the owner of three sugar plantations, Boisneuf stood to lose a great deal of wealth, status, and power with the end of slavery.

In May 1791, following an uprising of 350 free people of color in Saint Domingue, the National Assembly granted political rights to those who had been born of free parents. Enslaved workers took part in a revolt three months later, and the National Assembly responded by revoking the rights of the *gens de couleur,* who retaliated by attacking white colonists. Enslaved workers were active participants and leaders in the increasingly violent and widespread revolts, burning plantations, destroying crops, and torturing and killing slave masters in their efforts to end slavery and demand rights and respect.

French colonial elites worked to subdue these rebellions. In November 1791, Jean Payen de Boisneuf traveled to Philadelphia with a fellow deputy of the assembly, the Baron de Beauvois, to appeal to George Washington for help in the form of food, building materials, and a large number of weapons, including "eight thousand fusils and bayonets, two thousand mousquators, three thousand pistols, [and] three thousand sabres" (Babb 1954:90). The men met with Secretary of State Thomas Jefferson, who brought their appeal to Congress, but the United States government declined to make a significant contribution of food or weapons, provide military assistance, or otherwise get involved in the uprising in support of French colonists (Rivers Cofield 2006:274).

In March 1792, the National Assembly reinstated the rights of free people of color, then abolished slavery in the French colonies on February 4, 1794. At this point, Saint Domingue had experienced almost three years of rebellion, attacks, and destruction and had lost its status as the jewel in the French empire's crown. Former slave Toussaint L'Ouverture emerged as the leader of the slave rebellion, though Napoleon Bonaparte had him captured and jailed in 1802 and reinstated slavery in the French colonies and again revoked the rights of *gens de couleur*. However, enslaved workers continued their insurgency and established the free republic of Haiti in 1804. The combined efforts of enslaved Africans and free people of color toppled the most lucrative colony of one of the wealthiest countries in the world, displaying the strength of collective action and the fragility of the extractive plantation system. The Haitian Revolution was and remains the only example of enslaved people overthrowing colonial rule and the institution of slavery, and establishing an independent nation ruled by formerly enslaved people.

Motivated by slave rebellions and the Haitian Revolution, a large number of French colonists left Saint Domingue between 1791 and 1803. The first wave of displacements occurred after the slave revolt that began on August 21, 1791, in the northern plain of Saint Domingue, where enslaved workers reportedly destroyed sixty-four plantations; white colonists and soldiers retaliated by killing "all the negroes who fell in their way, amounting, by the Friday following, to the number of 15,000" (quoted in Gillikin 2014:58). During and immediately after this insurrection, colonists fled to other parts of Saint Domingue or elsewhere in the Americas, such as Cuba, Jamaica, and cities along the eastern seaboard of the United States. A second wave of migration occurred in 1793 after revolutionaries burned Saint Domingue's main port city, Cap-Français; most colonists went to the Atlantic Coast of the United States. This wave of migration comprised approximately 15,000 refugees, leading French consul Alexandre Hauterive to remark in his journal that they were like "a flood of impure lava." A third wave of migration occurred in 1803 on the eve of Saint Domingue's transition to the independent republic of Haiti, sending colonists to Jamaica or the eastern United States, and the final wave occurred in 1809 after Napoleon declared war on Spain, compelling the forced migration of those from Saint Domingue who had previously sought asylum in Cuba (Dessens 2007:15). A total of about 20,000 refugees came to the United States by 1791, most commonly to port cities such as Savannah, Boston, Charleston, Baltimore, New York, Philadelphia, New Orleans, and Norfolk. Some exiles also returned to France, but it was a less common destination, due to the expense, the lack of ties between longtime Dominguan residents and their country of origin, and the fact that slaveholders would not be able to bring their enslaved workers there (15). Most expected that their time away would be temporary, that they would return to Saint Domingue once the slave rebellions had been subdued and resume the way of life they left behind.

It was during these waves of upheaval and migration that the Vincendières, Jean Payen de Boisneuf, and twelve of their enslaved workers fled to the United States. By March 1792, slave rebellions had spread to the Artibonite River valley where the family's plantations were located. Jacob St. Macary, a *procureur* in the region, shared increasingly dire news with his employers in April of that year, writing that "one part of this plain has already followed the unhappy example of the insurrection by a large number of workshops that have shaken off the yoke," and "our situation becomes more and more critical, disorder is at its limit in our quarter and particularly in the Artibonite plain where there remains not a single white" (Palmer 2016:191).

The Vincendières and Boisneuf likely sold or lost their property before leaving Saint Domingue, though the Vincendières did inherit the estate of one of Magnan's relatives, and Boisneuf willed his colonial property—consisting of three sugar plantations, a house in Saint-Marc, and additional land—to Victoire Vincendière and her sisters, to repay them for their support following their arrival in Maryland (Rivers Cofield 2011:32). In 1825 France signed a treaty recognizing Haiti's independence in exchange for an indemnity of 150 million francs, paid by Haiti to compensate French colonists for the loss of their property and revenues in the Haitian Revolution. Victoire and her siblings received indemnity payments from the French government for the estates they inherited, but they received only 10% of the full value, and they did not receive payments for the loss of Étienne's properties (Birmingham and Beasley 2014:15). The fact that Boisneuf left his properties to members of the Vincendière family reveals his expectation that they would eventually be able to return to Saint Domingue and resume their previous way of life and recoup their fortune (Rivers Cofield 2011:32).

The family members arrived in the United States separately in 1793 and settled in different parts of the country. Records indicate that Étienne Vincendière departed from Saint Domingue aboard the *Governor Pinkney* in December 1792, arrived in Charleston, South Carolina, on February 1, 1793, and remained there for the rest of his life with his brother Henri (Hait

2016:23). It is unknown why he settled in Charleston rather than join most of his immediate family members. Étienne's daughter, Marie Francoise Pauline Bellemeau de la Vincendière (known as Pauline), married Louis Rene Adrien Dugas de Vallon in Paris in 1790, then the couple emigrated to Saint Domingue during the French Revolution, but they left for the United States shortly after. In 1792 they arrived in Charleston but settled in Georgia, where Pauline opened the Boarding School for Select Young Ladies. Following her husband's death in 1807, Pauline and her family moved to Augusta where they lived in the home that she and her husband had built there in the early 1790s and opened a seminary (Hartridge 1943:118–119).

Magnan Vincendière and at least three of her children were in Paris when the slave uprisings were beginning in Saint Domingue; her daughters Émerentiénne and Adelaide were receiving their education while her son Étienne had joined the royalist army. The French Revolution was ongoing, and the Reign of Terror would begin in September of 1793. A Madame de Sapinaud, possibly of relative of Magnan, reported that the revolutionary army was pursuing Magnan, who hid with her children on a farm. They escaped just before the revolutionaries arrived, and the army killed the farmer and razed the farm (Birmingham and Beasley 2014:12). It seems that Magnan and the children returned to Saint Domingue where they reunited with their remaining siblings (save for Hélène, who was born in Maryland) and boarded the *Carolina* bound for the United States. This ship typically served as transport between Charleston and Baltimore, so perhaps Magnan and her children escaped to Charleston to reunite with Étienne before continuing on to Baltimore, arriving there on October 25, 1793. It is not known why Étienne continued to live apart from the rest of his family.

Jean Payen de Boisneuf joined the Vincendières in Maryland around this time. A twentieth-century newspaper article described his journey as such: "He was in France when the Revolution broke in 1789 and was a member of the Constituent Assembly for the Province of Touraine. Coming to Frederick to visit his friends. the Vincendière family at Frederick Junction. En route to Saint-Domingue to settle his brother's estate. Boisneuf . . . decided to take up residence here" (Russell 2001:226). Sara Rivers Cofield (2005:5.6) provides additional context for Boisneuf's movements:

By 1793, Boisneuf was socializing with a group of French gentlemen in Philadelphia who would meet in the back of Moreau de Saint-Méry's bookshop to talk and laugh over supper cooked on an office stove (Childs 1940:109). A Republican sympathizer warned the

Revolutionary Minister to the United States about this Philadelphia crowd, saying that "the French Agents here have always associated with the most gangrenous aristocrats such as Marnesia, Cottineau, Toussard, Rochefonainte, Payan (Boisneuf), Beauviois, Wante—" (Childs 1940:163). Whether Boisneuf disliked the Republicans who controlled France in 1793 or they disliked him, it is clear that they did not get along. It is possible, in fact, that he was one "gangrenous aristocrat" who may have left France in order to save his head from the guillotine. Unable to return to the colony, and apparently unwilling to return to France, Boisneuf took up residence in Maryland. (Catterall 1968:55–56)

The Vincendières and Boisneuf also brought twelve enslaved people to the United States. A Maryland law passed in November 1792 titled *An Act Respecting the Slaves of Certain French Subjects* required the registration of enslaved persons within three months of their residence and limited the number of enslaved individuals that French colonists could bring with them. This law also prohibited the sale of enslaved workers brought from the West Indies for at least three years following their arrival in the United States. It is because of this law that we have a record of the twelve enslaved workers who accompanied the Vincendières to Maryland, including their names and ages. The following appear in a Declaration of Negroes dated December 24, 1793: Magnan Vincendière registered Janvier (age 24), François Arajou (age 20), Jane Sans-Nom (age 16), Veronique (age 16), and Maurice (age 15); her son Étienne Vincendière registered Marianne (age ~40), Cecile (Marianne's daughter, age 18), and Souris (age 15); Victoire registered one person, Saint-Louis (age 15); and Jean Payen de Boisneuf brought an additional three enslaved individuals: Pierre Louis (age 35), Lambert (age 5), and Fillelle (age 8) (Beasley et al. 2005:2.7). Two of these individuals, Janvier and Veronique, were sent to Étienne Vincendières in Charleston sometime after their arrival in Maryland (Rivers Cofield 2005:5.25). It is unknown whether the enslaved individuals were forced to come to the United States or if they had any choice in the matter, or what role they played in the Vincendières' lives. Perhaps the older individuals, Pierre Louis and Marianne, were selected because they were trusted and/or had particular skills that the Vincendières valued. Nathalie Dessens surmises (2007:42) that "The slaves who traveled with their masters were generally the most faithful slaves who, according to many accounts, had often prompted their masters' flight by warning them of danger, sometimes even saving their lives." On the other hand, sometimes this "loyalty" was a strategic move intended to maintain close ties with slaveholders to gain something for the enslaved person. Haiti's transition to an independent nation was violent and unstable; though the Haitian Revolution brought freedom and independence to the Black population of the island, it also wrought destruction on the land. Unsure of what their future in Haiti might look like or whether the nation might eventually be brought back under colonial rule, some enslaved individuals may have been motivated to leave for the United States and other parts of the Americas and Caribbean. Migration to the United States might bring an enslaved person closer to family members or friends who were already there, or closer to Canada, which had outlawed slavery through court decisions and antislavery acts since the 1790s.

The Vincendières, Boisneuf, and their enslaved workers would have arrived in Baltimore along with hundreds of other immigrants pouring in from Saint Domingue. Baltimore received fifty-three ships with 1,000 white refugees and 500 free and enslaved people of African descent in the summer of 1793 alone (Rivers Cofield 2002:33). This had a significant effect on the city's demographics; at one point French refugees constituted more than 12% of Baltimore's population (Babb 1954:382). Baltimore was part of an established trade route with Saint Domingue, having become the depot and clearinghouse through which Europe and West Indies exchanged their products in the 1700s. A number of ships bound for Baltimore were already in the harbor during the burning of Cap-Français, and French colonists flocked to them, seeking transportation to the United States.

It is likely that Baltimore also appealed to those fleeing Saint Domingue because of its status as the Catholic center of the United States. Catholicism was the official religion in Saint Domingue, so being in the Catholic cradle of the United States may have been appealing to Dominguans, either because of their religious devotion or because of the cultural familiarity that a Catholic community could provide in their new home. Colonial Maryland was founded by Catholics George Calvert, first Lord Baltimore, and his son Cecil and was intended to offer a shelter from the religious persecution of Catholics in Anglican England. In 1789, Baltimore was the site of the first general meeting of Catholic clergy in the United States, after which the clergy requested that Pope Pius VI establish a Roman Catholic See in the city, owing to the fact that of 25,000 Catholics in the United States, 18,000 lived in Maryland (Hall 1912:686). Following the issuance of a Papal Bull in 1788, Baltimore gained its first bishop and Catholic cathedral. The first Catholic seminary in the United States, St. Mary's, was established in Baltimore in 1791. Furthermore, the western Maryland region where the Vincendières eventually settled had a sizable Catholic community. The area north of Thurmont and around Emmitsburg was almost entirely settled by Catholics, who formed a Catholic parish in Emmitsburg in 1786, followed by the erection of St. Joseph's Church in 1793 and St. Joseph's College in 1809 (Tracey and Dern 1987:255). St. John the Evangelist Catholic Church was founded in Frederick, Maryland, in 1763.

Magnan Vincendière, her children, and Boisneuf left Baltimore shortly after their arrival and had settled in Frederick, Maryland, by December 1793. It is not entirely clear why the family selected Frederick, but their intention to establish a plantation and engage in agriculture likely motivated them to seek out arable land. Their new home in the Monocacy Valley boasted extremely fertile and productive land; Polish traveler Julian Ursyn Niemcewicz (1965:110–113) observed in the late 1790s that the land in western Maryland "flows with milk and honey," and the fields in the region, "groan under the weight of Indian corn, wheat, rye," while the meadows were "covered with clover." Western Maryland's wheat industry boomed thanks to a commercial link it had established with Baltimore, from which crops were exported to Europe. By 1790, Frederick was the top producer of wheat in the country (Fiedel and Griffitts 2005:24). In any case, the town was appealing enough to attract a number of French immigrants from Saint Domingue. It was reported that "refugees of the San Domingo uprisings and the French Revolution of 1793 were among the residents of a section of Frederick referred to as Frenchtown, Paris Street, or Little France," which was located on the 200 block of North Market Street (Ranck 1985:120). Furthermore, "Frederick Town became a mecca for Creole dancing masters and teachers. In August 1793, Messrs. O'Duhigg and Large, 'lately arrived in this Town, from St. Domingo,' opened a dancing school at Mr. Sturm's in Patrick Street" (Hartridge 1943:118). The Vincendières lived in the town proper before purchasing land to create L'Hermitage, and it is possible that they resided in this community of French residents.

Historical records show that white refugees from Saint Domingue received a great deal of support and sympathy upon their arrival in the United States. Americans pitied the refugees and their loss of property and stability, and quickly rallied around them, raising money to help them establish a new life in the United States and donating food and clothing. The federal government also allocated funds to states to support the refugees; however, those fleeing to the United States from Saint Domingue were also met with fear and trepidation. Americans remained cautious and distrustful of their new neighbors, who were in many ways quite alien and believed to have the capacity to introduce potential dangers to the country.

For example, the late eighteenth century was a time of great distrust of the French, particularly in the late 1780s and early 1790s. The French Revolution, which occurred between 1789 and 1799, was widely covered by American newspapers. Though Americans had undergone their own revolution fairly recently, they were horrified to learn of the violent behavior of the French revolutionaries. Some granted the French revolutionaries cautious support while condemning their brutal acts, but even this support was revoked once the Reign of Terror began in the early 1790s and imprisonment and massacres became significantly more common (Gillikin 2014:153–154). Furthermore, Americans feared that French nationals might lobby for universal emancipation, with one South Carolinian fretting that the "lower order of Frenchmen who fraternize with our Democratic Clubs (might) introduce the same horrid tragedies among our negroes, which has been so fatally exhibited in the French islands" (Egerton 2000:99). The American economy had a growing dependence on slavery, and slaveowners feared that French expatriates would bring the ideals of "Liberté, égalité, fraternité" to the United States and encourage abolitionism. Consequently, many Americans looked upon the French with distaste and suspicion. Furthermore, relations between France and the United States deteriorated in the late 1790s to the point that it seemed possible that the nations would go to war. In anticipation of this conflict, and the belief that French aliens living in the United States would ally themselves with France if a war occurred, Congress passed the Alien and Enemies Act on July 6, 1798, which gave the president the power to deport aliens who had (or were suspected to have) ties to wartime enemies (McDonald 1909:144). Though France and the United States never officially went to war, the escalating tensions that occurred in the 1790s had a negative effect on public opinion of the French.

Americans also kept their attention trained on the social and political developments occurring in the French West Indies in the late 1700s. White Americans particularly feared that enslaved individuals brought from Saint Domingue would spread revolutionary ideas to enslaved workers in the United States and foment rebellion. After witnessing years of revolts culminating in the Haitian Revolution, they were hesitant to welcome those who, in their mind, had engineered chaos and destruction in Saint Domingue. The 1792 Maryland law that required the Vincendières to register their enslaved workers from Saint Domingue also prohibited the sale of enslaved workers brought from the West Indies for at least three years following their arrival in the United States, explaining that "many of the slaves imported into this state by the French subjects or citizens . . . have been guilty of disorderly conduct, and are suspected to be dangerous to the peace and welfare of the city of Baltimore" (The Laws of Maryland 1811:396). White Southerners also reacted with anxiety to the influx of free people of color from Saint Domingue, fearing that their presence and influence could undermine the institution of slavery in the United States. Consequently, several states, such as Virginia, Maryland, Delaware, and Kentucky, prohibited the entry of free Black people.

The fact that French migrants from Saint Domingue tended to practice Catholicism also prevented them from being entirely embraced by Americans and assimilated into U.S. society. While it was true that Maryland had a sizable Catholic community, the mid-Atlantic region remained dominated by Protestantism, thanks to its settlers of German and Scots-Irish descent, and Catholics were much discriminated against. There was a long history of conflict between Catholics and Anglicans in the state, which led to a host of anti-Catholic laws whenever Protestants controlled the government. The Maryland Assembly addressed the "Catholic menace" in 1718 by removing the rights of Catholics until they pledged the supremacy of the British Crown and renounced the papacy, and in 1756, the Lower House of the Maryland Assembly enacted a provision for double taxation of Roman Catholics (Tracey and Dern 1987:247). Catholics were not permitted to build churches, though they could observe Mass in a private setting. In passing this legislation, the assembly was following the orders of the British Parliament, who charged the assembly with keeping the "strictest watch" on Roman Catholics to prevent them from thinking themselves "more fortunate and easy if their religion was established here" (Archives of Maryland 2018:456). Victoire Vincendière's niece, Ester Lewis Lowe, wrote in 1913 that Frederick's Protestant residents were "bitterly antagonistic" to Catholicism and "had taken so strong a hold on their prejudices as to control neighborly feelings." The Maryland Journal, a daily newspaper published in Baltimore, featured a letter on August 23, 1793, stating that foreigners of non-Protestant persuasion "will be considered as Dissenters by our laws, and may of course expect a treatment corresponding with the inferiority of that subordinate character" and "their churches . . . will have no more protection than if they were Mahometan mosques or Pagan temples" (cited in Hartridge 1943:120).

Thus the Vincendières and their enslaved workers entered an environment and society that was not always welcoming and was quite foreign to them. First, Frederick County had the largest white population of all the counties in Maryland. This was a significant departure from Saint Domingue's demographic profile, in which Black enslaved workers and free people of color far outnumbered the white population. Even at their lowest proportion, which occurred around 1810, white residents accounted for 62% of Maryland's population (Fields 1985:3). Between 1790 and 1820, the percentage of enslaved Black people in the overall population grew from 12% to 17% in Frederick, but it remained small compared with the white population (Grivno 2011:38). However, both Saint Domingue and Maryland had a large population of free people of color; in fact, the free Black population in Frederick County increased by 122% between 1790 and 1800, 71% between 1800 and 1810, and 127% between 1810 and 1820 (U.S. Census 1790–1820). Of Frederick's white population, 40–50% were of German descent, while the remaining percentage was composed of English, Scotch, Irish, Welsh, and French settlers (Beasley 2003:21). Given that German farmers tended to not rely heavily on slavery, typically owning fewer than twenty enslaved people, the enslaved population of Frederick County remained relatively small and grew more slowly than the white or free Black populations (Reed and Wallace 2004:22) (see table for population numbers).

Upon their arrival in Frederick, the Vincendières and their twelve enslaved workers lived in the town proper but soon began purchasing the land that would form L'Hermitage. At the time, much of that land was known as Locust Level and was owned by Daniel Dulany. Beginning in 1784, the merchant James Marshall became an independent agent for Dulany "to improve his Estate here (in Frederick) & other good services," including the facilitation of land sales, contracts, and evictions among his duties (Earley et al. 2005:81). On December 12, 1794, Marshall acted on behalf of Dulany to sell a portion of Locust Level to the Vincendières. Marshall initially contracted with Boisneuf, but by December 16th, the contract was finalized and signed by Victoire Vincendière for 457 acres of Locust Level for £4,113 (Earley et al. 2005:83). According to the contract, Boisneuf paid half of the purchase price (£2,579) as a deposit to Dulany in Baltimore on December 13th, on behalf of Victoire Vincendière and with her money. The deed for the land was conveyed on the 24th of March 1795, when Victoire Vincendière paid the remaining amount in full to Dulany (83). A few years later, on April 27, 1798, Victoire purchased an additional tract of adjoining land. She bought the 291 acres from James Marshall for £2,910. The combined 748-acre property would become L'Hermitage plantation. Between 1792 and 1828, Victoire Vincendière continued to purchase property in the local area, including a 201.25-acre tract called Hawkins' Merry Peep-O-Day in Berlin, Maryland

Table 2.1. Population of Frederick County, 1790–1830

	1790	1800	1810	1820	1830
White	26,937	26,478	27,893	31,997	36,706
Slave	3,641	4,572	5,671	6,685	6,370
Free Black	213	473	783	1,777	2,716

Source: U.S. Census 1790–1830.

(1796), a 37.75-acre tract called "Gleanings" (1811), a house lot in Frederick (1816), a 28.5-acre tract called "Resurvey on Tuscarora" (1821), 80 acres of a tract called Merryland (1823), and Lot 91 in Frederick (Rivers Cofield 2002, Hait 2016). Victoire's 1849 will reveals that she also purchased land in Wheeling, Virginia, and Martinsville, Ohio, and co-purchased land with Boisneuf in Jefferson County, Kentucky (Hait 2011:7).

In each of these transactions, Victore Vincendière took the lead and became the legal owner of each piece of property. In 1795, at the age of eighteen, Victoire Vincendière had been established as the head of household—an unusual position for a young woman whose parents were both still living. It is possible that putting the property in Victoire's name was a protective measure rather than a reflection of her genuine role in the family; Jean Payen de Boisneuf and Magnan Vincendière had a number of unpaid debts and may have placed "L'Hermitage and its assets under the name of Victoire, in order to protect the land from creditors who may have been seeking Payen or Magnan for repayment of these debts" (Birmingham and Beasley 2014:14). Multiple accounts report that Boisneuf supported the Vincendières, in part by purchasing property in Victoire's name (Russell 2001:229, Ranck 1985:119–120, Niemcewicz 1965), but it is not known how reliable those sources are. On the other hand, it is possible that Victoire Vincendière did make these land purchases without assistance from Boisneuf, if his debts were great enough to prevent him from providing financial support. It was not unusual for white women in Saint Domingue to manage their own affairs; they "frequently bought, sold, and rented property, including land and slaves, and entered into contracts with people of color, white men, and other white women. They formed and dissolved businesses, lent and borrowed money, issued receipts, and held and issued powers of attorney" (Palmer 2016:111–112). With this precedent in place, perhaps Victoire was fulfilling a role that was actually more ordinary than it might seem. Sara Rivers Cofield suggests that "It was not uncommon, however, for single women to help run the household within their own family in much the same way as a wife would" (2005:5.15). Victoire's niece indicated that her aunt played a central role in the care of her family, describing her as "a charming young girl who gave up an engagement of marriage with a young nobleman to remain with her mother and devote her life to the education of her brothers and sisters" (Lowe 1913:17). While the information about the Vincendières' financial dealings and land purchases is contradictory and inconclusive (see Rivers Cofield 2005 for a more detailed discussion of the evidence supporting potential scenarios), historical records make it clear that Victoire Vincendière helped run her household and was recognized as its head in financial and legal situations throughout the rest of her life.

The Vincendière household contained an ever-changing number of family members, friends, and enslaved workers. The 1800 census indicates that L'Hermitage housed 108 people, including 90 enslaved people and 18 free white people. The latter probably consisted of the Vincendières' immediate family, Boisneuf, and a number of other French refugees. Victoire's niece, Ester Lewis Lowe (1913:43), recalled that "the Hermitage Farm . . . was an asylum for many a penniless exile from France and Saint-Domingue":

> Owing to the Insurrection of St. Domingo, people of vast wealth became impoverished. Obliged to flee the country, they sought refuge in the United States and elsewhere, Amongst them was a friend of Aunt Victoire who was wandering in the South with two grandchildren. Aunt Victoire heard of their pitiable condition and sent them to come to the Hermitage, and there they remained. They grew up to be charming women.

According to the 1810 U.S. Census, "V. Vincendière" was the head of a household that included one free white male aged 16–26 years, one free white male aged over 45 years, one free white female aged under 10 years, one free white female aged 10–16 years, two free white females aged 16–26 years, one free white female aged 26–45 years, one free white female aged over 45 years, and 90 enslaved individuals (Hait 2016:1). The U.S. Census indicates that in 1820 "Victor" Vincendière headed a household in Frederick County, Maryland, with two free white males aged under 10 years, one free white male aged 16–26 years, three free white males aged 26–45 years, one free white female aged under 10 years, two free white females aged 16–26 years, two free white females aged 26–45 years, two "[f]oreigners not naturalized," 25 "persons engaged in Agriculture," one "perso[n] engaged in Manufactures," and a total of 52 enslaved people of various ages and genders, for a grand total of 63 people (2016:1).

What was most unusual about the L'Hermitage household was that it contained an enormous enslaved population. Around the time the family and their twelve enslaved workers came to the United States, about 85% of households in Frederick County did not own enslaved individuals, and those which did had an average of five to six enslaved workers (U.S. Census 1790). In 1800, the Vincendières had ninety enslaved workers, making the family the second-largest slaveholders in Frederick County (following Thomas S. Lee, who had 109 enslaved workers), and they had had one of the largest slaveholdings in the state of Maryland (U.S. Census 1800). By contrast, 70.5% of households in Frederick County had five or fewer enslaved residents at that time.

The Vincendière's slaveholding is especially striking considering that the family came to the United States in 1793 with just twelve enslaved individuals, then purchased seventy-seven additional workers within seven years. It is possible that the Vincendières did not maintain a population of ninety enslaved laborers for ten years as the census records suggest—genealogist Michael Hait (2011:12) estimates that the number was closer to fifty in 1810— but a population of fifty or more still would have been uncommon in western Maryland. Furthermore, the Vincendières had assembled a labor force that was significantly larger than needed for the size of their landholdings and the types of agriculture they practiced. Agriculture in western Maryland tended to take the form of small farms with diversified agriculture, using land for grains, vegetables, and grazing. Thomas Scharf's (1882:362–363) nineteenth-century account of Frederick County describes the abundance of agricultural products found on local farms, thanks to the rich, fertile soil in the area: "In quality the soils comprise the best varieties of clay limestone, mica slate, roofing slate, and red lands. Each of these soils has its peculiar excellence and adaptation to particular crops, but all of them produce large yields of wheat, rye, oats, corn, and the cultivated grasses, and as a consequence, the best cattle, sheep, horses, and other domestic animals . . . Orchards abound, and the apple and peach are extensively grown."

Like their neighbors in the county, the Vincendières (or, more accurately, their enslaved workers) operated a mill and an orchard, grew wheat and clover, and produced lime and plaster. Unlike their neighbors, however, the size of their slaveholding more closely resembled that of large monocrop plantations, such as the sugar plantations of Saint Domingue or the tidewater tobacco plantations in Virginia and Maryland. In 1790, half of all enslaved workers in Maryland lived in the southern counties (Calvert, St. Mary's, and Charles), where labor-intensive tobacco was the dominant agricultural product (LaRoche 2007:50). By contrast, the diversified farming of western Maryland required fewer workers for shorter periods of time. Sara Rivers Cofield (2002:53) notes that "Cereal crops such as grain, wheat, and clover dominated the area and fewer laborers were necessary for growing these crops than the tobacco that dominated Southern Maryland. Typical cereal plantations of 700–1000 acres had 12–25 slaves." Therefore it was common for farmers in western Maryland to use free laborers whom they could hire as needed, or a very small enslaved workforce, who could be hired out to work as domestic servants, perform odd jobs, or work in a local mill or iron foundry during lulls in agricultural activity (Grivno 2011:36, Brugger 1996:239–240).

Enslaved workers at L'Hermitage would have cultivated wheat and clover, and perhaps corn and rye, in fields that were located north and south of the main building cluster. They would have worked in fruit orchards on the property, which may have already existed or been planted by enslaved workers. The stone barn would have been the site of wheat-processing activities, including the storage of grain, the threshing of grain, and the storage of threshed grain (Earley et al. 2005). In addition, a lime kiln was located north of the slave quarters and likely would have been another work site for enslaved laborers (Bailey 2014). Lime production required a decent-sized workforce and time commitment to take care of "quarrying, fuel gathering, carting, loading, burning, unloading, bagging, transporting, and marketing of lime" (Harrington 1996:22). Lime was known to improve soil, and its strategic use was encouraged by French colonial planters and in the 1791 *Pennsylvania, Delaware, Maryland and Virginia Almanack*; this book was ubiquitous throughout the mid-Atlantic. It is possible that the Vincendières were influenced by these sources to use lime to enhance crop yields; an advertisement that Victoire posted in the Frederick newspaper in 1816 offering 458 acres for sale describes the land as having been "improved by clover and plaister of Paris" (*Frederick-Town Herald* 1816:3). In addition, perhaps the sale of lime was one of the Vincendières' commercial enterprises. It is possible that the Vincendières were engaged in small-scale commercial production of lime, as this kiln was larger than those found on similarly sized farms. Lime was a critical component of several industries that developed in eighteenth-century Frederick, including tanning and glass and iron production. The Vincendières may have sold their lime to local iron furnaces, such as the Fieldera Furnace (located three miles from Frederick Towne on Harpers Ferry Road), the Catoctin Furnace, and the Mt. Aetna Furnace (also known as the Antietam Furnace) (Reed and Wallace 2004:6).

However, even with the labor needed to run a mill and lime kiln, care for livestock, and cultivate an orchard and hundreds of acres of crops, the Vincendières should not have required ninety enslaved laborers. Comparable plantations in Manassas, Virginia, had only ten to twenty enslaved laborers (Rivers Cofield 2002:53). The Vincendières may have hired out their enslaved workers when they were not needed at L'Hermitage. The enslaved individuals may have engaged in several occupations outside of the plantation: domestic servants, artisans, or hired help on neighboring farms (Rivers Cofield 2005:5.22). Victoire Vincendière may have leased some of her enslaved workers to local glass or iron manufacturers, such as Catoctin Iron Furnace (Reed 2002). Saw, grist, and flour mills also operated in the region, and they may have provided additional employment opportunities (Beasley et al. 2001:9). In the late eighteenth and early nineteenth centuries, these industries were booming in Frederick County; by 1790, the county had as many as 47 tanneries, 80 grist mills, and 300–400 stills, along with two glass works, two iron furnaces, two forges, and two paper mills (Williams 1967, 267).

In addition, many enslaved workers were skilled laborers and artisans, talented in brickmaking, carpentry, metalworking, coopering, spinning, weaving, and masonry, among other areas. Skilled laborers produced utilitarian and decorative objects that were for use primarily on the plantation, but they also became profitable enterprises when sold by slaveholders. In addition, enslaved workers were hired out by their masters to perform skilled labor locally. Newspaper advertisements indicate that Pierre Louis, an enslaved man brought to Maryland by Boisneuf, was a perruquier, or wig maker/hairdresser who played the violin, and an enslaved man named Jerry had previous experience as a brick-maker and had been hired out to brickmaking plants within the state (*Baltimore Daily Intelligencer* 1794:3, *Maryland Gazette* 1795:3). Slaveowners sometimes apprenticed enslaved workers to artisans to learn a skilled trade, with the intention of increasing the worker's value and skills that could be brought back to the plantation. Records of the sale of enslaved people indicate that those with specific skills could command a higher price for their masters.

The Vincendières did not use their sizable enslaved workforce for a monocrop enterprise but engaged in the same type of agriculture as their neighbors; advertisements for the sale of their property indicate that they grew clover on the northern portion of L'Hermitage and operated a mill and orchard at Hawkins' Merry Peep-o-Day. In addition, enslaved workers likely cultivated wheat at L'Hermitage; a record book from the nearby

Bloomsbury Mill displays contracts with Victoire Vincendière to haul, store, and sell wheat (Reed and Wallace 2004:100). In addition, archaeological excavations in 2011 revealed a lime kiln on the L'Hermitage property; the Vincendières may have been participating in the plaster and lime industry and/or producing lime for their own purposes. (Bailey 2014). All these activities were common for the region; in this way the Vincendières were similar to their neighbors. However, it was the size of their slaveholding that set them apart.

The three properties held by the Vincendières in Frederick County, known as L'Hermitage, Hawkins' Merry Peep-o-Day, and Maryland, totaled 1,029.5 acres. It is not known whether the Vincendières' enslaved individuals worked all these lands, but at the very least there were fifty to ninety enslaved workers tending anywhere from 748 to more than 1,000 acres. Similar-sized cereal plantations of 700 to 1,000 acres typically had twelve to twenty-five enslaved workers (Rivers Cofield 2002:53). A sample of plantations within fifty miles of L'Hermitage shows that Long Branch, a 1,000-acre wheat plantation, had twenty to thirty enslaved workers at its peak, and Brownsville plantation had twenty-two enslaved workers for 1,000 acres, while Belle Grove, a plantation with a comparable enslaved workforce of 101 in the 1820s, consisted of 7,500 acres (Wayland 1937, Lanier and Harding 2006, Galke 2001:259). Even with multiple properties to attend to and crops to cultivate, the Vincendières likely did not require ninety enslaved workers to run a successful agricultural enterprise.

It is possible that the Vincendières hired out their enslaved workers when they were not needed at L'Hermitage. The 1820 census indicates that of the fifty-two enslaved people held by Victoire, only twenty-five were involved in agriculture. It was common in large rural plantations of the late eighteenth century to have several enslaved individuals with specialized or expert skills, in contrast to farms with small and medium slaveholdings where enslaved workers were expected to take part in a variety of tasks (Franklin 2020:115). Furthermore, presumably some of the remaining seventeen enslaved individuals worked in L'Hermitage's main house, while others may have been engaged in several occupations in the local area: domestic servant, artisan, or hired help on neighboring farms (Rivers Cofield 2005:5.22). In addition, Victoire Vincendière may have leased some of her enslaved workers to local glass or iron manufacturers, such as Catoctin Iron Furnace, located twenty miles north of L'Hermitage. Saw, grist, and flour mills also operated in the region and may have provided additional employment opportunities (Beasley et al. 2001:9). In addition, enslaved workers were sometimes apprenticed to artisans and craftspeople in order to learn a new skill or trade, which could then be utilized upon their return to their home plantation or used to justify a higher sale price for an enslaved (Birmingham and Beasley 2014:24). Historical records indicate that some of the Vincendières' enslaved workers had acquired valuable skills; an advertisement for one individual, Jerry, notes that he "was hired out to work at brick-making both at Annapolis and Baltimore-town," while Pierre Louis, who had been brought to Maryland by Boisneuf, was described as a "hairdresser by trade; can play on the violin" (*American Star* 1794:4).

It is possible that the Vincendières were trying to replicate the large-scale plantation system they were accustomed to in Saint Domingue. Sara Rivers Cofield posits that "the family felt that this system was required for their financial success in Frederick County. . . . They may not have realized that the large enslaved labor force might be a financial burden in Frederick County until after they had tried to support such a population for many years" (2005:5.22–23). Having seen how a large plantation with a massive enslaved workforce generated enormous profits in Saint Domingue, the family may have thought that they needed to do the same in the United States to regain their previous levels of wealth and material well-being. The family arrived in Maryland with a number of debts owed to creditors in Saint Domingue and France. Though their colonial plantations may have been lucrative, plantation owners still typically borrowed money from French merchants in order to establish or expand their operations (Dubois 2004:20). Having abandoned their Caribbean plantations due to the slave revolts in Saint Domingue, the Vincendières would not have had the collateral of their plantations to repay their debt (Birmingham and Beasley 2014:14). Ashli White's (2012:111) study of white French refugees' wills and inventories indicates that "many escaped with property, bringing only easily moved possessions. These items usually included silver, textiles, currency and slaves," with the latter being the most valuable due to their high resale value and the free labor they provided. The Vincendières may have thought that a large enslaved workforce would be the most cost-effective way to recoup their losses and repay their debts.

In addition, the Vincendières might have maintained an unnecessarily large quantity of enslaved laborers as a symbol of status and wealth according to French Caribbean colonial norms. Moreau de Saint-Méry (1985:22) observed in 1798 that "In Saint-Domingue, everything takes on a character of opulence such as to astonish Europeans. That crowd of slaves who await the orders and even the signals of one man, confers an air of grandeur upon whomever gives the orders. It is in keeping with the dignity of a rich man to have four times as many domestics as he needs." Moitt (1995:1024–1025) writes of Moreau de Saint-Méry, "He may as well have been talking about any of the Caribbean colonies during slavery. The number of domestics varied according to types of establishments and households, but there was a general tendency for slave owners to have more servants than they needed." French Jesuit missionary Jean Mongin (Harrigan 2021:229) observed of the French Caribbean colonies, "The house of a planter in Saint-Domingue is like a great lord's hôtel in Paris. There you can see majordomos, cooks, scullions, coachmen, grooms, valets and chambermaids, lackeys . . . Another set of domestics look after the farmyard and the vegetable garden. These sorts of slaves do a perfectly good job; I was surprised to see slaves lay out a great feast, and serve many tables with as much taste and refinement as the best caterers in Paris could do. However, the skill of black valets can be seen even more in mounting and riding horses. They are all excellent horsemen."

The connection between slaveholding and status was not unique to the Caribbean; Robert Olwell (1998:44) observes that the same was true in South Carolina at the time:

> Obviously, because slaves were valuable property, slave ownership was regarded as an important measure and marker of economic status among whites. As one visitor to the low country remarked, "if a man has not as many slaves as they, he is esteemed by them their inferior." But possession of slaves had a social and political meaning as well as an economic one. Ownership of a slave automatically made one into a master and, in a slave society, into a member of the ruling "class."

Many French refugees were destitute following their departure from Saint Domingue and sought to reclaim their wealth and status. The Vincendières may have wanted to communicate to their neighbors that they were members of the elite. However, given that large plantations and slaveholdings were not the norm in western Maryland, it is unclear how such signals would have been received.

The Vincendières acquired and maintained their property holdings for twenty-two years before Victoire began selling parts of L'Hermitage. More than half of L'Hermitage was advertised for sale in January 1816 and 1819 in the *Frederick Town Herald* and the *Baltimore Patriot & Evening Advertiser*, in which Victoire described the land as having "been improved by clover and plaster" (Earley et al. 2005:98). The timing of these sales could be attributed to several factors. Jean Payen de Boisneuf died in 1815, and Magnan Vincendière died in 1819; Victoire may have been less inclined to continue managing a plantation when she had had less assistance from her family members. In addition, financial reasons could have been the motivation: the Vincendières and Boisneuf owed debts to creditors in Saint Domingue, France, and Maryland. These could have been for financial reasons; the family had many debts, and a combination of crop failures and financial panics in the 1820s–1840s led to a widespread economic downturn (Rivers Cofield 2005:39, Grivno 2011:18). In addition, perhaps their large enslaved workforce was becoming untenable to support. Furthermore, Victoire's household was shrinking. By 1820, at least one of her brothers had died, and her remaining siblings were married, with only her sister Adelaide, Adelaide's son Enoch Lewis Lowe, and several family friends residing at L'Hermitage (Reed and Wallace 2004:97). On June 14, 1827, Victoire sold L'Hermitage to John Brien, an iron master and landowner in Frederick and Washington counties (Birmingham and Beasley 2014:13).

In 1822, Victoire began selling enslaved workers, and within the next five years she sold at least twenty-five individuals, including seventeen enslaved workers to a dealer from Louisiana, and others to dealers in Baltimore and Tennessee (Rivers Cofield 2011:39).[1] One of the enslaved individuals sold at this time was Fillele, who had been eight years old when Boisneuf brought her to Maryland from Saint Domingue. Another was Manuel, who had been brought to Frederick County by Pierre Laberon in 1794. The remaining fifteen individuals were likely the offspring of Manuel or Fillele. Manuel and Fillele's decades of service to Victoire and her relatives did not garner their eventual freedom; rather, Victoire still regarded them as valuable primarily for their financial potential. Between 1827 and her death in 1852, Victoire sold or manumitted all but three of her enslaved workers, who were eventually manumitted by her will (Rivers Cofield 2002:57–58). She moved to a townhouse in Frederick on Second Street near St. John's Catholic Church. In 1830, census records indicate that Victoire was living with five free white people, six enslaved people, and two "other free." In 1840, she was still listed in Frederick City with four free white people and four enslaved people. Victoire remained in Frederick Town until her death in 1854.

---

1   See Hait 2014 for further details about the enslaved workers who were sold and manumitted during this time.

3

L'Hermitage

A Nervous Landscape

In writing about the nervous landscapes of nineteenth-century Australia, Denis Byrne (2003) describes the ways in which European settlers imposed social control and constraints on Aboriginal people. After mapping the land, the colonizers imposed a grid upon it, which was initially only represented on maps, but later it became tangible and visible when wire fences were installed to mark the grid and land ownership. These fences ignored topography and the "unpublished and undrawn Aboriginal map of everyday practice" in order to divide and delineate space with precision and regularity (Byrne 2003:180). The grid system became ever more pervasive as time went on:

> The cadastral grid worked, indirectly, to train Aboriginal bodies to function within the geometry of the new economic order. The grid prevailed upon them to walk its straight lines and turn its 90-degree corners. This geometric discipline continued on inside the rectangles of the grid. When the Aboriginal Reserve at Purfleet was established in the valley in 1900, Aboriginal people were 'encouraged' to move there and to live on the 18 acre reserve in box-like wooden houses that were internally divided into square or rectangular rooms. Their children would go to school and sit within a grid of desks in a rectangular room, and when they died they would be buried in rectangular graves (the precise dimensions of which were stipulated in the Public Health Act) within a grid of other graves inside the rectangular bounds of the cemetery. (Byrne 2003:176)

These grids segregated land and races and, by extension, society (Byrne 2003:170). A hierarchical society and controlled space allowed white settlers to impose their will on the landscape, making use of the resources and bodies upon it to their advantage. As Kathryn Sampeck (2016) puts it, the reordering of space "segregated people into controllable spaces for achieving imperial schemes."

The Vincendières participated in a plantation economy that was similarly concerned with the manipulation and control of space, people, and resources. As with colonial Australians, slaveowners in the Americas were exceedingly concerned with their disciplinary power, which Patricia Hill Collins defines as a system of rules, hierarchies, and "techniques of surveillance" intended to produce "quiet, orderly, docile, and disciplined populations" (1990:294–307). The "grids" imposed by plantation owners in the United States and Caribbean took the form of fenced and segregated spaces, as in colonial Australia, as well as other methods of imposing order and control, all with the goal of making the plantation productive and profitable. Slaveholders devised a variety of methods to extract as much labor from their enslaved workers as possible, believing them to have an animal-like capacity for work. Sara Gruder, a formerly enslaved person, recalled in 1936 for the Federal Writers' Project that "I never know what it was to rest. I just work all the time from morning till late at night. I had to do everything there was to do on the outside. Work in the field, chop wood, hoe corn, till sometime I feels like my back surely break." In order to induce this level of productivity, slaveowners used a combination of physical, mental, and emotional abuse, applying coercion, threats, violence, and systems of rewards and punishment.

However, slaveholders also used less overt methods to control and coerce their enslaved populations. Robert Olwell (1998:7) observes that, "throughout human history, rulers have understood that their domination rests on more than force alone." Perhaps the best illustration of that observation in a plantation context like L'Hermitage is the way in which planters intentionally designed and constructed plantations in order to achieve multiple management goals.

For slaveowners, the formal layout of the plantation landscape was intended to "establish, maintain, and reinforce their status and power over members of the lower class" and facilitate "economic efficiency and surveillance of labor" (Bates 2014:119). An effective plantation layout would communicate the planter's power and dominance and "keep slaves, literally and figuratively, in their place" (McKee 2000:190). Plantation owners used the built environment to display their wealth and status to visitors, passersby, and enslaved people alike. The contrast between the planter's house—which was usually larger, sturdier, and had a variety of decorative elements—and the smaller, nondescript, enslaved worker's residences sent a clear message about one group's power over a subordinate group. Furthermore, slaveholders designed plantations to enhance productivity, arranging buildings, quarters, and fields to minimize the time it took to get to work areas and facilitate surveillance of enslaved workers. These strategies, which Stephanie Camp (2004:6) calls "geographies of containment," were intended to restrict movement and prevent enslaved workers from rebelling or escaping.

These concerns prompted slaveowners to turn plantation management into a science, devising and sharing methods and strategies that would maximize productivity and give them greater control over their land and laborers. In the eighteenth century, planters in the colonial Caribbean colonies wrote and circulated treatises on how to organize a plantation landscape, depicting "idealized plantations intended to yield maximum harvests through efficient layout and labor management" (Meniketti 2020). For example, Pierre Joseph Laborie's 1798 manual for operating a coffee plantation suggested that all the buildings should be arranged in an orderly and symmetrical manner and located "as much as possible within sight and reach of the mansion house" (36). These manuals included estate plans illustrating the ideal plantation layout that planters should emulate. In the 1770 publication *L'Art de l'indigotier,* maps and plans of indigo plantations show neat, even rows of buildings evenly spaced and arranged close to the main house.

These ideas around plantation organization and layout were not limited to Caribbean plantations. According to Theresa Singleton (2015:96), "the spatial organization of the nucleated plantation village became increasingly uniform, if at times formulaic, in its design and overall appearance," in large part due to the circulation of plantation designs throughout the Americas. Planters disseminated these plans through "correspondence, agricultural and other learned societies, publications, travel to other plantation regions, settlement of immigrant planters to new plantation settings, and so forth" (Singleton 2015:96). Thus plantations in the Western Hemisphere came to adopt many of the same design elements, including neoclassical attributes, strategies of self-surveillance, and improvements to slave quarters (Singleton 2015:97). The Vincendières incorporated many of these features into their design of L'Hermitage; perhaps they were influenced by the literature circulating in Saint Domingue and the United States at the time. Their plantation featured many of the neoclassical attributes that Singleton identifies on other plantations of the time, including "the elevated great house, a hierarchical order for buildings, a symmetrical layout of outbuildings and grounds," and "avenues leading to the grand entrance of the great house" (2015:97).

Though there are no maps or plans of L'Hermitage, the historical and archaeological sources reveal a great deal about the layout of the plantation. L'Hermitage's appearance reflected some elements of Caribbean plantation layouts that the Vincendières were familiar with, as well as the farms and plantations they observed in western Maryland. It is clear, based on the available evidence, that the Vincendières did not construct an exact replica of the Saint Dominguan plantations they would have been familiar with, but this is perhaps to be expected: upon their arrival in Frederick, they may have attempted to adapt to the local geography, environment, and architectural traditions.

A newspaper advertising the plantation for sale in 1820 provides a detailed description of the farm complex:

> The improvements are—a good two story Stone HOUSE with six rooms and a Cellar; a stone barn; stone stable, large enough for 15 horses; a good two story dwelling log house; a granary, corn, pigeon, meat log houses; ice house and others; a large well, which, altho' upon a hill, has never less than 20 ft of most excellent lime stone water, even in the driest seasons; a good and well situated garden, of four acres of fruit trees, of several kinds. (*Baltimore Patriot & Mercantile Advertiser*, May 11, 1820, Vol. 15, Issue 113:1)

The advertisement does not mention privies, industrial areas, and quarters for the enslaved individuals, which also would have been part of the plantation landscape (Birmingham and Beasley 2014:20). A 2005 archaeological study examined the area where the main house and stone barn are located and identified a privy, cistern, and an icehouse, all of which may have been constructed by the Vincendières (Beasley et al. 2005:3.14).

Three of the buildings constructed by the Vincendières (or, more likely, their enslaved workers) survived to the present day and remain on the landscape. These include the main house, secondary dwelling, and barn. The multipart, two-story, L-shaped stone, brick, log, and frame main house (Figure 3.1) was constructed in several sequences beginning in 1794 and ending in 1820. The initial construction date pre-dates the Vincendières' purchase of the southern parcel of L'Hermitage by four years, indicating that the family may have been residing there as tenants prior to purchase (Birmingham and Beasley 2014:19). Architectural studies identified its stylistic influences as "a combination of French Colonial and Caribbean Island, mixed with Early Federal which are manifest through the original hipped roof, the large airy rooms and high ceilings of the south wing, with its high, alcove, double-hung window" (GWWO 2003:3). The south wing has several large windows (five per room) that extend to the floor, and high ceilings, giving the room "an internal light-filled airiness that could be character-ized as having a 'Caribbean' or 'Island' quality" (GWWO 2003:12). How-ever, no other part of the house has this open quality, and the house lacks the open porches and shades that characterize Caribbean plantation homes. Two unusual features of the main house are the floorboards in the hallway, which run horizontally instead of front to back, and the placement of the parlor fireplace against the back wall instead of at the gable end (Reed and Wallace 2004:132). It is unclear what inspired this deviation from standard mid-Maryland architecture. Furthermore, in Maryland the main house dis-played the symmetry that is characteristic of the Georgian Order. While the overall layout of L'Hermitage displays some degree of symmetry and plan-ning, the dwelling is not symmetrical, possibly because "Georgian ideals represent an essentially Anglo-American style," which is not in French taste (Rivers Cofield 2002:54).

The secondary dwelling (Figure 3.2) is located northeast of the main house. It has two stories with a stone-walled first story and a log upper story and a hall-and-parlor plan on the first story (Reed 2004:147). It displays local styles, as "the front and rear sill logs lie in seats or indentations in the stone foundation walls," and the "wall logs are hewn on their side with their tops and bottom surfaces left rounded," both of which are typical for central and western Maryland (Reed 2004:163). The structure has two doors that face east toward the Georgetown Pike, but likely also included an elevat-ed gallery or porch to access the second-story entrance doors, which face west, toward the main house (Reed and Wallace 2004:147). Interior refine-ments, including plastered walls and ovalo-architrave moldings, are similar to those in the main house, suggesting that the two structures were con-structed around the same time. Several changes were made to this structure postdating its construction and were likely undertaken to weatherproof the structure, including the addition of a central pen chimney and the resizing of windows and doors. The secondary dwelling may have been used to ac-commodate the large Vincendière household, including other French refu-gees, and/or an overseer for the enslaved population (Lowe 1913:17, Reed 2002:69).

Figure 3.1. L'Hermitage/Best Farm main house, eastern elevation, 2022. Photo courtesy of the author.

Figure 3.2. L'Hermitage/Best Farm secondary dwelling, 2022. Photo courtesy of the author.

North of the main house is the rectangular, hipped-roof stone barn (Figure 3.3), constructed in the 1790s with local stone. It is possible that the barn was originally divided into three bays to form an English or "Yankee" barn, which has clear architectural differences from the German bank or "Swisser" barns that are so common in western Maryland (Beasley et al. 2005:3.13). This barn type was usually divided into three equal bays, which were alternately used for the storage of grain, the threshing of grain, and the storage of threshed grain. Typically, the middle bay contained the threshing floor, and each side bay served as storage for the respective stages of grain processing (Earley et al. 2005).

The slave quarters are no longer extant, but we have learned a great deal about them from archaeological investigations. As mentioned in the introduction, the slave quarters were initially located based on the 1798 travel account of Julian Niemcewicz, who observed "a row of wooden houses and one stone house with the upper storeys [sic] painted white" as he passed L'Hermitage on the Georgetown Pike (1965:111–112). Based on this information, archaeologists surmised that the traveler was describing the stone secondary dwelling and a slave village—the "row of wooden houses"—in the field in front of the dwelling and adjacent to the Georgetown Pike. Archaeological investigations were carried out in this field in 2003, 2010, 2011, and 2012 to identify and explore the slave quarters associated with the plantation complex. In 2003, systematic metal detecting and magnetic gradiometer surveys helped identify a domestic artifact concentration in this field. The deposit appeared as a large and dense "relatively continuous band extending approximately 400 ft north-south and 100 ft east-west, and covering about two-thirds of an acre" (Beasley et al. 2005:14.28); the long axis ran parallel to Route 355. Artifacts recovered included architectural materials (hand wrought nails, mortar and brick fragments), domestic objects (red and white paste earthenware and stoneware), and personal objects (diagnostic buckles, coins, and one-piece flat buttons) dating from the late eighteenth through early nineteenth centuries. The temporal period of the materials, the dense nature of the deposit, and the probable correlation to the "row of wooden houses" detailed in the Niemcewicz account led the archaeologists to propose this as the probable slave village location. Limited Phase II investigations of the site were conducted during the 2003 and 2004 field seasons to explore the domestic deposit, resulting in the identification of additional large features. Five features extended at least 55 × 31 feet along two axes that intercepted in a corner. Artifacts recovered from this area

Figure 3.3. L'Hermitage/Best Farm stone barn, 2022. Photo courtesy of the author.

were primarily architectural in nature. As these features were larger than a dwelling structure, they were interpreted as the footprint of an enclosure or paling fence associated with the slave village (Figure 3.4) (Birmingham and Beasley 2014:14).

The 2003–2004 surveys allowed archaeologists to roughly define the boundaries of the area to be further tested archaeologically. In 2010, 196 shovel test pits (STPs) were excavated in this area, with some STPs holding a great deal of potential, such as one from which we recovered more than 180 pieces of animal bone. Others indicated the presence of structural remains, as evidenced by large pieces of stone and mortar. The STP survey assisted us with the placement of 49 excavation units (EUs) over the course of two field seasons in 2010 and 2011, as well as an additional week of excavation in 2012. These excavations revealed a row of six stone-and-mortar chimney bases, five of which were partially excavated. Each structure was given an alphabetical designation (Structures A–F) for ease of discussion. Structure A is located furthest to the south, whereas Structure F is located at the northernmost area of the site (Figure 3.5). One in particular, designated as Structure B, was more fully exposed to reveal some of the interior, which was characterized by a C-shaped mortared hearth base, a builder's trench, and large amounts of charcoal and heated clay.

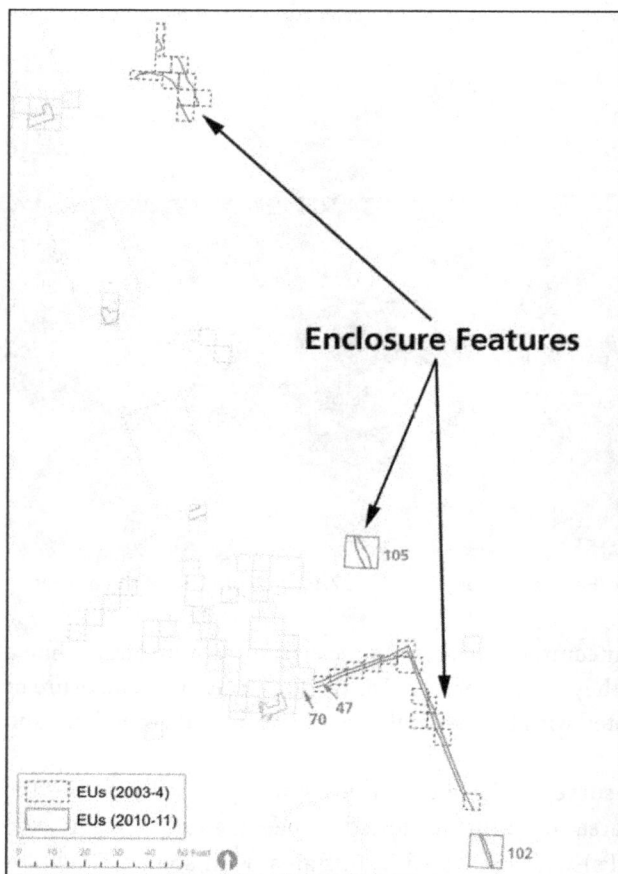

Figure 3.4. Map highlighting enclosure features discovered during the 2003–2004 and 2010–2011 archaeological investigations of L'Hermitage Slave Village. Map created by Tom Gwaltney. Image courtesy of the National Park Service.

Limited excavations were conducted in the yard area in front of and adjacent to the slave quarters. Although the stone hearths and piers proved to be the most substantial features uncovered in 2010, we also exposed a trash midden, an outdoor activity area, and linear soil stains that represent the footprint of a large enclosure. The midden was found northwest of Structure B and was partially excavated, revealing a layer of architectural debris (likely resulting from a demolition event) and, below that, numerous faunal, kitchen, and vegetal materials, including cow and pig skeletal fragments, charcoal, and utilitarian and tableware fragments. The activity area was located east of Structure F and contained a concentration of faunal remains and kitchen-related artifacts such as utilitarian tablewares; based on this assemblage it is likely that this area served as an out-kitchen or activity area "used for large-scale processing or rendering" (Birmingham and

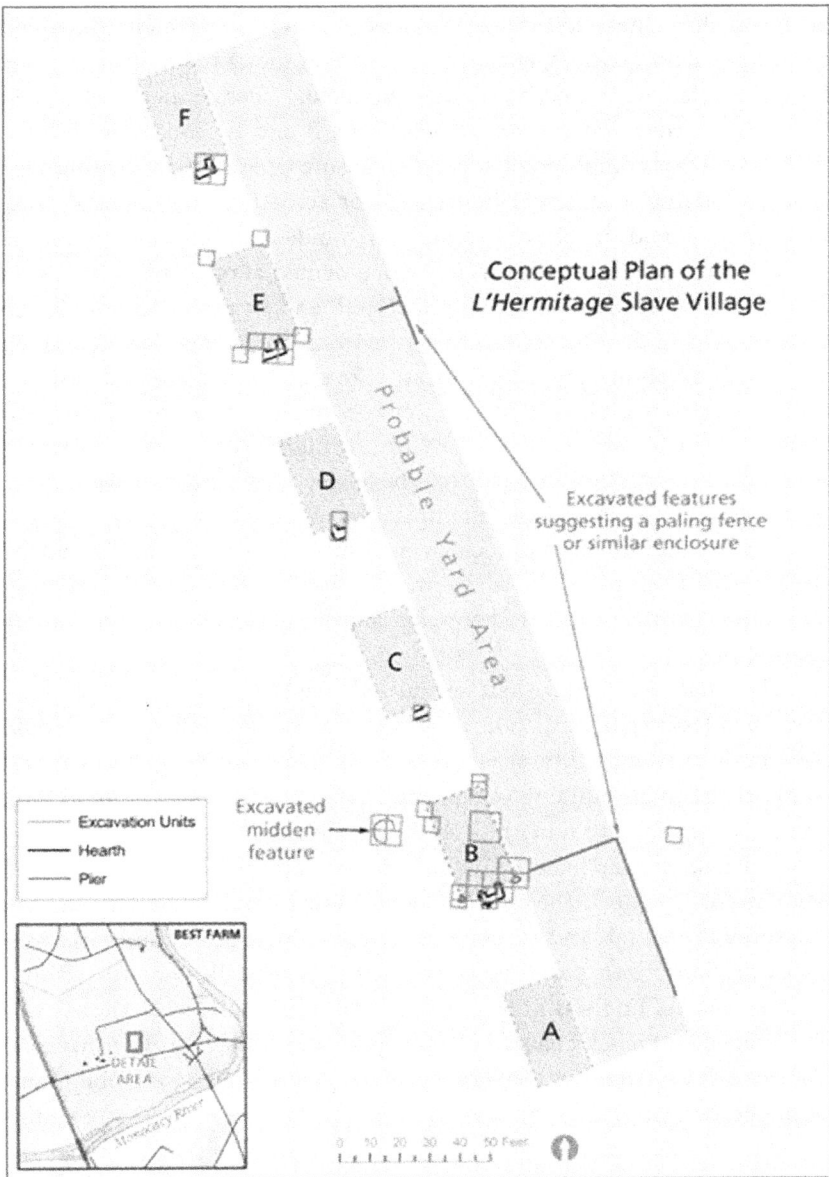

Conceptual Plan of the
L'Hermitage Slave Village

F

E

Probable Yard Area

D

Excavated features
suggesting a paling fence
or similar enclosure

C

Excavation Units
Hearth
Pier

Excavated
midden
feature

B

BEST FARM

DETAIL
AREA

Monocacy River

A

0 10 20 30 40 50 Feet

Figure 3.5. Conceptual plan of L'Hermitage Slave Village, based on 2010–2011 excavations. Map created by Tom Gwaltney. Image courtesy of the National Park Service.

Beasley 2014:56). The enclosure feature was further exposed in 2010 and 2011, revealing linear soil stains. The fence ran north-south alongside and east of the slave quarters, enclosing a yard that measured at least 280 feet long and 31 feet wide. In two areas, perpendicular lines connected the main fence to the southern corners of Structures B and E, indicating that the fenced area was composed of smaller enclosures, perhaps delineating yard space belonging to different households or activities. These fenced areas may have defined the slave yard and surrounded garden plots or animal pens; this use of space has been well documented at other plantation sites such as Poplar Forest and Rich Neck (Heath and Bennett 2000, McFaden et al. 2003) and documented in first-person accounts (e.g., William Hugh Grove's observation in 1732 that Chesapeake slaveowners allowed enslaved individuals "to plant little Platts for potatoes or Indian pease and Cimnells [squash], which they do on Sundays or [at] night" [Grove et al. 1977:25]). Joy Beasley (2005:18.15) suggests that the fence may have also played a strategic role in the Vincendières' attempts at manipulation and control, arguing that "another function of such an enclosure may have been to shield the slave village from public view" to prevent the interference of "meddling" locals and "isolate the enslaved population from the local Frederick County community."

L'Hermitage would have had several dedicated work areas, though those have been less explored than its domestic spaces. Enslaved workers would have performed agricultural labor in fields that were located north and south of the main building cluster and slave quarters, as well as in fruit orchards (location unknown). In addition, a lime kiln was located north of the slave quarters and likely would have been another work site for enslaved laborers (Bailey 2014). The lime kiln, which was partially excavated in 2011, measures 10 feet tall and 13 feet across at its widest point, and features a concentration of ash and lime bordered by stone walls constructed in a beehive shape. Lime was known to improve soil, and its strategic use was encouraged by French colonial planters and later in the 1791 *Pennsylvania, Delaware, Maryland and Virginia Almanack*; these books were ubiquitous throughout the mid-Atlantic. It is possible that the Vincendières were influenced by these sources to use lime to enhance crop yields, and perhaps the sale of lime was one of their commercial enterprises.

Slaveowners regarded the spatial arrangement of the plantation as one of the key methods to demonstrate and reinforce control over their enslaved workforce. Spatial organization could be used by slaveholders as a tool of control and manipulation, and in fact, as Singleton suggests, "nearly every aspect of plantation space resulted from conscious decision making on the part of planters to maximize profits, exercise surveillance and reinforce the subordinate status of enslaved people" (2001:9).

Acts of domination and resistance are not always tangible or explicit; they can be subtle and must be interpreted rather than identified. For example, archaeologists have looked to the landscape and material culture to detect evidence of power negotiations. As Delle suggests, archaeologists should examine social and material spaces to understand local systems, negotiations of power, and the ways in which "spatial manipulations were used to create and reinforce systems of oppression and were in turn resisted" (1998:146). Others have pointed out that spatial analysis of landscape design and the arrangement of slave housing can reflect racist ideology, the creation and enforcement of difference or otherness, social relationships, power relationships, and security motives, and a desire to highlight one's wealth and status (Epperson 1990, 1999; Agorsah 1999; Armstrong 1990; Schein 2006). Vlach (1993:1) points out "the design of a plantation estate was an expression of the owner's tastes, values, and attitudes," and this particular arrangement promoted supervision, control, and function. The spatial layout of the slave quarters in relation to other buildings could signify the way that slaveowners regarded their enslaved workers and strove to exercise control over them.

Spatial analysis has proven to be an effective tool for examining structural inequality, negotiations of power, and the dynamics of plantation life at L'Hermitage as well as other historic plantations (cf. Armstrong 1992, Delle 1998, Epperson 1990, Joyner 2003). The spatial arrangement can indicate the plantation owner's desire to "assert domination over and difference from slaves" by keeping the enslaved workers separate from the main house but close enough to facilitate surveillance (Epperson 1999:171). Thus the spatial arrangement of a plantation can reflect the intentions of the owners and a desire for control over their environment and enslaved individuals. By keeping the main buildings and slave quarters within a relatively small distance from each other, the slaveholder could monitor his workers and squelch any sign of rebellion. The spatial organization ensured that enslaved workers were less likely to gain power and participate in any kind of insurrection (Joyner 2003:15). The arrangement of structures at L'Hermitage can be interpreted as a conscious effort to maintain order and hierarchy on the plantation. An examination of the spatial layout of L'Hermitage can reveal a great deal about structural inequalities and the dynamics of plantation life. The plantation displays a level of landscape planning unlike most small-scale family-run farms in the region, and likely signals the Vincendières' desire for conformity and rigid control over their landscape.

One spatial technique that reinforced the social hierarchy was to elevate the main house so that it dominates the landscape. According to Upton (1988), the planter's house would occupy higher ground than other buildings, allowing it to be seen from a long distance, and set apart from the surrounding countryside by fences and terraces. As the largest domestic structure on the property, the planter's house served as a center of power constructed to dominate the landscape visually. At L'Hermitage, the main house and its cluster of farm buildings stood on the higher ground of an inland terrace, above a wide floodplain. The main house faced the Georgetown-Frederick road from its perch above the gentle concave of the fields to the east of it, through which ran a small, probably ephemeral, stream (Earley et al. 2005:16).

In addition to exercising control over the arrangements of buildings, plantation owners regulated the dimensions and appearance of these buildings, sometimes in minute detail. According to Vlach (1993:164–165), planters specified the dimensions for the structures, and their orders were carried out by enslaved workers or hired carpenters; the identical, uniform housing "stifled the individuality of the slaves by limiting their social development and 'familial identities' and . . . were, foremost, the planters' instruments of social control." By controlling house size, location, and construction, plantation owners could influence the comfort level, health, and relationships of their enslaved workers (Maryland-National Capital Park and Planning Commission 2009:16). During the archaeological investigation of the slave quarters of L'Hermitage, we discovered five stone piers and one possible pier and post holes surrounding the perimeter of Structure B, which may have been log or frame. Based on these findings, we determined the stone hearths would have been located on the exterior of the southern elevation of each of the structures, which would have measured approximately 19 × 34 ft. and had one or one-and-a-half stories and wooden flooring supported by the stone piers. The lack of slate or other roofing materials indicates that the roof was likely composed of wooden shingles or boards. In addition, very little flat glass was recovered, "indicating that windows may have been shuttered without glass panes, or that glass panes were carefully removed prior to structure demolition" (Birmingham and Beasley 2014:58).

In addition, the slave quarters were spaced and oriented in such a way that reveals careful planning and a focus on order and symmetry. The six structures are arranged in a linear fashion oriented northwest, and the dis-

Best Farm Slave Village Geometry Relative to the Main and Secondary Houses

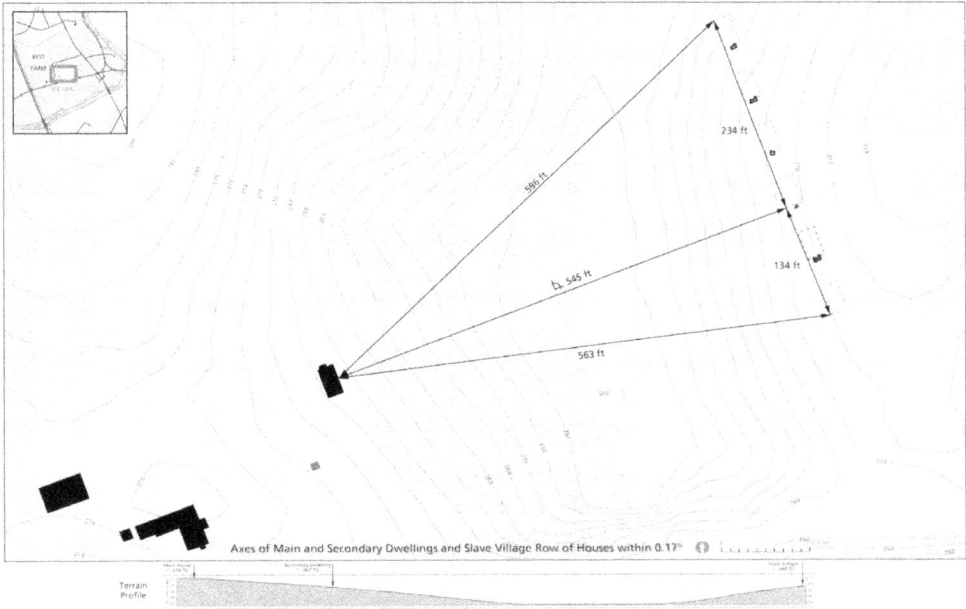

Figure 3.6. L'Hermitage plantation layout, showing the slave quarters in relation to the main buildings. Map created by Tom Gwaltney. Image courtesy of the National Park Service.

tance between each hearth is evenly spaced at 66 feet, or a chain (a common surveyor's unit of measurement in the eighteenth and nineteenth centuries).

Furthermore, all the hearths in the quarters are aligned, almost exactly, with the main houses on the property. In fact, the axis of the main house and the nearby secondary dwelling are within 0.17 degrees of each other, and the secondary dwelling and the slave quarters are aligned within 0.07 degrees of each other. The enclosure feature east of the slave quarters is aligned with the dwellings, and portions of it terminate or turn a corner at the corner of each structure (e.g., at B and E) (Figure 3.6). Along with being on a similar axis to the slave quarters, the secondary house is nearly centered in relation to the row of dwellings. The center of the secondary structure is 563 ft (approximately 8.5 chains) from the southernmost point of the row of slave quarters and 596 ft from the northernmost point.

It was hypothesized that a seventh dwelling may have stood at the south end of the row, leaving a lighter footprint not detected during the archaeological investigations; the presence of this dwelling would increase the overall symmetry of the layout. During the 2011 field season, a previously discovered enclosure feature was further exposed to reveal that it continued farther south than anticipated. This indicated to the archaeologists that the slave village was perhaps larger than expected, providing additional evidence for the existence of a seventh dwelling. During the summer of 2012, the question of the seventh dwelling was investigated through traditional archaeological methods. The excavation of this area revealed no sign of the substantial stone-and-mortar feature that characterized Structures A–F. Furthermore, no soil features were detected save for four plow scars. The lack of any unique or distinguishing features in this area, along with the dearth of artifacts, are not indicative of a substantial dwelling such as those detected in previous field seasons. However, this does not rule out the possibility that the area was occupied by another structure or facility, such as a well or outbuilding. Only further investigations will have the potential to answer this question definitively.

The Vincendières may have been influenced by plantation designs in the United States. At Carter's Grove Plantation in Williamsburg, Virginia, the façade of the log slave quarter is symmetrical and oriented at the same angle as the mansion (Epperson 1990:34). This design reinforces to visitors that strict limits were placed on the "cultural autonomy" of those who occupied the slave quarter (34). Similarly, at Monticello (Kelso 1984), rigidity and precision are characteristic of Jefferson's design of Mulberry Row, where the slave quarters were located. Not only did Jefferson create all the plans himself, he was so committed to having total control over the appearance of his landscape that his plans sometimes included measurements to be carried out to four or five decimal places (Dalzell 1993:545). Likewise, the slave quarters at L'Hermitage demonstrate a similar attention to detail.

While the Vincendières may have been influenced by the plantation designs of the surrounding area, they may have drawn on their previous experience in Saint Domingue as well. Several sources indicate that linear and symmetrical layouts were not unique to the United States. In both the United States and the Caribbean, plantations were distinguished by a rigidly defined plan and linear housing arrangements that had been informed by economic and power relations between planters and enslaved workers. Manuals written in the colonial Caribbean advised eighteenth- and nineteenth-century planters on the most efficient layouts and probably contributed to uniformity within and across planters. In Leonard Wray's 1848 planter's manual, the author observes that "It of course occurs, that the more compact and perfect the general arrangements are, the more satisfactory and economical its working details will prove" (307). Studies of maps of eighteenth-century Jamaican, Cuban, and Antillean plantations revealed that centrally located slave quarters with regular, linear layouts were most common between 1790 and 1840; a period that coincided with evolving notions of social engineering and "amelioration" of plantation conditions (Higman 1988:244). As William Beckford noted in 1790, "It is the custom now to have them [the negro-houses] built in strait lines, constructed with some degree of uniformity and strength" (7). Regimented housing layouts were especially common on Jamaican sugar and coffee plantations, particularly those where space was limited or the slave quarters were built close to the main house or on a slope (Higman 1988:244–245). Of course, this information must be applied to L'Hermitage plantation with caution, as it largely stems from British plantations in Jamaica, rather than French plantations in Saint Domingue or Maryland, but the potential for shared elements across Caribbean islands should not be discounted. In any case, it is clear that the Vincendières had contemporaries in the Caribbean whose plantations were arranged similarly to L'Hermitage, with an eye toward increasing profits and surveillance.

The relationship of this row of houses to the secondary dwelling indicates a degree of planning and a desire to arrange the landscape to promote uniformity and control. Furthermore, the plantation buildings are arranged in a manner that facilitates surveillance. Such surveillance had both functional and symbolic significance. Practically speaking, slaveholders wanted to ensure that enslaved workers were performing the labor assigned to them, and they also had an economic interest in monitoring the people whose labor was so essential to the successful operation of their enterprise (Knottnerus et al. 1999:22). From the main and secondary houses at L'Hermitage, one can observe the barn, slave quarters, and surrounding fields. In addition, the outdoor activity area/detached kitchen feature is located to the east of the row of structures but is clearly visible from the main building cluster between Structures E and F. It is quite possible that the Vincendières or the plantation overseers monitored the activities conducted in this area.

Although the elevations of the main house, the secondary dwelling, and the slave village are about the same, the topography dips between the secondary dwelling and the slave quarters, ensuring that the line of vision between these two areas was unencumbered. From the main house and secondary dwelling, the enslaved workers could be easily monitored, and therefore controlled more strictly by the Vincendières.

The concept of panopticism is worth consideration in the case of L'Hermitage. Arising in the European philosophical tradition with Jeremy Bentham and further developed by Foucault (1980), this idea was concerned with social control and discipline; for Foucault, "spatial effects determine social relations" (Fontana-Giusti 2013:15). The ideal panopticon design allows an observer to monitor subjects without being seen, thereby creating a sense of perpetual invisible omniscience. Subjects internalize the authority's gaze and begin to self-monitor and apply self-discipline. As Foucault described it:

> Hence the major effect of the Panopticon: to induce in the inmate a state of conscious and permanent visibility that assures the automatic functioning of power. So to arrange things that the surveillance is permanent in its effects, even if it is discontinuous in its action; that the perfection of power should tend to render its actual exercise unnecessary; that this architectural apparatus should be a machine for creating and sustaining a power relation independent of the person who exercises it; in short, that the inmates should be caught up in a power situation of which they are themselves the bearers. What matters is that he knows himself to be observed. Bentham laid down the principle that power should be visible and unverifiable. Visible: the inmate will constantly have before his eyes the tall outline of the central tower from which he is spied upon. Unverifiable: the inmate must never know whether he is being looked at any one moment; but he must be sure that he may always be so. (1980:179)

Subjects internalize the authority's gaze and begin to self-monitor and self-discipline. "And, in order to be exercised, this power had to be given the instrument of permanent, exhaustive, omnipresent surveillance, capable of making all visible, as long as it could itself remain invisible" (Foucault 1980:203). This type of psychological control would be useful on plantations where owners tried to break down the individuality of their enslaved laborers and create submissive workers. Various surveillance studies have employed the panopticon as an analytical tool in order to explore how social control operates on certain bodies and in certain spaces, as well as to conceptualize disciplinary power and the ways that it comes to be internalized by some (Browne 2015:38). Epperson has applied panoptic theory to plantation sites such as Monticello, Gunston Hall, and Ferry Hill. The last, a 700-acre plantation in Washington County, Maryland, has characteristics of the panopticon in that the enslaved workers were made to feel watched at all times by way of the landscape design (Epperson 1990:43). From the main house, the planter could see the activities of all the enslaved workers, though they could not see him (Epperson 1990:45). Panoptic theory has also been applied to sites such as the Jamaican coffee plantations studied by James Delle (1998). There, the overseer's house was centrally located to facilitate perpetual surveillance of the slave quarters and the daily labor efforts.

In addition to spatial techniques, slaveowners had a variety of other strategies for controlling and disciplining enslaved laborers. First, slaveholders like the Vincendières exerted control over their enslaved workers by controlling their living conditions, including housing and food. Slaveowners demonstrated their denial of enslaved workers' humanity by keeping them in inferior conditions: "Under the master or mistress' care, enslaved Africans were subjected to various forms of domestic terrorism. Among them was the willful neglect of their basic human needs (food, medical care, and clothing/shoes). Intentional withholding and deprivation of these basic needs to control slaves and enforce labor for New World advancement was a glaring mark of domestic terrorism" (Harrison 2009).

McKee (1992) points out that slave quarters had the dual purposes of providing shelter and reminding enslaved workers of their subordinate status (195); the structures were meant to be "orderly but lowly-appearing, so slaves can live without challenging the plantation system" (200). The houses were constructed in such a way that took care of the needs of health, procreation, nursing, surveillance, and discipline (McKee 1992:200). The housing provided to enslaved workers was often inadequate or subpar, as slave narratives attest:

> We lodged in log huts, and on the bare ground. Wooden floors were an unknown luxury. In a single room were huddled, like cattle, ten or a dozen persons, men, women, and children. All ideas of refinement and decency were, of course, out of the question. We had neither bedsteads, nor furniture of any description. Our beds were collections of straw and old rags, thrown down in the corners and boxed in with boards; a single blanket the only covering. Our favourite way of sleeping, however, was on a plank, our heads raised on an old jacket and our feet toasting before the smouldering fire. The wind whistled and the rain and snow blew in through the cracks, and the damp earth soaked in the moisture till the floor was miry as a pig-sty. Such were our houses. In these wretched hovels where we penned at night, and fed by day; here were the children born and the sick—neglected. (Mintz 2009:92)

[. . .]

Our houses were but log huts—the tops partly open—ground floor—rain would come through. My aunt was quite an old woman, and had been sick several years; in rains I have seen her moving from one part of the house to the other, and rolling her bedclothes about to try to keep dry—everything would be dirty and muddy. I lived in the house with my aunt. My bed and bedstead consisted of a board wide enough to sleep on—one end on a stool, the other placed near the fire. My pillow consisted of my jacket—my covering was whatever I could get. My bedtick was the board itself. And this was the way the single men slept—but we were comfortable in this way of sleeping, being used to it. I only remember having but one blanket from my owners up to the age of nineteen, when I ran away. (Mintz 2009:93)

Although an accurate description of L'Hermitage slave quarters is difficult to produce, it is likely that the dwellings were made of wood and had dirt or wood floors. The lack of interior chimneys indicates that these were single-pen structures. The open floor plan would indicate that the structures at the L'Hermitage slave village were designed as barracks, meant to house the enslaved population en masse. Barracks were used as slave housing within the United States and were also used on coffee plantations within Saint Domingue. It is unknown how many of the individuals enslaved at L'Hermitage resided within the village. It is possible that some of the enslaved individuals resided in outbuildings, in the basement or attic of the main house, in the secondary house, or in the loft space above the log kitchen building. Additionally, due to the lack of any historic documentation regarding the households of the enslaved population at L'Hermitage, it is unknown whether they were separated into the structures by family group or gender.

Notably, the position of the hearths within L'Hermitage slave quarters would have made the buildings uncomfortable for the enslaved individuals during periods of extreme seasonal variation. Not only would one hearth have been insufficient to heat a 12 × 18 ft. (or whatever) structure such as those uncovered at the slave village, but the weather patterns associated with the mid-Atlantic United States would have made the position of the hearth on the southern elevation problematic. While external end chimneys were common in the mid-Atlantic region to help dissipate the humid and often oppressive heat of summer, the location of the chimney is critical for the adequate heating of the structure during the winter months (Noble 1984:49).

Winds in the region generally blow from the northwest to the southeast; regional construction methods dictated that hearths should be located on the northern or western elevations of structures for adequate insulation. The location of these chimneys on the southern elevation of the structures likely meant that the hearths did not warm the drafty structures adequately during the winter. It is likely that the Vincendières knew that the structures were inadequately weatherproofed. Evidence identified during the Historic Structure Reports for the Best House (L'Hermitage) and the Secondary House indicate that the Vincendières made several tactical errors in the construction of their dwellings (GWWO 2003). The original wing of the Best House exhibited several distinctly Caribbean elements and was constructed with 11-foot ceilings, multiple large six-over-six light windows set in deep alcoves, and shallow fireplaces. In future building episodes the high ceilings, shallow fireplaces, and large windows were not repeated, while shallower 9-foot ceilings, smaller and fewer window openings, and deeper, larger fireplaces were added. Similar changes were made to the Secondary House; after its initial construction, a central wall and chimney were added, making it a two-pen rather than one-pen building, with the window and door openings substantially decreased in size. These changes were likely more than a shift in stylistic preference, as the changes consistently suggest methods undertaken to weatherproof these buildings from Maryland winters (Birmingham and Beasley 2014:73). The archaeological evidence suggests that the Vincendières did not make similar changes to the structures occupied by the enslaved population, which in turn indicates the kind of control the family had over their enslaved workers' living conditions; the Vincendières could keep these individuals in an uncomfortable, unhealthy environment.

The ceramic assemblage could indicate the Vincendières' influence over enslaved individuals' consumption of material goods. The majority of ceramics recovered from the slave village were locally made, undecorated red paste earthenwares (57%), followed by white paste earthenware (41%). Stoneware, yellowware, porcelain, and tin-enameled earthenware each made up around 1% of the assemblage. Some of the red paste earthenware sherds were under-fired or defective at the time of manufacture, and were clearly potters' seconds. These vessels would have been the most inexpensive available on the market at the time, with potters' seconds likely free or cheaper than the properly constructed wares (Parker and Hernigle 1990:69, Heath 1999a:59).

A number of refined, English-made earthenwares were also recovered. These wares were composed mainly of annular, painted, shell-edged, and undecorated creamware (n = 1,684, 29%) and pearlware (n = 546, 9%). A total of 12 decorated and undecorated whiteware fragments were also identified. The ceramic assemblage located at the slave village site contained a large variety of earthenware types, both imported and locally made, that were manufactured throughout the late eighteenth to early nineteenth centuries. One interesting aspect of the assemblage is that it could easily resemble the household wares of middling or small planters in the region. It is unclear if the more expensive decorative earthenware vessels were purchased by the enslaved individuals with earnings from side-work, or if the Vincendières provided these goods to the enslaved population. It is possible, due to the lack of obvious matching ceramic decorative patterns, that the vessels were acquired in a piecemeal fashion after the Vincendières broke items within their tableware sets or upgraded to the newest, most fashionable items (Samford 2007:99). The presence of refined earthenware and porcelain tableware shows that individuals had access to more expensive ceramic types, although it is unknown whether these were hand-me-down or purchased items (Birmingham and Beasley 2014:78).

Food was also a significant means of controlling enslaved populations on plantations. In many areas a good deal of the slaves' diet was provided from rations distributed by the plantation. Enslaved workers also made use of private gardens, livestock, local markets, hunting, fishing, and trapping. A typical slave diet included pork, chicken, beef, sheep, goat, fish, wheat, corn, oats, and molasses (Reinhart 1984, Yentsch 1994:212–213). Regardless of the source, enslaved people rarely had adequate food; a former slave, Annie Hawkins, wrote of her experience that it was "a constant misery to us . . . I never had no white folks that was good to me. We all worked jest like dogs, and had about half as much to eat, and got whupped for everything" (Federal Writers Project 1941:131).

Our knowledge of the diet of enslaved workers at L'Hermitage is incomplete, as it is based primarily on faunal remains discovered during excavation. The presence of utilitarian hollowware and other vessels indicates that the enslaved workers prepared and stored their own food. Five bone and ferrous metal utensil fragments and two ferrous knife and fork fragments were recovered during the excavation, indicating that the enslaved population was provided with or purchased at least a limited number of utensils. Interviews from the Works Progress Administration's (WPA) slave narratives indicate that enslaved individuals utilized utensils of a variety of materials, including wooden spoons and knives that would not survive in the archaeological record (Covey and Eisnach 2009:61). Additionally, slave narratives indicate that some enslaved persons were forced to eat with their hands, or to create utensils with shells, gourds, or broken ceramics. None of the ceramic fragments or well-preserved shells recovered from the site exhibited evidence of secondary use; further, it seems likely due to the prevalence of ceramic and metal cooking vessels and utensils that the enslaved population at L'Hermitage possessed at least a limited number of cast iron pots, forks, knives, and metal storage containers.

Faunal materials recovered from the slave village give some indication of the types of foods consumed by the enslaved population, including lower-quality cuts of beef, pork, and mutton. Specialized analyses of the faunal remains were not undertaken due to budgetary constraints, but some general conclusions regarding these materials can be drawn. It is clear that the individuals on the site were consuming a high number of domesticated animals, mainly cow, pig, and sheep/goat. The majority of the faunal assemblage consisted of unidentified mammal remains (n = 1,070, 34%). It was apparent that the enslaved individuals living at the site were primarily consuming second cuts of meat. While the archaeological record does not account for the cuts of meat that lack bones, such as bacon, sausage, or other rendered meat products like dried or pickled meat, the presence of skulls, vertebrae, and lower phalanges within the artifact assemblage closely resembles other enslaved diets within the Chesapeake region (Crader 1990:700), albeit with a greater number of identifiable cow bones (n = 114) than pig bones (n = 52). The presence of cow and pig skeletons either reflects on-site butchering, as skulls were often discarded during the initial butchering process, or skulls given to the enslaved population as an additional protein source (Lyman 1977:71). Cow and pig foot phalanges, metapodials, and carpals indicate that the knuckles and feet were consumed. Further analysis of the skull remains could indicate whether tongue extraction or headcheese production was undertaken. A number of the faunal remains exhibited evidence of butchering, such as chopping, scraping, and sawing, as well as purposeful breakage visible through fracture patterns. These marks likely represent the initial butchering of the animals, as well as secondary butchery for use in stews and for marrow extraction (Crader 1990:706). Many of the in situ faunal remains were fairly complete bone elements, but a high volume located within feature contexts is fragmentary, suggesting the fragmentation of various long and flat bones within stews (Birmingham and Beasley 2014:81). One-pot meals and stews were a common staple for the enslaved diet; as Singleton states, "carcasses cut into small portions, highly fragmented bones, or bones from which the meat has apparently been sliced all suggest that meats were boiled, in stews or soups for example, rather than roasted. The making of stews was perhaps a culinary preference, but it may also have been a creative way of using pieces of meat considered undesirable by slaveholders" (Singleton 1991:162).

Enslaved populations often supplemented their diet with wild game and flora (Samford 1996, 2007; Covey and Eisnach 2009). Preliminary data show that some avian species, as well as small game mammals like raccoon, were used to supplement the enslaved diet at L'Hermitage. There is also evidence that the enslaved population was fishing and collecting in the Monocacy River; fish scales and bones ($n = 14$), and freshwater mussel shells ($n = 15$) were identified within the assemblage. Small fragments of seeds ($n = 2$), nut shells ($n = 8$), including walnut, and two fruit pits further indicate that the enslaved population was supplementing their diet with locally available plants and fruits; it is possible that some of these fruits were obtained from the orchards located on the plantation (Birmingham and Beasley 2014:82). Although no flotation was performed on the samples taken during the excavations, it is possible that seed or plant remains could shed light on the types of crops raised by the enslaved on the larger plantation or in their personal garden plots, which were likely located within the enclosure feature (Birmingham and Beasley 2014:82). A large number of oyster shells ($n = 362$) were recovered from both feature and plowzone contexts. Oysters were not local to the area, but would have been imported from the Chesapeake Bay or Alexandria regions during the cooler months of the year (Beasley et al. 2010:130; Parker and Hernigle 1990:181). Oysters were imported from these areas along the Georgetown Road, which connected bustling economic centers and was the likely cause of high oyster shell counts identified from other contemporaneous, local sites (Beasley et al. 2001:130). It is unclear whether oysters were purchased directly by the enslaved individuals or provided by the Vincendières.

The enslaved diet at L'Hermitage is a particularly interesting subject when examined in tandem with the primary documents related to the Vincendière occupation of the Best Farm. Frederick County Court Dockets indicate that in November of 1797, Jean Payen de Boisneuf was tried and found guilty of "not providing sufficient Meat and Cloathing [sic] for his Slaves" (MSA 1797:97; Reed 2004).

Plantations were typically violent places, and L'Hermitage was no exception. The archaeological and historical record revealed instances of physical and spatial violence enacted against enslaved workers there. Since the proprietors at L'Hermitage had derived their livelihood from a regime of forced human labor, they probably arrived in Maryland accustomed to using such violence to maintain control. Slaveowners' brutal treatment of enslaved individuals was not only acceptable, but also encouraged: "Terror, or naked power, was at the core of the institution of slavery. . . . Whites were encouraged to keep firm discipline and to punish slaves frequently and harshly. Indeed, whites frowned on overseers and planters who were deemed to be lenient toward their slaves" (Burnard 2004:149–150). For example, in Saint Domingue it was permissible for a enslaved individual who struck his/her master/mistress to be hanged, and for white colonists to kill any person of African descent who showed any sign of rebellion (Loix, Ordonnance des Administrateurs, Article 21, March 27, 1721, cited in Moreau de Saint-Méry 1785:726) or refused to stop when encountered on a road (Loix, Ordre Concernant des Nègres de la Dependence du Cap, November 12, 1691, cited in Moreau de Saint-Méry 1784:502)—all because colonists were "concerned about threats to public order and continued existence of the colony posed by slaves," and the basic objectives of slave laws were to "preserve order in the colony, maintain and develop its wealth and continue its dependency on the mother country" and ultimately maintain social control (Midlo Hall 1971:81). Colonist Hilliard d'Auberteuil (1779:273) expressed the sentiments of white planters when he said that "In Saint Domingue, interest and security require that we crush the black race under so much contempt that whoever descends from it should be covered with indelible scars until the sixth generation." Planters "believed they could control any rebellion through harsh estate discipline. They were wary of what slaves were doing but were convinced they could effectively repress slave discontent. Few believed there was a limit to the amount of repression slaves would endure" (Burnard 2004:261).

The most potent account of abuse at L'Hermitage was recorded in 1798 by the Polish writer and politician Julian Niemcewicz, who saw the plantation as he traveled from Georgetown to Frederick in June 1798. He wrote in his journal that:

> This is the residence of a Frenchman called Payant [*sic*: Boisneuf], who left San Domingo with a substantial sum and with it bought two or three thousand acres of land and a few hundred negroes whom he treats with the greatest tyranny. [MMB4] One can see on the home farm instruments of torture, stocks, wooden horses, whips, etc. Two or three negroes crippled with torture have brought legal action against him, but the matter has not yet been settled. This man

is 60 years old, without children or relatives; he keeps an old French woman with two daughters; she, in sweetness of humour, even surpasses him. This charming group has caused about 50 legal actions to be brought. They foam with rage, beat the negroes, complain and fight with each other. In these ways does this man use his wealth, and comforts his life in its descent toward the grave. (1965:111–112)

Evidence that the refugees attempted to perpetuate their Saint Domingue lifestyle is found in their treatment of the slaves at L'Hermitage. Disciplinary practices varied from plantation to plantation, but mutilation, whipping, and other violence has been recorded throughout the Caribbean and plantation areas of North America (Blackburn 1997). Atrocities committed against enslaved workers were by no means limited to French colonials, nor does the research indicate that the French in general were crueler than slaveholders from other countries, but the losses that the proprietors of L'Hermitage suffered upon their unwilling expulsion from Saint Domingue may well have escalated the violence they employed in Maryland.

What Niemcewicz described would have been a miserable and violent existence for the enslaved laborers, as well as a jarring scene for the mainly English and German Protestant neighbors passing by the plantation. In his firsthand account, as mentioned, Niemcewicz describes "instruments of torture, stocks, wooden horses, whips, etc." These particular torture devices were utilized quite frequently during colonial and postcolonial times and would have been publicly recognizable by individuals throughout the nineteenth century (Brackett 1889:138; Friedman 2005:35). Stocks and wooden horses were used frequently in domestic and military settings in English, French, and American society and were also later employed in both Union and Confederate prisons during the Civil War (Casstevens 2004:99). The goal of public, corporal punishment "was to reteach and retouch the erring soul, and it used, as means to this end, confession, public humiliation, and infamy" in order to enact reform (Friedman 2005:35). By placing instruments of torture in public view of a well-traveled road, the Vincendières were displaying an unusual public message to both the enslaved population and their neighbors. The devices Niemcewicz highlighted were particularly barbaric. Stocks consisted of large, hinged wooden boards used to restrain an individual by the legs, hands, and/or head, for a prolonged period of physical and mental torture and humiliation (Casstevens 2004:98). Wooden horses were a particularly brutal form of punishment. The wooden horse was constructed of a wooden frame with four legs and a triangular roof-shaped, sharp body. Victims of this device were forced to straddle the sharp body and were often tied down or strapped with weights to prohibit movement (this was referred to historically as "riding on a rail") (Casstevens 2004:99; Farmer 1889:448). While stocks and wooden horses did not generally inflict lethal damage to an individual, death was possible due to exposure to the elements or lack of food and water.

Niemcewicz also mentions the presence of "whips," which were a commonly used method of punishment on American plantations, as well as a sanctioned legal punishment issued by civilian and military courts throughout the nineteenth century (Brackett 1889:138–139; Casstevens 2004:110–111). Whipping left permanent physical scarring on individuals and could permanently maim or blind the victims. The threat of whipping was used as a mental and physical means of control by plantation owners and overseers, as "practically every slave either had been whipped, knew another who had been whipped, had witnessed whippings, or had seen the scars of earlier whippings," thus they feared the experience through both direct and indirect association (Harrell et al. 2005:363). Although no archaeological evidence of these torture devices has been located, it is assumed due to the accuracy of Niemcewicz's account in terms of the location of the slave quarters that they did exist. This style of slavery, characterized by openly acknowledged physical, sexual, and mental abuse, is more commonly associated with antebellum slavery on farms, plantations, and cities in the southern United States and within the Caribbean. In Saint Domingue, between one-third and one-half of the slaves who survived the passage from Africa died within a few years of residence; 10% of plantation slaves died of "overwork, malnutrition, disease, and harsh treatment every year" (Dubois and Garrigus 2006:8, 13). Infanticide, suicide, abortion, and self-mutilation were common among the enslaved (Geggus 1982:25; Moreau de Saint-Méry 1985[1798]:65, 273–274). Violence against slaves was the rule in this colony, and punishments were meted out "publicly to terrorize other slaves, forcing them to watch and sometimes participate" (Dubois and Garrigus 2006:14).

Saint Domingue had a reputation for being tolerant of particularly brutal treatment of enslaved workers. In her characterization of colonial Saint Domingue, Fick (1990:36) states,

One might well argue that the ruthlessly labor-intensive, capitalistic nature of Caribbean slavery necessitated the extraction of maximum labor from the slave in the shortest period of time and that, to do this, the utilization of fear and the creation of an atmosphere of terror were requisite. Yet at the same time, in colonial Saint Domingue there seemed to be an indeterminate line between economic interest, on the one hand, and pure self-indulgent sadism, on the other. Where the one began and the other left off in these cases was hardly clear.

Haitian writer and politician Baron de Vastey devoted his essay *The Colonial System Unveiled* to cataloging the horrifying brutality of Saint Dominguan slavery that he observed. This unsettling account describes more than 100 instances of enslaved workers in the colony being tortured and killed—burned alive, mutilated, flogged to death, sexually assaulted, held in iron masks and iron collars—and insists that this is the norm:

> I can anticipate your response: you will reply to me, with your usual arguments and bad faith, that such acts of cruelty rarely happened; you will go on to tell me that since time immemorial there have been monsters who have defiled themselves with misdeeds of this sort, and that just because Barré Saint-Venant is one such monster, I should not conclude from this that all colonists are indiscriminately monsters. Yes, they all are, more or less; they all committed such horrors, participated in them and contributed to them. In any case, the number of colonists who acted in a decent and human fashion is so small that it is not worth making them an exception to the general rule. (Bongie 2014:107–108)

In fact, the perpetuation of these norms was necessary to the maintenance of their plantation and lifestyle:

> For the slaveholder, psycho-social survival required interpreting the plantation context in a fashion that led all whites and blacks to believe that white dominance was God-ordained white destiny. Indeed, slaveholders had to construct their own meaning, as they constructed the meaning of those they enslaved. Within that construct, white privilege, which was their birthright, was inextricably linked to the devaluation of the black bondsmen they owned. (John 1999:44)

It is entirely possible that Boisneuf and the Vincendières thought their actions at L'Hermitage were tame compared with what they witnessed in

Saint Domingue, and were generally unaware that their practices would contrast so starkly against the social mores of the Maryland community. Maryland itself was not an area known for extensive public torture of enslaved individuals, particularly in the postcolonial period (Brackett 1889:1). As Frederick Douglass stated,

> It is generally supposed that slavery, in the state of Maryland, exists in its mildest form, and that it is totally divested of those harsh and terrible peculiarities, which mark and characterize the slave system, . . . but there are certain secluded and out-of-the-way places . . . where it can be indecent without shame, cruel without shuddering, and murderous without apprehension or fear of exposure. (1855:61–62)

In Maryland, torture and mistreatment of enslaved people was an activity conducted in private and with the utmost secrecy. The citizens of Maryland, as reflected through the body of the Maryland State Legislature in the years from the American Revolution to the Civil War, were equally divided over the issue of emancipation (Brackett 1889:52, Frey 1991:218). In 1789, a bill outlining the gradual emancipation of enslaved individuals, with the caveat that slaveowners be reimbursed for their losses by the state, lost by a margin of two votes (Brackett 1889:54). While some counties in Maryland were decidedly pro- or antislavery, central counties like Frederick were evenly divided. This equal division would have made it especially important for communities to downplay the issue so that social, political, and commercial interests of neighbors were not impeded. The practice of slavery within the United States represented a broad spectrum, from enslaved individuals who were treated so mildly "as almost to blur the distinction between slavery and freedom," and those who were treated with violent brutality (Harrell et al. 2005:363). The majority of enslaved persons experienced events that fell in the middle of this spectrum; however, it should be emphasized that all enslaved individuals experienced the inhumanities of chattel slavery with its "denial of basic freedoms and its everyday humiliations and unrewarded labor" (Harrell et al. 2005:363). Despite the fact that lines between freedom and subjugation were sometimes blurred in the north, and the form of slavery in these areas often appeared to be milder, "slaveholders in such societies could act with extraordinary brutality precisely because their slaves were extraneous to the main business," and "because they desired to set themselves apart" from their subordinates (Berlin 2003:9). Boisneuf and the Vincendières were clearly at the end of the spectrum representing brutal treatment of the enslaved population. This proclivity toward brutality may have been due to their origins in the violent and slave-reliant system in Saint Domingue; however, the style of slavery they practiced was so foreign to their Frederick neighbors, and passersby like Niemcewicz, that the state was persuaded to take legal action against them (Birmingham and Beasley 2014:27).

In 1797, the State of Maryland brought Victoire up on charges for assaulting an enslaved individual named Rosina Cecille, and also for "Especially cruelly and immercifully beating her slave Jenny" (MSA 1797:65). Jenny's case was dismissed by a grand jury, and Rosina Cecille's case was also struck off, but Victoire did have to pay at least $272 in court fees (MSA 1797:65, Reed and Wallace 2004:99). Similarly, the 1797 Criminal Dockets charged Boisneuf on six separate counts for "Cruelly and immercifully beating and whipping his slave[s]" Harry, Jerry, Abraham, Stephen, Soll, and George. Nine witnesses testified against him, but these cases were also dismissed, possibly because it was not illegal to beat an enslaved laborer in Maryland (MSA 1797; Rivers Cofield 2005). Although physical punishment of enslaved people had been institutionalized in Maryland for at least 100 years, the existence of these cases indicates that the practices at L'Hermitage were severe enough to be considered criminal (Rivers Cofield 2006:278–280). Boisneuf was not acquitted of all cruelty charge: another long list of witnesses came forward in a case brought on behalf of the enslaved individual Shadrack Hinton, and this time a jury found Boisneuf guilty of "Excessively, cruelly, and unmercifully beating, etc. of his slave Negro Shadrack" (MSA 1797:91; Reed 2004:99).

Regardless of whether the cases went to trial, they can be interpreted as verification that the enslaved population at L'Hermitage was physically abused, as reported in the Niemcewicz account. While the whips and horses mentioned in the Niemcewicz account could have been used for animal herding or general farm activities, the reference to stocks is not easily dismissed. Stocks may have been readily visible from the road, and they would have been recognizable to travelers as a device designed specifically for confining humans (Rivers Cofield 2005:5.28).

There is also an example of an attempt to limit the interactions between L'Hermitage's enslaved workers and local residents of Frederick. Victoire Vincendière placed a notice in the January 16, 1806, issue of the *Frederick Town Herald* forbidding anyone from interacting with her enslaved workers without her written permission, saying:

TAKE NOTICE: I do hereby forewarn all persons whomsoever from dealing with my slaves from this date, without their having leave in writing from me. If any person or persons should hereafter disregard this notice, I will put the law in force against them. V. Vincendière

> January 11 (*Frederick-Town Herald,* 1806, p. 3).

While we cannot say with certainty why she placed this ad, Birmingham and Beasley (2014:35) postulate that some of Victoire's anger could have resulted from her earlier legal troubles, and from the later petition for freedom by enslaved worker Pierre Louis, which were caused and assisted by members of the local community. It is also possible that these activities were impacting the economic viability of the Vincendières, or compounding their numerous debts and troubles. Victoire could have also been concerned that the enslaved laborers were planning escapes, as two others, François (Cayou) and George, attempted escape in the years following this notice. What is clear is that communication of the enslaved individuals outside the plantation was making life difficult for the Vincendières and Payen. It is probable that the enslaved individuals were using these connections as a resistance against slavery.

Ultimately, the Vincendières held nearly all the power at L'Hermitage, as they had the ability to impose their landscape design and rules on their enslaved laborers. These characteristics could reflect the Vincendières' insistence on forced control and order regarding their landscape, as well as their desire to closely monitor their enslaved workers. The methods used to manipulate the landscape were tools to exert dominance and further oppress the enslaved population. This desire could have stemmed from a fear that the slave uprising that occurred in Saint Domingue would be repeated at L'Hermitage. By controlling the architecture and landscape, the Vincendières could actively attempt to stifle the individuality and autonomy of their enslaved workers. This may have been especially important to the Vincendières, who, as discussed in chapter 2, had escaped a slave uprising in Saint Domingue and were likely concerned with the discipline and control of their enslaved workers to prevent another such event. After having lost land and family members in the Haitian Revolution, the Vincendières may have feared rebellion and therefore implemented harsher treatment and more strict control (Beasley et al. 2005:5.30).

4

Reading Nervousness in the Historical and Archaeological Record

As evidenced by the comparative examples I provided in chapter 3, the Vincendières were not unusual in their strict and deliberate arrangement of their plantation, nor their violence toward and mistreatment of their enslaved workers. In this chapter, I consider the motivating factors behind such actions. Without a doubt, the Vincendières' behavior was part and parcel of the colonial project. As a system of societal and economic organization, colonialism "depended upon racializing and dehumanizing colonized peoples or constructing them as unruly populations to be disciplined, worked upon, managed, ruled, or otherwise 'civilized'" (Go 2016:21). Any violence, abuse, and social control enacted by the Vincendières was underwritten by racism and racial hierarchies developed during the colonial era. White colonizers used racism to justify the use of enslaved Africans for free labor and to label Black populations as inferior, nonhuman beasts of burden, which in turn was used to justify all manner of cruelty. Once constructed, this concept generated several unquestioned truths for white slaveowners: that there was no limit to the abuse that enslaved workers could endure, that an enslaved individual was something between an animal and a machine, that such a nonhuman does not deserve human rights, that the sole worth of an enslaved person resided in their labor and what they could produce. Undergirding all these beliefs was a sense of complete ownership and entitlement on the part of slaveowners. Frantz Fanon describes this proprietary gaze, saying, "The white man wants the world; he wants it for himself. He discovers he is the predestined master of the world. He enslaves it. His relationship with the world is one of appropriation" (1952:107). W.E.B. Du Bois writes in *Black Reconstruction* that such beliefs of total dominion have been ubiquitous among white people and legally supported by American slave codes that designated enslaved individuals as "purely and absolutely property" (1935:7). The plantation system was founded upon and operated by those principles, and as white slaveowners and residents of colonial Saint Domingue and Maryland, the Vincendières were steeped in these concepts and beliefs.

Furthermore, the Vincendières' Catholic beliefs may have encouraged or justified their practice of slavery. The Vincendières' Catholicism is well documented; they were actively involved in Saint John the Evangelist Roman Catholic Church in Frederick, and historical research indicates that they had financial dealings with the Reverend John Dubois, founder of St. John's, and with the Church itself (Rivers Cofield 2002:56). Moreover, when Victoire sold L'Hermitage in 1827, she moved to a townhouse in Frederick less than a block away from St. John's Church (Rivers Cofield 2002:56). The Vincendières' devout Catholicism is perhaps most poignantly expressed in the memoirs of Victoire's niece, Esther Polk Lowe (1913:12), who wrote that "They were strictly religious Catholics and at that period there were few of such—of their social standing—in Frederick." Esther Lowe drew a direct connection between the Vincendières' religious beliefs and charitable work, writing that "Self-sacrifice was their rule of life. They were most generous and appeal from any charity was never unheeded, unless it savored of protestant progress, and in that they were as stern as rocks. No Protestant churches was considered by them as such. During the cholera, Aunt Victoire had tents erected just outside of Frederick where Irish laborers on the B&O road, then in the course of construction were cared for and nursed at her expense" (1913:10).

In assessing the Vincendières' Catholicism, Katherine Birmingham says, "The matter of the Vincendières' fervent religious beliefs is not easily reconciled with their treatment of the enslaved population" (2014:19). However, Catholicism and slavery were in fact very compatible. The Catholic Church assisted the development of the slave trade in Latin America and the Caribbean beginning in the 1500s. According to Richard Miller (1957:18), Catholic countries were "the prime movers in the revival of slavery in the Old World and the introduction of it into the New World." The five major countries that dominated slavery and the slave trade in the New World were either Catholic, or still retained strong Catholic influences, including Spain, Portugal, France, England, and the Netherlands (18).

Catholicism was the official religion of Saint Domingue, where the Catholic Church maintained a constant presence from before it was a French colony and even after it achieved independence. The Church played an active role in colonial politics and society, and Catholicism was incorporated into Saint Domingue's laws and policies. The Code Noir, which sought to regulate master-slave relations in all the French slaveholding colonies of the Caribbean, features Catholicism as a central element of the preamble and the first fourteen articles, which require baptism and religious instruction of enslaved people, provided for their marriages and burials, and prohibited the exercise of any other religion than Roman Catholic faith. The incorporation of Catholicism into the Code Noir was a strategic move intended to alleviate concerns that slavery was un-Christian.

The Catholic Church justified slavery with a series of papal bulls, beginning with Pope Nicholas V's *Dum Diversas* (1452), which authorized the European invasion of Africa, Asia, and the Americas and sanctioned perpetual enslavement, and Pope Alexander VI's *Inter Caetera* (1493), in which the Church morally sanctioned the development of the transatlantic slave trade. It was in the interest of the Church to condone slavery, as it was enslaved labor that funded missions and other Church activities and built Catholic churches and other properties.

The Society of Jesus participated in slaveholding from the sixteenth to the nineteenth centuries, and by the mid-eighteenth century Jesuits owned about 2,000 enslaved people in the British and French colonies of northern America (Collins and Dial 2020). French Jesuits became involved in the Atlantic slave trade in the mid-seventeenth century through sugar production, using this highly profitable and labor-intensive crop to fund their Caribbean missions. French colonial plantations made extensive use of enslaved labor from Africa. By the mid-eighteenth century, Jesuits ran multiple cash crop plantations with enslaved labor across the Caribbean (Collins and Dial 2020).

Jesuits in the United States acquired enslaved laborers in the late seventeenth century and continued to own and trade enslaved people throughout 1800s. Over the course of the nineteenth century, the Jesuits in northern America owned, rented, and received as payment in kind on term more than 700 people. The Jesuits concentrated most of their enslaved labor at six plantations across Maryland (Inigoe's Manor and Newtown Manor in St. Mary's County, St. Joseph in Talbot County, St. Thomas Manor in Charles County, Bohemia in Cecil County, and White Marsh Manor in Prince George's County) but also had a large population of enslaved workers in Louisiana.

While some Catholics condemned slavery, many tended to accept that slavery was the natural world order and even benefited Africans as it saved them from their "heathen" ways. One Jesuit priest in the colonial Caribbean wrote that

> The slavery of the blacks will seem to you inconsistent with the holy laws of Christianity, but you will change your mind once you reflect on the priceless good fortune they have in being illuminated by the purest lights of the true religion. This is an advantage they would not have had in their land, all of which is immersed in the thickest darkness of paganism. (Harrigan 2021:218)

To Catholic slaveholders, particularly Jesuits, enslaved people were possessed not for the good of the master, but for the benefit of the enslaved. God had given enslaved people to the master because these "inferior" people needed to be governed by someone of higher wisdom and social status if they were to achieve eternal salvation (Murphy 2001). Catholic support of slavery was rationalized by white supremacist notions that Black people were subhuman and the Church was improving their lives by introducing them to Catholicism. While Jesuit slaveholders may have condemned violent and abusive treatment of enslaved people, they considered "benevolent" slavery to be acceptable. Furthermore, when Jesuits refrained from or abandoned the use of enslaved labor, they nearly always did so for financial reasons or because of legal prohibitions, rather than out of principled opposition. The Jesuit order in the United States did not participate in the nineteenth-century abolition movement, and some Jesuits openly countered this movement with arguments that slavery was socially and morally beneficial for Black people. (Collins and Dial 2020). Given the ubiquity of these beliefs throughout Saint Domingue and Maryland, it stands to reason that the Vincendières may have relied on Catholic teachings to support their purchase and sale of enslaved people and their exploitation of enslaved labor.

Inextricably bound in the racism and colonialism of the time was a deep fear of colonized and enslaved subjects, a fear that slaveowners attempted to mitigate through manipulation, control, and violence. Planters were "obsessed with containing and controlling slaves . . . they lived in constant terror of their slaves" (Midlo Hall 1971:52). Slaveowners perceived their enslaved workers as a threat to their safety, status, and wealth, even while enslaved labor provided those very things. Though white slaveowners possessed a great deal more structural, legal, and social power than enslaved people, their enslaved workers still managed to find spaces to rebel, resist, and exercise autonomy in ways large and small. These acts of assertion and resistance—or even the threat of them occurring—put slaveowners on edge. Their lack of trust in enslaved laborers had far-reaching impacts, including the passage of restrictive laws, increased violence and abusive treatment of enslaved people, and implementation of strict practices of control on plantations.

The Vincendières' cruel and controlling behavior toward their enslaved population was undoubtedly linked to a global system of white domination, and I argue that it can be further attributed to their fear of losing the rewards of that domination. While their behavior was not unusual for its time, I contend that their reasons for acting as such may be attributed in part to their specific experiences in Saint Domingue. After having enjoyed an upper-class existence in Saint Domingue, the Vincendières lost their property, home, livelihood, wealth, and way of life in the events leading to the Haitian Revolution. Following this experience of rupture and loss, the Vincendières may have been fearful of rebellion and therefore implemented harsher treatment and stricter control. Moreau de Saint-Méry wrote in 1789 of slaveowners in Saint Domingue, "the reason for the concern of the planters was very simple, of course. They feared that the servile problem would get out of hand and that the white régime would be overthrown" (1985:270). The Vincendières may have taken these fears with them when they immigrated to Frederick and established another plantation, where they were again vastly outnumbered by enslaved people. The strictly controlled L'Hermitage landscape, including the uniform slave quarters and precision of layout, may reflect the Vincendières' attempts to increase security and protect their assets, while their harsh discipline and mistreatment of their enslaved workers may have been intended to assert their power and keep enslaved people in a subordinate position. Such measures may have been particularly important to the Vincendières who, after having experienced slave uprisings in Saint Domingue, may have been especially concerned with the discipline and control of their enslaved workers to prevent another such event. Fear, anxiety, and insecurity around potential loss of status, stability, and wealth, and potential resistance and rebellion on the part of enslaved workers, may have manifested in both material and violent ways on the L'Hermitage landscape.

Colonial and plantation environments (which were often one and the same, as in Saint Domingue) have frequently been characterized as fraught with anxiety and paranoia (e.g., Wilson 2008, Cobb and Sapp 2014, Delle 2014), where there was "the seemingly constant fear and concern of colonizers with the threat of violence on the part of the colonized" (Green 2002:813). Likewise, Harald Fischer-Tiné (2016:1) argues that

> the history of colonial empires has been shaped to a considerable extent by negative emotions such as anxiety, fear and embarrassment, as well as by the regular occurrence of panics. This is perhaps most obvious if we zoom in on the group of the ruling colonial elites. Contrary to their well-known literary and visual self-representations, Europeans who were part of the imperial enterprise were not always cool, calm and collected while 'running the show' of empire. Quite the reverse: one of the seemingly paradoxical effects of the asymmetries characteristic of the situation coloniale, which put a minuscule elite of culturally alien colonizers in a position to exercise power over an often numerically stronger 'native' population, was the fact that anxiety, fear and angst became part of their everyday experience.

Plantation environments were characterized by a situation in which white planters "had established an awesomely productive economy in which they made enormous profits. On the other hand, they made those profits within a highly distorted social structure that included a mass of exploited, brutalized, and resentful African slaves" (Burnard 2004:138). The awareness that enslaved workers were not cooperating of their own free will but through coercion, and that they could resist or rebel at any time, produced anxiety in slaveowners. They expected resistance from their enslaved workers but could not predict when it would occur or what form it would take, lending a sense of danger and vulnerability to the plantation landscape (Peckham 2015:24).

Planters and colonists attempted to appear as though their power was safe and secure, but "such acts of self-assertion only thinly concealed a subterranean—and no less constant—strain of doubt. Beneath the pomp and ceremony, anxiety was perennial to empire" (Jackson 2016:73). Elites give the appearance of being in control, but they were actually often acting defensively or reactively: "colonial discourse only *seems* to be successful in its domination of the colonized. Underneath its apparent success, this discourse is secretly marked by radical anxiety about its aims, its claims, and its achievements" (Huddart 2005:5).

Ironically, the very same conditions required in a successful plantation and/or colony were those that were anxiety-provoking. In his assessment of eighteenth-century Jamaican plantation societies, Trevor Burnard points out that white colonists "had established an awesomely productive economy in which they made enormous profits. On the other hand, they made those profits within a highly distorted social structure that included a mass of exploited, brutalized, and resentful African slaves." The result was a society in which fear was, as the historian Bryan Edwards argued, "the leading principle upon which the government is supported" (Burnard 2004:138).

Many of these fears stemmed from the fact that, for slaveowners, enslaved Africans were the Other, an unknown entity, and therefore unpredictable, a great source of nervousness and anxiety. As Trevor Burnard points out, "The uncertainty of whites' position in the island was heightened by their profound lack of knowledge about Africans and African society" (Burnard 2004:142). Unity among slaves, shared customs and languages unknown to slavemasters, and the retainment of a culture that slaveowners could not access or engage created a great deal of fear of the unknown (Murphy 2011:2). "The degree of unity among slaves and the danger that that unity posed to whites who knew little and understood less of African customs and language" (Burnard 2004:43); "the discovery of slaves retaining their own culture, a culture to which slave owners could not access nor engage, created a great deal of fear—namely of the unknown" (Murphy 2011:2).

According to Homi Bhabha, this fear of the unknown was the primary cause of colonial anxiety. Colonists stereotyped the Other (e.g., African slaves) in order to satisfy "the colonial desire to know the inscrutable natives in their peculiar or different specificity"; however, this fixed and oversimplified perception of the Other is constantly disrupted by the colonized: "And every time the colonized announces its desire or breaks out of its objectified positions (that is, whenever it *speaks!*), such as in the times of armed anti-colonial resistance, the colonial imaginary breaks round this fault," resulting in uncertainty, insecurity, and anxiety (Thakur 2012:250). "Because it is not self-evident that colonial relationships should exist at all, something needs to supply an explanation for colonialism. One explanation has often been the supposed inferiority of the colonized people. Through racist jokes, cinematic images, and other forms of representation, the colonizer circulates stereotypes about the laziness or stupidity of the colonized population. These stereotypes seem to be a stable if false foundation upon which colonialism bases its power, and are something we should perhaps simply dismiss. However . . . their stability is not quite as assured as it seems, and that the strange anxieties underlying stereotypes can be productive for critics writing against colonialism" (Huddart 2005:35). The system of stereotypes and classification is established to give the illusion of order and control, but any such system must confront anomalies and inconsistencies—a destabilizing experience (Douglas 1966:36–39). For slaveowners, daily life on a plantation was full of these contradictions: enslaved individuals were portrayed as "savage and inhuman," yet at the same time they were valued for their skills and abilities; they were said to have a "debilitated mental capacity" yet planters also believed them capable of plotting rebellions (John 1999:45). Colonial administrators "pathologized native populations as naturally violent, secretive, ignorant or hyperemotional, lending themselves to a continual state of anxiety over potential loss of control" (Peckham 2015:5). According to Lacan (following Freud), anxiety is the result of when "the Other is too close, and the order of symbolization . . . is at risk of disappearing" (Harari 2001:xxxii), anxiety as "the feeling of being helpless in a hostile world" (Slater 2013:2) or "the feeling that one is living among enemies" (Moehle and Levitt 1991:177).

Thus the precarity of the master-slave/colonizer-colonized relationship is revealed, making it uncertain whether slaveowners ultimately have total knowledge of and control over their enslaved workers. On the one hand, colonial discourse recognizes colonized subjects (or any "Other") as difference; something "patently foreign and distant" (Bhabha 1994:73). On the other hand, it inserts the colonized into some familiar category ("black," "uncivilized," etc.). This is what enables the colonizer to believe that they know the colonized and thereby allow them to manage, regulate, or rule. Colonial discourse admits of something foreign but then rejects the difference by classifying it as something familiar. It tries to make the unknowable "entirely knowable and visible," seeking to fulfill its fantasy of coherence (Bhabha 1994:70). Enslavers and colonizers experienced a constant tension "between not knowing and yet knowing, between recognizing difference but disavowing it" (Go 2016:53). According to Terrence Epperson (1990:29), "All forms of domination are characterized by a fundamental contradiction between the exclusionary impulse represented by the need to create the 'Other' as different and alien and the need to incorporate the 'Other' into a single social and cultural system of domination."

A large plantation required significant numbers of workers in order to be productive and profitable, meaning that enslaved laborers often far outnumbered their captors. These unbalanced population ratios became a source of anxiety for enslavers, who were surrounded by large numbers of people they had deemed alien, unknown, and potentially violent. Therefore enslaved individuals could actually pose a threat; there were things they could feasibly do which would jeopardize the lives and livelihoods of their owners and risk the loss of that initial investment. In Saint Domingue, the white population grew 30% between 1681 and 1731, while the enslaved population grew 1,050% during this time (Garrigus 2006:32). The Vincendières were part of the racial minority not only in Saint Domingue but again in Frederick on their own plantation.

Ultimately, slaveowners were dependent on enslaved labor for their wealth. Dependence inherently results in a vulnerability on the part of the dependent. Charles Ball, a former slave, pointed out that, "There is, in fact, a mutual dependence between the master and his slave" (Taylor 1999:390). Dependency on another puts one in a vulnerable position; slaveowners were dependent on slaves for their livelihood and wealth. "This class of people across the Americas," notes Murphy, "had gained and were continuing to gain substantial riches because of slavery. However this wealth necessitated the co-operation of slavery for it to continue. It was not only their lives that were at threat; their livelihoods and their status in society (both of which were highly prized at the time) were dependent on slave complicity" (Murphy 2011:2). C.L.R. James (1963) points out that France was economically dependent upon its overseas colonies, such as Saint Domingue. The colonies provided them with enormous profits, but because those profits were made with a coercive system, it was ultimately a system founded on fear (Burnard 2004:138).

Indeed, the loss of the enslaved workers themselves would have significantly affected the Vincendières' financial security. As with most slaveholders, "Their own personal income and all the power and prestige that came from that were reliant on their successes in the plantation," and the co-operation of slavery was necessary in order to maintain their livelihoods and their status in society (Murphy 2011:2). Murphy states, "The financial investment of slave owners should also be remembered; the cost of purchasing slaves was not cheap. Slaves then were not commodities; they were investments that needed to be protected in order to yield any kind of profit. Not only that, they were risky investments; success (and wealth) were by no means guaranteed." Credit was necessary to operate plantation estates and maintain a planter's lifestyle, but to live on credit instead of currency put planters in a precarious position (Meniketti 2020:10).

The Vincendières were already in a precarious financial position, so further losses of their income could be enormously detrimental in their attempt to regain security and status and maintain their class standing following the loss of their property in the Haitian Revolution. Boisneuf and the Vincendières were involved in several legal cases regarding unpaid debts. Their legal troubles were not confined to Maryland but extended throughout the Atlantic world (Birmingham and Beasley 2014:14). Many of these debts may have originated due to the collapse of the plantation system in Saint Domingue, and they stayed with them throughout their lives. These debts likely influenced the decision to place L'Hermitage and its assets under the name of Victoire, in order to protect the land from creditors who may have been seeking Boisneuf or Magnan for repayment of these debts (Birmingham and Beasley 2014:15). The family and their associates had debts that followed them from Saint Domingue. Although plantations in the colony were some of the most lucrative in the world, plantation owners still borrowed money in order to get their operations off the ground, or expand their productivity (15). The reputation of the colony for producing landowners of great wealth, as well as the thriving economy toward the end of the eighteenth century, made the business of plantation management in the West Indies particularly competitive (15). Plantation owners often borrowed large sums of money from French merchants in order to expand their businesses. These loans were usually paid off over time, and in the case of a default the plantation was confiscated. The slave revolts rendered this system of loan default particularly difficult, however, as plantation owners no longer had the collateral of their plantations, instead having to pay in cash or goods. For individuals like Boisneuf and the Vincendières, these debts placed them in a difficult financial situation, as they had lost their lands and crops and needed to start over as refugees in another country, likely with new lines of credit. These debts complicated the lives of refugees, especially those like Boisneuf, who sought to continue to enjoy the lifestyle to which they were accustomed (15).

In all, these individuals were involved in an unusually high number of lawsuits involving their failure to pay for goods or services, or repay loans. It seems likely that Boisneuf and the Vincendières believed they should either be allowed to prolong their debts until they regained their properties in Saint Domingue, or have their debts forgiven entirely since their major assets were no longer under their control (Birmingham and Beasley 2014:16). It is more likely that Boisneuf was merely prolonging his financial obligations until the end of the conflict in Saint Domingue. Boisneuf, Étienne, and family friend Pierre Laberon still bequeathed their assets in Saint Domingue to relatives during the period after the revolt. It appears that many refugees believed that the slave revolt in the colony would fail, and that their assets would be returned to them. However, this would not come to fruition for the Vincendières, to whom the French government gave only 10% of the value of their property (Birmingham and Beasley 2014:16).

As plantation owners in Saint Domingue and the United States, the Vincendières may have experienced the fears described above, particularly after having experienced the slave uprisings that preceded the Haitian Revolution. There was no better illustration of the collective power of enslaved workers, for the Vincendières and others, than the Haitian Revolution and events leading up to it, which they had witnessed and may have been significantly affected by. Saint Dominguans experienced near-constant slave revolts and rebellions in the 1790s, which contributed to an environment of instability and insecurity for planters. Slaves practiced guerrilla warfare, escaped in large numbers (*marronnage*), and participated in massacres and mass destruction of Saint Domingue's cities and plantations. "Colonists lived in fear of being suddenly ruined by the loss of all their slaves. Planters going to bed at night owning 100 or 200 slaves could not be sure of waking up the next morning with even one" (Midlo Hall 1971:65). Sometimes slave resistance was smaller and subtler, but still had definite repercussions for slaveowners. Other forms of resistance included "partial revolts, conspiracies, plots to kill the master, suicide, infanticide, voodoo, poisonings" (Fick 1990:75). (Figure 4.1).

Poisonings in particular caused a great deal of panic in Saint Domingue. In the late 1700s, there were widespread reports of slaves poisoning their masters. In his writings on Saint Domingue, Moreau de Saint-Méry (1985:36) claimed that a quarter of the enslaved workers brought from Africa were sorcerers proficient in "the odious art of poisoning." It remains unclear how pervasive the practice actually was; perhaps the paranoia and panic were partially manufactured or fueled by rumors. But regardless of the veracity of these stories, they caused mass hysteria and witch hunts on Saint Dominguan plantations (Midlo Hall 1971:68–75, Burnard and Garrigus 2016:103–112, Gaspar and Hine 1996:248, Fick 1990:66–74, Moreau de Saint-Méry 1985:273). As Carolyn Fick points out, "what the masters believed their slaves capable of doing, what they thought the slaves could and would do, was equally as important as that which the slaves actually did or did not bring about through poison" (1990:67). When poisonings did occur, they were usually motivated by the desire to be free: "slaves who administered poison often did so in a highly calculated manner. . . . Some slaves would consciously administer small doses of poison in their master's food or drink as an initial warning. If the master's cruelty persisted, the doses could be increased and finally induce death" (Fick 1990:71).

In addition to threats to their health and physical safety, planters experienced violence and the destruction of their surroundings. Étienne Vin-

Figure 4.1. *Incendie du Cap. Révolte général des Nègres. Massacre des Blancs.* [Burning of Cap-Français. General revolt of the Negroes. Massacre of the whites.]. Engraving of a 1791 slave revolt created in Paris, 1815. Courtesy of the Library Company of Philadelphia.

cendière reported fleeing Saint Domingue "to avoid being murdered by the assassins armed by the Civil Commissioners Polverel and Sonthonax against all the planters of . . . St. Domingo" (South Carolina Will Book D 1800–1807). The diary of Mrs. Enoch Lowe recalls, "Aunt Victoire told me that her uncle was one of the victims of the Insurrection, having been shot by a native whilst seated at the dinner table" (Lowe 1913:17).

The physical destruction of Saint Domingue during the slave uprisings also had an enormous effect on those who witnessed it. Written accounts describe an environment of "ruins," "desolation," and "horror" (Gillikin 2014:239). "On landing, we found the town a heap of ruins. A more terrible picture of desolation cannot be imagined. Passing through streets choked with rubbish, we reached with difficulty a house. . . . The people live in tents, or make a kind of shelter, by laying a few boards across the half-consumed beams; for the buildings being here of hewn stone, with walls three feet thick, only the roofs and floors have been destroyed" (Sansay 2007:61, quoted in Gillikin 2014:239).

A personal account by M. Le Clerc, written in 1791, describes the violence and destruction he witnessed:

From a distance, it looked like universal desolation. Our ruin was complete. One person hardly recognized the site of his own plantation, the other the plantation of a friend he sought in vain. What the fire had spared, hands even more destructive than the flames had reduced to dust. We felt as though we were marching on the ruins of the world. Sad playthings of fate, the plantation owners mixed in with the main body of the army dragged themselves along, lost in contemplation of their misery. Soldiers and civilians, all shared our sufferings; no black, no animal, no living creature interrupted the silence of these deserts, broken only by the rumbling of the cannon and the slow and measured pace of the troops. (Quoted in Popkin 2008:97–98)

The Vincendières' experience with the slave uprisings in Saint Domingue demonstrated to them that the power and control of the white and wealthy were not absolute, thus they had reason to feel nervous and uneasy when they rebuilt a plantation with an enormous enslaved workforce that far outnumbered them.

Slavery funded their livelihood yet was also inherently dangerous, as their plantation was filled with "a people they both despised and feared" (Burnard 2004:19). Slaveowners knew that enslavement was an oppressive practice and feared what enslaved workers would do if given the opportunity for revenge: "Slaveholders . . . expected that the dehumanizing institution of black enslavement would compel those held in chains to attempt acts of bloody revenge. Advocates for the enslavement of black Americans understood that subjugation of another person required two essential ingredients: a culture willing to sanction oppression and a government that commanded a monopoly on the legal distribution of violence and was capable of enforcing it" (Paulus 2017:4).

Dominguan slaves were believed to be dangerous, as they might spread revolutionary ideas and incite rebellion among slaves of the American South. As refugees flooded the country, fear spread that slaveholders in the United States might suffer a similar uprising if they did not keep the slaves arriving from Saint Domingue under tight control. White Virginians referred to the enslaved refugees as "infected with the contagion of liberty," and Louisiana prohibited importation of Saint Dominguan slaves altogether (Rivers Cofield 2011:32). The U.S. government passed laws ending the country's participation in the international slave trade in 1807 due to this fear of Black Saint Domingans inciting insurrections: "During debate about enforcing the ban, one Pennsylvania congressman asked the House of Representatives 'to look at St. Domingo' as a reason to end the slave trade. The Haitian Revolution illustrated that slaves might 'learn the rights of man' and become 'proficient in the art of war' in order to obtain their freedom" (Paulus 2017:36). The transgression of these borders and boundaries, of there being a "pollution" of ideas or persons, or of "matter out of place," was viewed as dangerous in eighteenth- and early nineteenth-century America (cf. Douglas 1966). These fears were not entirely unfounded; "in the decade of the 1790s, slave uprisings in the United States increased by 150%, and many Americans blamed the refugees (Babb 1954:242–243). In order to maintain control, various states with a high number of refugees passed laws to regulate them" (Rivers Cofield 2011:32). In some cases they tried to make excuses for why Saint Domingue's enslaved people were able to rebel: the owners were too harsh, whites had carelessly allowed slaves to hear the rhetoric of freedom and equality, outsiders had infiltrated the slave society and provoked enslaved people to revolt.

In fact, slave revolts did occur in the United States that were likely inspired by the Haitian Revolution, but revolts actually had a much longer history that predated the Haitian Revolution: "There were at least 18 revolts in Maryland which began in the 1680s, and continued through 1688, 1705, 1738, 1739, 1805, 1814, 1817, and 1830, and occurred throughout the United States in 1831, 1835, 1840, 1845, 1855, and 1856; the only revolt recorded in 1857 occurred in Maryland" (LaRoche 2007:24). Furthermore, "In 1739, at least 200 insurgent conspirators led a systematic revolt in Prince George's County . . . careful planning and organization with a considerable period of preparation marked this type of revolt." The aim of establishing the "Negro" state revealed careful planning and a calculation of the numbers of reliable and trusted insurgents. Conspiracies were constantly rumored, uncovered, betrayed, and thwarted. In 1740, Maryland courts received depositions from several African Americans in Prince George's County "relating to a most wicked and dangerous Conspiracy having been formed by them to destroy his Majesty's Subjects within the Province, and to possess themselves of the whole Country." In 1753, the state again had to cope with "a conspiracy among Blacks to kill whites." As Vincent Harding notes, this fight was for Black possession of "the whole Country." Blacks closely followed the outbreak of the French and Indian War, hoping that the "French will give them their freedom." Frederick County, Maryland, reported insurrectionary movements among slaves after French soldiers and their Ohio Valley Indian allies routed General Edward Braddock in 1755. These stirrings for liberty, occurring twenty years before the American Revolution, suggest that Black people had deep seated desires for freedom derived independently of the political conflicts of the 1770s (LaRoche 2007:24–25).

Slave rebellions in the United States increased by 150% in the 1790s, a trend that was blamed on the "dangerous ideas" spread by enslaved workers from Saint Domingue (Babb 1954:242). A resident of Norfolk, Virginia, observed that, "Our negro Slaves have become extremely insolent & troublesome" due to their "associat(ion) with French Negroes from St. Domingo (with whom the place is also overrun)" (Egerton 2000:96). The extent of the influence of the French colonies is uncertain, but it is clear that organized slave resistance was becoming more prevalent in the early nineteenth century. In 1800, Gabriel Prosser, a blacksmith, and his brother Martin, a slave preacher, planned a major rebellion in Virginia, for which they recruited at least a thousand slaves (Mullin 1972). In 1811, 500 slaves took part in the German Coast Uprising in Louisiana. Five years later 1,300 formerly enslaved people joined Native Americans to battle U.S. Army troops in Florida (Turner 1905). In 1822, freed slave Denmark Vesey planned an insurrection in Charleston, South Carolina, but was caught—along with thirty-four other slaves—before carrying out the plot (Egerton and Paquette 2017). It was around this time that Victoire Vincendière began downsizing L'Hermitage's enslaved workforce. After they had seen four major rebellions organized in just over two decades, it is possible that the Vincendières responded by reducing their enslaved workforce. Grivno postulates that it was a combination of financial and security reasons that inspired plantation owners like the Vincendières to sell or manumit their enslaved workers:

Not only was slave property deemed unprofitable, it was becoming untenable. During the late eighteenth and early nineteenth centuries, Pennsylvania was transformed into free soil and a haven for runaway slaves through the workings of its gradual emancipation act and the implementation of anti-kidnapping statutes and a personal liberty law. Faced with an economy that was in the doldrums and fearful that their slaves would escape northward, slaveholders on the sectional border began to rid themselves of their human chattels. Frederick County's slave owners manumitted 630 people between 1790 and 1819 but did so out of motives that were far from altruistic. For most masters and mistresses, manumission was a desperate attempt to shore up their authority, not an expression of political or religious sentiments. (Grivno 2011:46)

Slaveowners in the United States never saw a major slave rebellion or revolution like that of Saint Domingue, and therefore they were not confronted with the violent consequences of their exploitative plantation econ-omy in quite the same way as Saint Dominguan slaveowners living through the Haitian Revolution. However, the only successful slave rebellion—in that it achieved its final aim of the overthrow of slavery—was that in Saint Domingue.

The consequences of this rebellion were widespread: the event served as a deeply felt reminder to all those with an economic interest in slavery of the potential risks involved. The rebellion would also have tapped into the second concern of anybody with an interest in slavery; the massacre of 2,000 white residents would have made it clear just how precarious their situation was:

> With the fall of white power in Saint-Domingue, the United States found itself neighbors with the only black-led nation in the Western Hemisphere. The wealthiest colony in the New World now belonged to those who had been brought there in shackles. The vulnerability of slavery as an institution had been exposed. American slaveholders detected their greatest horrors turning into reality merely a few hun-dred miles away. They feared that the ideology of the Haitian Revo-lution might spread to the continent, that the fires of insurrection might consume the South next. (Paulus 2017:16)

This fear, as a result of the Haitian rebellion, would have been felt all the more as it became apparent that the rebellion was an inspiration for many more (albeit unsuccessful) rebellions. For example, the Bussa rebellion of 1816 saw 400 enslaved workers from plantations across Barbados unite in a rebellion aimed at bringing about the ending of slavery. The rebellion lasted four days before ultimately failing, but it served as a demonstration once again of the potential power that enslaved Africans could possess. White slaveowners in the United States and Caribbean feared the spread of revolu-tionary ideas inspired by the Haitian Revolution and the birth of new ideas during the Enlightenment and French Revolution of 1789. The emergence of potentially damaging new ideas that challenged the status quo and the very ideas underpinning slavery were a threat to the fundamental organiza-tion of plantation societies.

The U.S. government passed laws ending the country's participation in the international slave trade in 1807 due to this fear of Black Saint Domin-gans inciting insurrections: "During debate about enforcing the ban, one Pennsylvania congressman asked the House of Representatives 'to look at

St. Domingo' as a reason to end the slave trade. The Haitian Revolution illustrated that slaves might 'learn the rights of man' and become 'proficient in the art of war' in order to obtain their freedom" (Paulus 2017:36).

The fears of slaveowners in the United States were further stoked by the fact that enslaved workers did engage in all sorts of acts of resistance, resilience, and persistence, on large and small scales. The historical and archaeological records display many examples of the ways in which enslaved people attempted to assert their humanity and autonomy. Some have argued that practices such as Hoodoo and other religious or magical traditions can be interpreted as resistance to dominant hegemony (Cochran 1999, Wilkie 1995). Evidence of such practices includes the water-ground and hand-ground porcelain triangles, Native American lithics, cowrie shells, and pierced coins found on Oakley Plantation in West Feliciana, Louisiana, that could be interpreted as religious artifacts representing efforts to manipulate supernatural powers and assert some measure of control over a life dictated by oppressive forces (Wilkie 1995:140). Items reflecting personal use, individuality, and independence among enslaved individuals include handmade pottery and pipes, tools, reworked mass-produced or natural items, coins, beads, cowrie shells, pierced coins, polished stones, clothing fasteners, reed-stem pipes, brooches, medallions, mouth harps, and haircombs (Reinhart 1984, Singleton 1995). These have been interpreted as symbols of resistance as they could have been used to "promote group cohesion and self-identity" (Orser and Funari 2001:62).

Little evidence reflecting the religious beliefs or affiliation of the enslaved individuals at L'Hermitage was identified in the archaeological record or primary sources. While some of the enslaved individuals were Catholic, additional religious beliefs are difficult to identify through the archaeological record. For nearly thirty years, archaeologists in the Middle Atlantic region have sought evidence of ethnic markers denoting cultural affiliations between enslaved individuals and African or Caribbean roots. Through some known spiritual practices, objects of interest on archaeological sites tend to focus on the presence of blue glass beads, incised utensils or pots, reworked European goods like pierced coins, and unusual objects like minerals, prehistoric objects, or quartz crystals (Klingelhofer 1987, Stine et al. 1996). Artifact caches have been used to extrapolate the spiritual beliefs of enslaved individuals at a number of slave sites within the Atlantic world (Galke et al. 1992, Patten 1992, Logan et al. 1992, Orser 1994). A large cache of quartz crystals under an overturned bowl at the Charles Carroll House in Annapolis, Maryland, was found to reflect the Central West African roots of the enslaved individuals who worked there (Logan et al. 1992). At the Utopia site in Virginia, brick and spiritual object-filled cache piles found within structural floors were interpreted as spiritual shrines. Similar brick piles uncovered in two interior hearth features at the L'Hermitage slave village were not associated with other objects of proposed spiritual significance. The majority of objects identified with the potential for spiritual meaning were found in disturbed contexts. One blue bead was identified within a plowzone context on the site, but no other beads were identified; 1/8″ screening of feature soil failed to recover more beads during the excavation.

A prehistoric projectile point, quartz crystal, unidentified mineral, and Spanish reale were identified within the buried "A" context of the outdoor activity area but were not cached in an in situ context. Two silver reales found in the northwest pier of Structure B may have been intentionally placed there; this cannot be confirmed since the pier had been robbed of its limestone supports, likely during the demolition of the structures. Additionally, the reales were not pierced, making it difficult to determine if these coins were used for spiritual purposes. As with many other sites in the region, such as the Nash site at Manassas National Battlefield, the probable spiritual remains found at the L'Hermitage slave village are inconclusive and cannot be associated with the specific West African cultures and the documented occurrence of specific spiritual practices of individuals at sites like Utopia and the Charles Carroll House (Galke et al. 1992, Samford 2007:166, Logan et al. 1992). In the case of the L'Hermitage slave village, the ethnic origins of the enslaved individuals, including those brought from Saint Domingue, are uncertain, and as such cannot further elucidate "ethnic markers" until more historic documentation about the enslaved population is uncovered (Birmingham and Beasley 2014:86–87).

However, we did discover artifacts that could be interpreted as representing enslaved workers' means of maintaining a sense of individuality and exercising personal choice. The archaeological record of enslaved individuals often includes a variety of items used for personal adornment. As Heath states, "men and women ornamented their clothing and themselves to display personal taste, to attract potential spouses, and to celebrate important events in their lives" (1999b:53). The enslaved laborers at L'Hermitage certainly utilized jewelry and other objects for adornment; the runaway slave advertisement for Pierre Louis (discussed in this chapter) indicated that he wore "a gold ear-ring in one ear" (*American Star* 1794). Jewelry and beads were associated with supernatural or religious powers, although these associations can be difficult to prove without knowing the origins or spiritual beliefs of the enslaved individuals living at the site (Parker and Heringle 1990:215, DeCorse 1999:148). While most of the materials used for adornment likely did not survive in the archaeological record due to decreased likelihood of their disposal and material type, several were identified during the excavation of the L'Hermitage slave village. One carved oyster shell pendant was recovered from the northeast pier associated with Structure B. While the origins and creation of the object are a mystery, this handmade, likely slave-made, decorative item is an interesting manifestation of cultural expression. It is unclear whether this object was fashioned to express spiritual or cultural beliefs, or for individual artistic motives. One small, blue handmade bead was identified in the area of Structure E within the plow-zone. It is possible that the use of quarter-inch screens over the majority of the site area decreased the rate of recovery for beads; however, eighth-inch screening of feature soil did not identify any additional beads within the site area. Two brass copper alloy decorated buckles were identified in the area of Structure B. One of these buckles was a shoe buckle, and the other likely a breech or hat buckle, although they could have been reused for any purpose. One watch fob fragment was identified at the site. Based on the runaway advertisement for Pierre Louis, it is clear that at least he, and likely other enslaved individuals, possessed watches (Birmingham and Beasley 2014:84).

Glassware made up 14% ($n = 2,416$) of the total L'Hermitage slave village assemblage, and several wine bottle bases and tumbler bases located within feature soils provide evidence that the enslaved individuals had access to these glasswares, although it is unknown whether they were reusing discarded bottles and vessels or purchasing them elsewhere. Many of these vessels were wine bottle fragments, indicating that the enslaved population either had access to wine, or were reusing emptied bottles as containers. The consumption of alcohol has been interpreted as representative of slave resistance in other plantation contexts (Smith 2008, 2004, Burton 2015, Fesler and Franklin 1999, Otto 1984); alcohol was a means of fostering a sense of community and group identity among enslaved individuals, and it was a means of labor resistance as drunkenness led to decreased productivity (Barker 1996).

Additionally, L'Hermitage was located close to the Pennsylvania border, and therefore close to a free state, which put the Vincendières at a greater risk of losing enslaved workers who attempted to gain freedom. A growing number of enslaved individuals escaped to Pennsylvania in the 1780s and 1790s, in spite of a stipulation in the state's law saying that runaway slaves from nearby states were not entitled to "any relief or shelter," and that slave-masters "shall have like right and aid to demand, claim and take away his slave . . . as he might have had in case this act had not been made" (Grivno 2011:45). In 1828, slaveholders in Frederick County complained that they had suffered "serious losses" from slaves escaping into Pennsylvania and cautioned that "the evil seems to be growing, and unless a speedy stop can be put to (it), much greater evils can be anticipated" (Grivno 2011:46). Within a few years, self-protection and refugee societies had been formed by free African Americans in Maryland and Pennsylvania to receive escap-ees going from Frederick to Franklin County in Pennsylvania and protected them from slavecatchers (LaRoche 2007:128). Running away did not always mean leaving permanently, though: sometimes enslaved workers went into the woods or visited friends and family at nearby plantations for a few hours or overnight before returning to their residence. For example, Lan-caster County Court records from 1722 recount the activities of an enslaved laborer named Madagascar Jack who lived and worked at Carter's Grove Plantation in Williamsburg, Virginia, noting that he "hath for some time past lain out hid & lurked in swamps and woods & other obscure places both here and in Maryland killing hogs & committing other injurys to his Majestys good subjects" (quoted in Epperson 1990:29). Perhaps some of the enslaved workers at L'Hermitage engaged in this type of temporary leave-taking; in 1800, neighbor Rebecca Dulaney sued Victoire Vincendière and Jean Payen de Boisneuf for damages after the trespass of enslaved individu-als on her property (Hait 2011:34).

In any case, attempting escape was a gamble for enslaved persons, as the threat of capture put those individuals in danger of serious beatings and torture, or the threat of torture to friends, family members, or loved ones who were left behind. For many enslaved individuals, escape was impracti-cal; familial and community obligations and connections were not easily severed. The majority of runaway slaves were men between the ages of six-teen and thirty-five, who were forced to cut ties to their families; slave nar-ratives indicate that these men felt intense guilt and loneliness for the rest of their lives after leaving their communities behind (Gutman 1976:265). Additionally, individuals were often unsure of where they would go geo-graphically and how they would support themselves; as one former slave stated, "We knew we could run away, but what then?" (Escott 1979:72). State laws in Maryland regarding runaways and the return of runaways located in other states were particularly harsh, requiring payment of any individual who aided or encouraged an enslaved individual in escape to reimburse the owner for the price of the slave, or be imprisoned for one to six years (Brackett 1889:79–80). Free blacks were required to carry papers on them at all times, especially during ship travel, and all ship captains were required to check their vessels for stowaways for fear of hefty government fines (Brackett 1889:75, 82–83).

On February 12, 1793, the United States Congress passed the Fugitive Slave Act of 1793, which allowed for the arrest of any runaway enslaved person. This act also made the penalties of assisting the escape of an enslaved individual cost prohibitive for the majority of the population, despite any moral objections they might have. It also ensured that runaway slaves could be sent back to their owners across state and territory lines. In addition to fear of substantial state and federal penalties for aiding escapees, the return of runaways was often rewarded with cash, thus providing encouragement for free individuals to keep an eye out for those who left the plantations (Brackett 1889:79–80, Escott 1979:72). Plantation owners or their legal representatives placed advertisements in newspapers around the area, as well as in areas that were suspected hiding places for the escaped individuals, including Pennsylvania (Brackett 1889:85). Enslaved individuals caught after attempting escape were often sold to southern plantations (Brackett 1889:81). Thus, escape was not an easy or a safe decision and came at great cost to the individuals who attempted it.

Historic newspaper advertisements show that at least five enslaved individuals ran away from L'Hermitage in an attempt to gain their freedom. In 1795, an advertisement was placed in the *Maryland Gazette* detailing the escape of a slave named Jerry. It reads:

Ran away from the subscriber, living near the middle ferry on Monocacy, Frederick county, about two weeks ago, a negro fellow named JERRY, about 25 years of age, a very stout well made negro, about 5 feet 7 inches high. He was bought of Doctor Davidge last spring, who formerly lived in Annapolis, where this negro was raised, who, in his master's absence to Britain, was hired out to work at brick-making both at Annapolis and Baltimore-town; at one or an-other of those places it is supposed he may be found. It is supposed that he carried off with him a bay horse and bridle; the horse is about fourteen hands high, and branded on the left buttock something like [upside-down T]. Whosoever takes up the said negro and puts him into gaol in Baltimore or Anne-Arundel county, shall receive SIX DOLLARS REWARD, and if brought home and delivered to me TWELVE DOL-LARS. 31- J. DELAVENCENDIERE Frederick county, December 1, 1795. (*Maryland Gazette* 1795:3)

Details about Jerry's life can be gleaned from this advertisement, including: his life in Annapolis, physical build, age, and skills as a brick-maker. In order to assist in his escape, Jerry stole a horse and horse tack. Jerry was thought to be returning to one of two cities, Baltimore or Annapolis, familiar to him based on his previous owner. It is unclear if these details were simply inferred by the Vincendières due to Jerry's past, or if some other individual, like the overseer or another enslaved individual, provided them. While there is no solid evidence regarding Jerry's capture, two years later a man named Jerry was cited in a court case as subject to "unmerciful beatings and whippings" brought against Boisneuf in 1797. It is uncertain if this is the same individual. An advertisement in the December 8, 1810, edition of the *Federal Gazette* provided information about the escape of François, also known as Cayou. It is likely that he was one of the enslaved individuals brought to Maryland by Magnan Vincendière in 1793. The advertisement reads:

Forty Dollars Reward Ran away in March 1809, from the plantation known by the name of L'Hermitage, the property of Miss V. Vincendière, near Frederick-Town; a French Negro Man called FRANCOIS, and only known by the name of Cayou. He is of common size, rather of a red colour, small eyes and deep heavy browed, big lips and large mouth, he has two of the incisive teeth wanting, speaks broken English and slowly, his tone of voice is harsh; he has been seen at Annapolis, some time ago, it is expected that he has got into the seafaring business. Whoever will secure said negro in any of the gaols of this State, or bring him back either to his Misstress on the plantation, up to the subscriber, corner of Frederick & Second sts. Baltimore, shall receive the above reward. P. LAFONT. N.B. Masters of vessels and other persons, are forewarned not to receive said negro on board, or give him shelter, as the law will be enforced against any person so off ending. (*Federal Gazette* 1810:1)

It is unknown if François (Cayou) was ever captured, or if he gained his freedom.

An enslaved worker named George ran away from L'Hermitage in July of 1811. It is possible that this is the same George referenced in the 1797 charge against Boisneuf for "unmerciful beatings and whippings." The advertisement states:

20 Dollars Reward. Ran away from the sub-scriber, living on Monocacy, near Marshall's Ferry (Georgetown road) three miles from Frederick-town, Maryland, on Saturday morning 29th July inst. a Negro man, named GEORGE, about 35 years of age, and 5 feet 4 or 5 inches high; strong built, narrow forehead, thick lips, small eyes, stammers and looks down when spoken to, walks quick and short steps. Whoever brings him back to the subscriber living as above state, or to Mr. P. Lafont, corner of Second and Frederick streets, Baltimore, or secures him in gaol and gives notice either to the subscriber or M. Lafont, will receive the above reward. Victoire Vincendière N. B. Masters of vessels and other persons are forewarned not to receive said negro on board, or give him shelter, as the law will be enforced against any person so off ending. July 26. (*Federal Gazette* 1811:4)

No further information regarding George could be located, and it is unknown if he was successful in his quest for freedom. It is likely that Jerry, François, and George ran away from L'Hermitage in order to escape the harsh treatment they received at the hands of the Vincendières and Boisneuf. These enslaved laborers were not only trying to escape a tyrannous and violent life, but were also seeking the self-determination that came along with freedom.

The fourth enslaved laborer that ran away from L'Hermitage, Pierre Louis, had a long and hard-fought battle, ultimately resulting in his freedom from bondage. Pierre Louis was one of the enslaved individuals registered by Boisneuf for importation into the United States on December 28, 1793. Pierre Louis was born ca. 1758 in Saint Domingue. Before his arrival in Maryland, he was the slave of Pierre Payan, brother of Jean Payen de Boisneuf. Pierre died in Saint Domingue in 1791, at which time Boisneuf took ownership of Pierre's assets as the executor of his brother's Saint Domingue estate; during this time Boisneuf was residing at his estate in France. Upon his arrival in the United States, Boisneuf chose to import Pierre Louis from Saint Domingue to the United States. On March 22, 1794, Pierre Louis chose one of the most straightforward and perilous methods to gain his freedom: he ran away from L'Hermitage. Two advertisements in French were placed—one in the *Baltimore Daily Intelligencer* on April 2, 1794, and the other in the *American Star* (a Philadelphia publication) on May 1, 1794. The ad from the *Daily Intelligencer* reads (translation):

Twenty Gourdes Reward Maroon has left on 22 of this month, after robbing the undersigned (his master), came from St. Domingo making his home in Frederick town. The Negro slave PIERRE LOUIS, he is about age 35, a weak temperament, height about 5 feet 8 inches, and large eyes, when he left he had a white hat, but it is unclear what he is wearing [because] he stole a large number that he carries in a packet. He has a small ring in one ear. He is peruquier, plays violin, and he speaks French & English poorly; in addition to the clothes that he stole, he also carries a gold watch & a violin. It is expected that he has taken the road to Baltimore, or Georgetown to try to get a passage to Charleston. Whoever takes the Negro, if it is ten miles from Frederick-town, will have six Gourdes reward, if forty miles, twelve Gourds & if out of the State of Maryland Twenty Gourdes. Contact Castinave & Walker, in Baltimore. (*Baltimore Daily Intelligencer* 1794:3 [translation by Michael Hait])

Another advertisement was placed in the *American Star,* but in English. It reads:

TWENTY DOLLARS REWARD. RAN AWAY from the Subscriber, living in Frederic-Town, Maryland, on the 22d of March, a NEGRO SLAVE, named PIERRE LOUIS, after robbing his master, Mr. Payen Boisneuf, from St. Domingo. The negro is about 35 years of age, of a weakly countenance, apt to cough sometimes, about 5 feet 8 inches high, with large eyes. His cloaths is uncertain; a gold earring in one of his ears; he is hair-dresser by trade; can play on the violin; Speaks bad English and French, and carried with him a gold watch. Whoever takes up the said negro when 10 miles from home, Six Dollars; if 40 miles, Twelve Dollars; and if out of the state, the above reward, paid by Mr. John Vaughan, merchant, Philadelphia; or by Messrs. Cazenave and Walker, merchants, Baltimore. PAYEN BOISNEUF. (*American Star* 1794:4)

These advertisements indicate that Pierre Louis was skilled as a wig maker and/or hairdresser and musician, and was at least partially bilingual. In his initial advertisement placed in early April, Boisneuf had a suspicion that Pierre Louis's ultimate goal was to reach Charleston, South Carolina; as Michael Hait speculates, this may have been because Pierre Louis was trying to reunite with one of the slaves of Étienne Vincendière (2011:102–103). The placement of the two ads in the *American Star* on May 1 indicates that Boisneuf believed Pierre Louis to be located in Philadelphia. Pierre Louis's escape was short-lived, as he was picked up in May 1794 as a vagrant—a homeless beggar—on the streets of Philadelphia, Pennsylvania (Nash 1998:57). In the years following the influx of Saint Domingue refugees to the United States, a number of slaves from that colony were picked up as vagrants. Philadelphia was one of the main centers of French refugee life in the United States at that time; while it is unknown how or whether Pierre Louis knew this, it was more likely that he could have started a life as a French speaker within that city (Nash 1998:46). Unfortunately for Pierre Louis, the Fugitive Slave Act of 1793, as previously described, required the Philadelphia courts to return him to Boisneuf in Maryland (Hait 2011:104).

Pierre Louis's attempts to gain his freedom did not stop after his return to L'Hermitage; instead of giving up, he tried a different tactic: a lawsuit. Although Maryland law declared that black individuals were assumed to be slaves unless proven otherwise, this created a loophole that allowed the presumed slaves to petition for their freedom and bear the burden of proof thereof (Brackett 1889:37). The Maryland Act of 1796 specified that slaves could file petitions for freedom in the county court of the jurisdiction in which they or the owners resided (MSA, Laws of Maryland 1811:358). It is unknown how Pierre Louis knew of or had access to these legal avenues, but on March 31, 1797, he filed a petition for freedom against Boisneuf and Victoire (MSA, FCC March 1797 no. 239). Later that year, during the November term, Boisneuf and L'Hermitage neighbor James Marshall filed recognizances at £120 each to allow Pierre Louis to attend the court to have his petition heard, since petitioners were treated as slaves until the court ruled otherwise (MSA, FCC November 1797 no. 5; Brackett 1889:162). During this period, it was unusual for the court to require that the owner of a petitioner file a recognizance (Brackett 1889:162). It seems as though requiring Boisneuf to file this recognizance was indeed a tactical decision on behalf of the court, as Boisneuf violated this order and had to appear in court to provide evidence as to why the case "should not be forfeited" (Hait 2011:104; FCCD March 1797). Frederick County Court finally heard Pierre Louis's case in the November 1798 term (FCCD November 1797). Victoire served as Boisneuf's witness. George Murdock, a leading Frederick citizen, served as a witness for Pierre Louis, while Joshua Dorsey, an active local attorney and prominent local citizen, served as his attorney. Selections from the transcript of the Frederick County Court proceedings state:

That your petitioner is now held in Slavery by Monsieur Payen Bois-neuf. . . . That your Petitioner was brought into the State of Maryland from the Island of Saint Domingo in the year seventeen hundred and ninety-three and is now held in Slavery as aforesaid. Your petitioner further sheweth that he is entitled to his freedom your petitioner therefore prays you Honors to take his case into consideration and grant him such relief as your honors may think right and your Petitioner will pray. The Court then reviewed Payen's failure to adhere to the earlier recognizance , and the case at hand, including Pierre Louis's request to recover twelve shillings and five hundred and eighteen pounds of tobacco from Payen in order to cover his court costs.

The case continued:

That the Petitioner was the Slave in St. Domingo of Piere Payan the Brother of the Defendant who was a Native and resident of St. Domingo and held the said Petitioner as his Slave until the said Piere Payans death which happened in January 1791 in St. Domingo That the said Defendant was appointed Executor and Testamentary Representative of the said Piere Payan but had not taken out letters Testamentary That the Defendant caused the said petitioner to be brought from St. Domingo to George Town in Montgomery County in the State of Maryland where he was landed on the 4th day of November 1793. . . . That the said Piere Lewis never was used as a domestic or house Slave by the Defendant before he was brought to america upon this Evidence as above stated the Petitioner was entitled to his freedom To which Opinion and direction the Defendant prayed leave to except.

Although the Frederick County Court (through the twelve jurors deciding the case) granted Pierre Louis his freedom, Boisneuf immediately filed an appeal that was heard in Annapolis, Maryland by the General Court of the Western Shore in October of 1799. The court upheld the earlier decision, making Pierre Louis a free man. Pierre Louis's case was made on the grounds that Boisneuf had imported him illegally. During his life in Saint Domingue, Pierre Louis was the servant of Payen's brother. Although Boisneuf inherited his brother's property including his slaves, upon the brother's death Pierre Louis never actually served Boisneuf. The 1792 law governing the importation of slaves from Saint Domingue was quite specific about only importing personal domestic servants, thus, Boisneuf was found to have broken the law (Laws of Maryland 1792:686–687). Although Pierre's earlier attempt at escape was stymied by the passing of the Fugitive Slave Act of 1793, his petition for freedom was successful based on more fortunate timing. The Maryland Act of 1796 allowed enslaved individuals the right to file petitions for freedom in the county court of the slaves or master's residence (MSA, Laws of Maryland 1811). While it is possible that Pierre Louis could have filed a petition for freedom based on more archaic laws, his chances of success and court assistance were likely increased due to the contemporary legal precedent.

It is unclear how Pierre Louis was acquainted with the particularities of the petition for freedom. His attorney, Joshua Dorsey, was admitted to the Frederick County bar in 1785, and he served in the Maryland House of Delegates for up to two terms beginning in 1791 (Scharf 1882:416, 478). According to the Maryland Court Dockets, Dorsey represented both enslaved individuals and plantation owners in court. Pierre Louis's main witness, George Murdock, was a slaveowner himself (U.S. Census 1790, 1800). While it remains a mystery as to why these individuals helped Pierre Louis, and whether or not Pierre Louis made his own inquiries about his legal rights, what is clear is that he had access to the greater community. It was likely this access that allowed him to obtain his freedom (Birmingham and Beasley 2014:33).

It was not unusual for enslaved laborers to develop networks outside the smaller plantation community. Enslaved laborers were often involved in small-scale economic activities and engaged in general, daily communication with community members, passersby, and business owners. As part of their duties, enslaved laborers could have been rented out to other farms or businesses, which would put them in contact with others in the community. As mentioned previously, enslaved individuals would be sold away from established networks in other areas, thus expanding their connections and knowledge of the world. It was through these networks that Pierre Louis might have established his relationship with his attorney and character witness in support of his petition for freedom, and how the escaped individuals may have planned their escapes. Enslaved individuals often created relationships with slaves owned by other individuals. Historic documentation indicates that Fillette, one of the enslaved women brought from Saint Domingue, may have been in a relationship with a slave named William, who was the property of John T. Shaaff. William, Fillette, and her four children were purchased on the same day by Nicholas Wilson and transported to Louisiana together. In a later document Fillette and William were recorded as married; however, it is unknown if they had a relationship prior to their sale to Nicholas Wilson (Hait 2011). Many enslaved individuals in central and western Maryland found themselves isolated due to smaller farms and landholdings typical in the region (as compared with the larger enslaved populations found on farms and plantations that grew staple crops). The smaller regional population of enslaved people employed on farms in Frederick County gave the enslaved fewer opportunities to gather and create networks. However, due to their location, the enslaved individuals at L'Hermitage may have had more opportunity to network based on their proximity to the Georgetown Road. The slave village at L'Hermitage was located in front of the main plantation house. This placed the quarters in very close proximity to the well-traveled Georgetown Road, which linked Georgetown with Fredericktown. The slave village was just north of the Monocacy River, close to the Middle Ford Ferry Crossing, where numerous travelers would have rested during their long and tiring journeys. Given these factors, it is likely that the enslaved at L'Hermitage had ample opportunities to communicate with free persons and other enslaved individuals, expanding their economic and personal networks. This communication could have taken place within the notice of the Vincendières, or at night when it was more difficult for the overseers to track their movements. The enslaved's proximity to the public road and ferry crossing may have also allowed some covert alliances to be formed (Birmingham and Beasley 2014:35).

The cultivation and sale of crops was another way in which enslaved workers asserted their autonomy and agency. The enclosure features discovered at the slave village site could have served a "functional purpose for the enslaved population, as well as an ideological purpose for the Vincendières" (Beasley et al. 2005:18.14). It was common for the enslaved to maintain their own vegetable gardens to supplement their diets (Hilliard 1972; Phillips 1966). These plots may have been individual or communal. Crops were used to feed enslaved populations and for sale at local markets, and they served to offset planters' investment in food and rations (Covey and Eisnach 2009:73). Furthermore, the yard space immediately in front of the slave quarters could not be viewed from the main house or secondary dwelling, giving enslaved workers some privacy away from the eyes of the Vincendières. Due to limited time and resources, we could not fully explore the L'Hermitage slave village, but a study to locate activity areas, pathways, gardens, animal pens, wells, evidence of yard sweeping, or privies would help us understand how the enslaved utilized their yard space, and how they viewed and functioned within their prescribed landscape (Birmingham and Beasley 2014:54).

Slaveowners reacted to enslaved workers' acts of resistance, rebellion, and disloyalty—real or perceived—with harsh discipline and cruel treatment. Their fears and paranoia motivated slaveowners to assert even more control over the environment and respond with increasingly strict, harsh measures toward enslaved workers. Those in positions of power tend to have the means to alter their environment, and to do so as a defense or reaction to fear. In some ways, this power is an illusion: "Because of the view that elites, through their control over resources, have the most power at their disposal, it is often assumed that they are the ones exercising power proactively and expansively. But it needs to be stressed that elites, especially in the face of change, tend to defend their interests and privileges as a reaction to external challenges to their position. The elite may apply its power to resist pressure to maintain the status quo, at least in certain domains. Hence, colonial elites who have lost their hegemony—their initial dominance over virtually all (public) spheres of life—have to move from exercising power over others directly to more strategic uses of their remaining resources to prevent them losing their power base and privileges" (Salverda 2010:117). These strategies often took the form of extremely violent reactions and brutalization for the most insignificant offenses. According to Delle (2000:3), it is precisely during these times of "capitalist crisis," when elites feel that their economic systems and white supremacy are threatened, that they "accelerate their attempts to reorganize the spaces of production, thus to secure and maintain their positions of socioeconomic dominance." Or, as Salverda and Hay (2013) put it, geographies are reshaped when elites face challenges to their dominance.

Slaveowners turned to racist ideologies, slave codes, and harsh discipline to keep their enslaved workers subdued and provide themselves with "a desperate sense of security" (Fick 1990:67, Knight 1970). Harrison posits that "Shock and fear tactics were necessary methods for enforcing labor and paralyzing the slave community to ensure the slavers' footing and security in the New World. The more slaves lived in fear and uncertainty the stronger the slaver and overseer's grip on their bodies, minds, and souls" (2009:67). Slaveowners' brutal treatment of enslaved individuals was not only acceptable, but also encouraged: "Terror, or naked power, was at the core of the institution of slavery. . . . Whites were encouraged to keep firm discipline and to punish slaves frequently and harshly. Indeed, whites frowned on overseers and planters who were deemed to be lenient toward their slaves" (Burnard 2004:149–150). For example, in Saint Domingue it was permissible for a slave who struck his/her master/mistress to be hanged (Code Noir, Article 33), for white colonists to kill any person of African descent who showed any sign of rebellion or refused to stop when encountered on a road (Loix, Ordonnance des Administrateurs, Article 21, March 27, 1721, cited in Moreau de Saint-Méry 1785:726; Loix, Ordre Concernant des Nègres de la Dependence du Cap, November 12, 1691, cited in Moreau de Saint-Méry 1784:502)—all because colonists were "concerned about threats to public order and continued existence of the colony posed by slaves," and the basic objectives of slave laws were to "preserve order in the colony, maintain and develop its wealth and continue its dependency on the mother country" and ultimately maintain social control (Midlo Hall 1971:81). Colonist Hilliard d'Auberteuil expressed the sentiments of white planters when he said that "In Saint Domingue, interest and security require that we crush the black race under so much contempt that whoever descends from it should be covered with indelible scars until the sixth generation" (1779:273).

Slaveowners also became more violent and controlling in the response to slave resistance: "when resistance occurred, slaveholders responded with vicious rapidity, as much to subdue their own fears as to smother revolution. Whether an act of perceived insolence was punished with a whipping, or whether an insurrection was quelled by hanging the leaders, the motive was always to keep the slaves in total subjection" (Orser 1991:40). Furthermore, planters "believed they could control any rebellion through harsh estate discipline. They were wary of what slaves were doing but were convinced they could effectively repress slave discontent. Few believed there was a limit to the amount of repression slaves would endure" (Burnard 2004:261). Slaveholders became more controlling over enslaved workers' living conditions in response to fears of uprisings. This was indicated materially; for example, by the end of the eighteenth century, the enslaved population at Rich Neck plantation in Virginia was eating a smaller variety of wild animals, and whites were eating less fish and meat that mirrored contemporary cuts. Maria Franklin (2004) hypothesizes that enslaved populations were starting to be controlled more closely at that time, so white slaveowners would have been attempting to rein in the use of firearms by the captives. Franklin asserts that this is a reflection of increased control due to white fear of, and reaction to, revolts and uprisings across the diaspora, such as the 1791 Haitian Revolution.

The "exceptional cruelty" with which the Vincendières treated their slaves may have been borne of this paranoia. The family may have had a genuine fear of their labor force, and this fear may have compelled them to make an example of any perceived offense committed by a slave. Furthermore, revenge and pride may have played a role as the family attempted to perpetuate their way of life despite the revolution that had taken it from them (Rivers Cofield 2006:283). Perhaps they were influenced by the colonial mentality in which "any brutality exercised by whites toward blacks could be excused by the fundamental necessity of keeping blacks subdued. Only in this way could white fears be assuaged. Such assumptions, of course, were a license for sadism and tyranny among all whites, not just those inclined to psychopathic behavior. Whites knew that they had the full support of the state and white public opinion for whatever they did toward slaves" (Burnard 2004:33). Consequently, slaveowners like the Vincendières could behave with impunity and assuage their fears in whatever way they deemed necessary.

Though the lengths to which they went to maintain control over their enslaved workers reveals the reality of their power, the Vincendières may have seen themselves as victims of an unfair attack, who lost everything—wealth, property, status—without just cause. From the perspective of Boisneuf and the Vincendières, these were crimes perpetrated by individuals whom they had been conditioned to see as highly inferior beings—mere chattel to be exploited as a means to a profit. The revolution created a situation ripe for a volatile emotional response from the refugees (Rivers Cofield 2011:35). Written accounts from that time demonstrate that refugees from Saint Domingue were more likely to cast themselves as "passive victims" than "active participants in the great events they recount" (Meadows 2000:94–95). These post-exile narratives shaped the belief among refugees and their descendants that the revolutions had "reversed their family's fortunes, separated members of the family, and caused all their hardships" (Meadows 2000:95). Refugees from Saint Domingue reportedly came to the United States around the time of the Haitian Revolution "destitute, bewildered, despairing, inflamed with race prejudice, passionately and fanatically opposed to the revolution and all its works in the island" (Childs 1940:16). Winston Babb (1954:388) surmises that "As a group, the refugees must have been, in modern psychological terms 'on the defensive.'"

Slaveowners' victim mentality and fear of potential harm perpetrated by enslaved workers were ironic in two key ways. The first is that while enslaved workers were capable of causing some level of harm—from inconvenience to destruction—to slaveowners, they were generally in far greater danger on a legal, social, and personal level. Enslaved workers had far more to fear, were more at risk, and were more oppressed on a day-to-day basis than their captors. Massive violent uprisings were not a daily occurrence, but the physical and mental abuse of slaves surely was. Slaves had objectively far less power, less security, and more to fear. In spite of whatever forms of rebellion, resistance, or resilience were displayed by enslaved workers, slaveowners basically always had the upper hand and the power to control their enslaved workers, exerting enormous influence on their physical, emotional, and psychological well-being. As Trevor Burnard notes, slavery was characterized by "disorganization, instability, and chaos," where enslaved workers "lived in a world of radical uncertainty. They were always vulnerable to the depredations of whites and fellow slaves" (2004:179). Enslaved workers' lack of autonomy meant that every day had the potential for abuse, starvation or malnutrition, disease, injury, sale and separation from family, and death (Young 1997:14). Undoubtedly the enslaved inhabitants of L'Hermitage were in a much more precarious position than the Vincendières, vulnerable in terms of both their structural power and their physical safety.

Furthermore, slaveowners' fears were often unfounded. The United States did not experience major slave uprisings, widespread poisonings, or other forms of upheaval that slaveowners so feared. In fact, the practice of chattel slavery lasted more than two centuries, a testament to the power of the system and the individual slaveowners who participated in it. As Robert Peckham points out, "the socially constructed nature of panic is demonstrated by the asymmetry between actual mortality figures and the fear elicited by the threat" (Peckham 2015:23). However, even though the perceived threats to slaveowners' safety and security were not always real or did not come to fruition, they motivated particular thoughts, beliefs, and behaviors enacted in the pursuit of security. As Hofstadter argues, "the paranoid style has to do with the way in which ideas are believed and advocated rather than with the truth or falsity of their content" (1965:4).

The crucial difference between the experience of fear and anxiety by slaveowners vs. enslaved people is that enslavers had power to react to their anxiety by implementing entire systems, institutions, and laws to make them feel more secure. Slaveowners and enslaved workers were both subject to situations that provoked a sense of vulnerability and precarity, but only slaveowners had the power and resources to assuage their fears through changes on a structural or material level. Indeed, the mark of being in a position of power is to be able to manipulate one's environment to ensure one's own safety and security. Slaveowners could structure the plantation landscape around their comfort, values, and needs, in contrast to enslaved workers who also had fears and insecurities that were generally more real and urgent, but they did not have the same power to manipulate their environment.

When reviewing the ways in which slaveowners and colonizers put great effort into securing their position and power and protecting their property and wealth through discipline and control of their enslaved workforce, a second irony becomes obvious. The fears of slaveowners like the Vincendières stemmed from the very system they had created and upheld. The Vincendières were in fact the architects of their own precarity; they chose to participate in a system of radical inequality—and an institution that condoned cruelty, violence, rape, and even murder—and to live in environments where they were dependent on the labor and subordination of others in order to maintain their quality of life. Political elites and slaveowners like the Vincendières used a variety of strategies to suppress their enslaved population in order to quell their own fears, including corporal punishment and control over living conditions, but they did not attempt to give up slavery and their investment in the plantation economy. A formerly enslaved person, Olaudah Equiano (1789), describes the ways in which slaves were abused and dehumanized by slaveowners and asks, "above all, are there no dangers attending this mode of treatment? Are you not hourly in dread of an insurrection?" He goes on to say that the balm for this anxiety is clear: "[B]y changing your conduct, and treating your slaves as men, every cause of fear would be banished. They would be faithful, honest, intelligent and vigorous; and peace, prosperity, and happiness, would attend you" (Equiano 1789). By contrast, the Vincendières created another "nervous landscape" in Maryland, despite having witnessed the demise and destruction of their plantations in Saint Domingue. Given the fears, vulnerabilities, and anxieties widely experienced by plantation owners in the United States and Caribbean, one wonders why the Vincendières persevered in their participation in the plantation economy. Did they ever question the plantation system that had failed so spectacularly in Saint Domingue? Why imitate those conditions in the United States, develop another plantation, purchase an enormous enslaved workforce, and maintain it for thirty-five years? Why not move to a small family farm, like their neighbors in Frederick, or move into the city center, as Victoire Vincendière did toward the end of her life? Perhaps the family was far too invested in trying to regain the status, wealth, and lifestyle they had lost in Saint Domingue, perhaps they turned toward that which was comfortable and familiar in an unfamiliar place. Perhaps the Vincendières believed that they could ultimately find a way to have total control over their plantation environment and enslaved workers, the control that they lost in Saint Domingue. We will likely never know the reasons behind the Vincendières' decision to purchase and develop L'Hermitage, but they clearly made a choice to uphold a dehumanizing, exploitative system rather than embarking on a new alternative.

Though slaveowners held most of the power in the master-slave relationship, their power was often not absolute. Plantations were the site of constant tension and negotiation—a dialectical relationship that played out over the landscape at all times (Thomas 1998:531). John Blassingame (1972:211) characterized the institution of slavery as "one continual tug of war." Planters tried to exert economic and social control over the people they owned, while enslaved workers tried to assert themselves in the face of this dominance. Trevor Burnard (2004:10) describes the dynamic as such:

> Whites had most of the power in society and exercised that power ruthlessly, but they did not hold a monopoly over power. Slaves possessed little power, but what they had, they used, sometimes to extraordinary effect. Masters did not always win; slaves did not always lose. But masters always had the upper hand, primarily because they controlled the coercive powers of the state.

Any time enslaved individuals engaged in acts of resistance or asserted their agency or humanity, enslavers were forced to reckon with the fact that they were not omnipotent, and that enslaved people were human beings with skills, intelligence, and resilience, who could and would exercise autonomy and seek freedom if they had the chance. Enslaved people's resistance efforts revealed the fragility and vulnerabilities of white slaveowners, as did the latter's show of force. After all, if slaveowners felt secure in their position, why would they be compelled to work so hard to maintain it? Ultimately, slaveowners' feelings of paranoia, anxiety, and fear were linked to the realization that their power and authority were never complete, and that enslaved people were never totally powerless (Thomas 1998:532). The fragility of one's position reflects the precarity of power, which, according to Judith Butler, "relies on a mechanism of reproduction that can and does go awry" (2009:ii). Butler's words echo the nervous landscape concept. According to Byrne (2003), nervousness is the result of "gaps in the grid," and the realization that one's power is not, in fact, absolute, nor can one count on the security or stability of the "grid." To be in a vulnerable or precarious position demonstrates that one's power is not absolute: "elites cannot take their position for granted, but also that one elite rarely controls all resources, such as land, financial means, parliamentary control, knowledge and access to force" (Salverda and Hay 2014:237). Du Bois's (1920) exploration of the fragility of the powerful led him to conclude that white colonizers and empire-builders were "super-men" and "world-mastering demi-gods" with "feet of clay."

It is clear that the Vincendières restricted their enslaved workers' agency and autonomy in many ways, and I interpret their extreme measures of control as a sign of their insecurity around the real or perceived precarious nature of the plantation dynamics and their fear of losing their status, wealth, power, and bodily integrity. Judith Butler argues that precarity—the condition that "Anything living can be expunged at will or by accident; and its persistence is in no sense guaranteed"—results in the creation of social and political institutions to "minimize conditions of precarity" (2009:ii). In the case of the Vincendières, I argue that their fears manifested in several different attempts to exercise control, including their treatment of enslaved workers and their manipulation of the landscape. Conceptual artist Jenny Holzer wrote in one of her *Inflammatory Essays* (1979–1982), "Knowing you have power has to be the biggest high, the greatest comfort. It is complete security, protection from hurt." I interpret the Vincendières' cruel and domineering actions, as well as their continued participation in slavery in the United States, as motivated by this desire for security, comfort, and protection, which the family was willing to pursue at the expense of human life and liberty.

While I understand the Vincendières' behavior to be shaped by racist and classist systems and structures in their environment, I have proposed an interpretation that gives attention to the circumstantial and psychological factors that motivated the family's cruel behavior. Racist measures were carried out to protect the privileged status and economic and political dominance of white Europeans, who feared that enslaved and free people of color, when in the majority, would realize their potential power and revolt. The system (racism) and the emotion (fear) went hand-in-hand in contributing to brutal treatment of enslaved workers.

I thought of the Vincendières when I came across the concept of the vulnerability cycle, a phrase coined by therapists Scheinkman and Fishbane (2004). They describe a phenomenon in which individuals have vulnerabilities, sensitivities, or trauma from past experience that can be triggered by the dynamics of a relationship, resulting in "intense reactivity and pain" (Scheinkman and Fishbane 2004:281). These vulnerabilities

> include experiences of loss, abandonment, abuse, betrayal, humiliation, injustice, rejection, or neglect, and feeling insecure, disempowered, unprotected, or inadequate. When vulnerabilities are triggered . . . the individual tends to perceive risk and anticipate pain. He or she then reacts to the actual or perceived hurtful behavior of the other person in an automatic way, as if the present situation is in essence the same as a stressful situation experienced in the past, or in a context outside the relationship. In the moment when vulnerabilities are triggered . . . there is a collapse of meanings between present and past, or an overlap of meanings from two different contexts. These overlaps can confuse the individual, stimulate pain, and trigger self-protective modes of reacting. (281)

Scheinkman and Fishbane explain that such reactions can be counter-productive and even violent. While such reactions are understandable in context of the past trauma, they are neither justified nor excusable. Similarly, the Vincendières' experience in Saint Domingue—which may have resulted in a lasting effect on their feeling of safety and security—did not justify or excuse their cruelty toward their enslaved nor their participation in chattel slavery.

By highlighting the Vincendières' potentially traumatizing experiences, I am not arguing that those experiences were somehow equally or more difficult than those of their enslaved workers.

Judith Butler (2005) has asked whether it is an act of violence to highlight white trauma, and this project has forced me to wrestle with the ways that we can talk about white trauma in an ethically responsible way, one that provides context and an explanation for behavior, but not a justification or excuse. Because to talk about the legacy of slavery is also to talk of "white trauma" and acknowledge, as Tracey Walker argues (2012:171), that "everyone implicated in slavery was traumatized." My focus on the Vincendières' anxiety is not meant to indicate that they were more vulnerable than their enslaved workers, or that their emotions or experiences are more important or interesting. Undoubtedly the enslaved inhabitants of L'Hermitage were in a much more precarious position, vulnerable in terms of their lack of structural power and physical safety. As Trevor Burnard (2004:17) notes, slavery was characterized by "disorganization, instability, and chaos," where enslaved workers "lived in a world of radical uncertainty. They were always vulnerable to the depredations of whites and fellow slaves." In spite of whatever forms of rebellion, resistance, or resilience were displayed by enslaved workers, slaveowners generally always had the upper hand and the power to control enslaved people, exerting enormous influence on their physical, emotional, and psychological well-being.

My intention in focusing on the Vincendières' relationship to vulnerability and nervousness is to respond to Toni Morrison's charge to investigate "the mind, imagination, and behavior of masters" (1992:12). A critical analysis of oppressors' experiences and motivations can help address silences in the historical record, silences that persist in the present and contribute to ongoing structural inequality. To discuss enslavement without addressing the enslaver or portraying them as "shadowy figures" is to deny "the importance of the perpetrator in slavery's memory" (Walker 2012:169).

Indeed, I think there is a tendency to look at the cruel and oppressive behavior of slaveholders and dismiss them as evil monsters or an alien Other. I see how easily this narrative could be applied to the Vincendières—one could portray them as wealthy Catholic foreigners whose behavior was bizarre and out of control in comparison to the supposedly gentle German Protestant farmers around them. This is similar to the way that modern media categorizes those who commit horrific crimes as outsiders, foreigners, mentally ill, or misunderstood loners. I want to contextualize the actions and attitudes of plantation owners, *not* to garner sympathy for them, but to avoid these easy characterizations and distancing mechanisms. Nancy Scheper-Hughes and Philippe Bourgois (2003) argue that to characterize perpetrators as different or "other" as distinct from the "normal" human population obscures the pervasiveness of violence at the micro and macro levels. They state:

> Torturing and killing are as cultural as nursing the sick and wounded or burying and mourning the dead. We reject the view that violence is fundamentally a question of hard-wiring, genes or hormones, while certainly accepting that these contribute to human behavior, accelerating, amplifying, or modifying human emotions. But *brute* force is a misnomer, and it is the very *human* face of violence that we are trying to unravel here. Sadly, most violence is not "senseless" at all. (2003:3)

European and American slaveowners were not uniquely hard-wired to create and participate in a racist system; cultural conditioning shaped their beliefs and actions. Several scholars have written about the psychological effects of participating in a dehumanizing system, which left slaveowners and colonizers without empathy, humanity, or compassion. Toni Morrison (quoted in Gilroy 1993:178) argues that "Slavery broke the world in half, it broke it in every way. It broke Europe. It made them into something else, it made them slave masters, it made them crazy. You can't do that for hundreds of years and it not take a toll. They had to demonize not just the slaves but themselves." The writer and abolitionist Olaudah Equiano, who was enslaved until his early twenties, also argues this point, saying,

> Such a tendency has the slave-trade to debauch men's minds, and harden them to every feeling of humanity! For I will not suppose that the dealers in slaves are born worse than other men—No; it is the fatality of this mistaken avarice, that it corrupts the milk of human kindness and turns it into gall. And, had the pursuits of those men been different, they might have been as generous, as tender-hearted and just, as they are unfeeling, rapacious and cruel. (1789)

Martinican writer and political leader Aimé Césaire (2000:41) described the effects of colonization on the colonizer's mind, a phenomenon that closely parallels that of slavery and enslavers:

> They prove that colonization, I repeat, dehumanizes even the most civilized man; that colonial activity, colonial enterprise, colonial conquest, which is based on contempt for the native and justified by that contempt, inevitably tends to change him who undertakes it; that the colonizer, who in order to ease his conscience gets into the habit of seeing the other man as an animal accustoms himself to treating him like an animal, and tends objectively to transform himself into an animal.

Writing more generally about the psychology of the privileged classes and whiteness, Aida Hurtado is concerned with the "daily practices and psychological processes" involved in the exercising of whiteness and privilege, arguing that privileged, supremacist beliefs such as those described above "[take] psychological work to maintain. . . . it takes cognitive training not to empathize or feel for your victims" (1996:130; 149). What these authors convey is a commitment to understanding the beliefs and emotions in order to interrogate and understand domination, oppression, and white supremacy, in a plantation context and beyond.

To understand the behavior of the Vincendières and other slaveholders not as "senseless" but as partially motivated by a sense of fear, insecurity, entitlement, and a desire to remain at the top of the socioeconomic hierarchy and protect their power, status, and resources, and to understand that plantation owners didn't behave as they did just because it was their role but because there were multiple factors motivating their actions, is to have a deeper understanding of plantations, power dynamics, and humanity. To humanize and understand slaveowners' beliefs and actions is not to sympathize with and excuse them, but to illustrate how powerful the combination of fear and racism can be. The Vincendières' investment in their own supremacy, power, and privilege, and their investment in accumulating wealth and resources, prevented them from acknowledging and attending to the humanity, safety, and security of Black individuals. Even after seeing the consequences of participating in chattel slavery in Saint Domingue, the Vincendières attempted to replicate the system and perpetuate the violence, cruelty, and trauma that went with it.

It is important to consider how "ordinary people" exercise power over others, because as Hurtado (1996:124) says, "We are all potentially in the oppressor category, because whether we have power over others varies from context to context and is primarily determined by race, class, and gender." An understanding of these dynamics can help disrupt them in the present. By initiating this conversation about power and fear, we can link past events to oppressive practices, events, and policies in the present. As Paul Farmer (2004:309) points out, "Those who look only to powerful present-day actors to explain misery will fail to see how inequality is structured and legitimated over time. Which construction materials were used, and when, and why, and how?" Making connections between the past and the present demonstrates that the former isn't "over" and the latter doesn't exist in a vacuum.

5

Monocacy National Battlefield

A Nervous Landscape in the Present

The tensions and anxiety that played out on the Best Farm landscape were not simply relegated to the L'Hermitage period; the current landscape is also characterized by a kind of tension and therefore could be characterized as a nervous landscape even today, in terms of the tension between multiple and competing narratives at Best Farm (Bailey 2013). Monocacy National Battlefield has long been recognized as the site of an important Civil War battle, and considerable energy has been invested in educating the public about it. The emphasis on the Best Farm's Civil War connections is clear from the Monocacy National Battlefield website and public literature, as well as from its planning documents, all of which tie the site's significance to the 1864 battle and the subsequent memorializing and commemorative efforts (e.g., NPS 2009, Reed and Wallace 2004). However, in the past decade, archaeologists have pursued multiple research projects at Monocacy National Battlefield in order to expand interpretation of the site and provide broader context for the battle, with the most recent being the excavations undertaken to explore the slave village associated with L'Hermitage. Though the data have not yet been fully incorporated into Monocacy National Battlefield's interpretive materials, they form the basis of an alternative to the traditional battlefield narrative.

The promotion of certain values and ideals necessitates the omission of others that do not support the dominant ideology. In this case, the institution of slavery detracts from the promotion of a successful battle. Consequently, very little is remembered about African American history through the interpretation of the Best Farm, and a sanitized or distorted version of the past is created (Leon and Rosenzweig 1989:xix). Furthermore, this contributes to text that is selective, biased, and simplistic (Gatewood and Cameron 2004:207). As Lonnie Bunch points out, the desire to omit—"to forget disappointments, moments of evil, and great missteps—is both natural and instructive" (2007:2). It indicates which aspects of our history are considered shameful, unmentionable, or unimportant. Although slavery was one of the dominant forces in American life for almost 250 years, providing the basis of political and economic power, few institutions address this history and its legacy to the public (Bunch 2007:3). Bunch makes the observation that much of our struggle to find racial equality has been significantly influenced by slavery; therefore, race relations can never be fully addressed until we recognize their roots in a comprehensive, accessible fashion (2007:4). Furthermore, Shackel points out that if we leave minority histories out of the national public memory, we create a "consensus history" that lacks the richness of a more complicated, multicultural history (2005:24). It is for this reason that Ira Berlin charged NPS with the task of making "a history in which all Americans can see themselves" (2000).

This tension is an inherent part of the commemoration and memorialization of sites, structures, and landscapes. Commemoration is a selective process that memorializes certain aspects of lived experiences, particularly those elements that a community finds value in retaining and will make the past agreeable (Lowenthal 1996:148). One key characteristic of memory and the past is that they are produced and constructed. They undergo constant invention and reinvention; there is no single objective truth, or if it exists, it is never passed down without many alterations. As Lalone (2003:72) points out, "Historical representations vary depending on time period, political climate, intended audience, circumstances of presentation, and producer's background and intent." The past is often improved in some way; it is "always altered for motives that reflect present needs. We reshape our heritage to make it attractive in modern terms, we seek to make it part of ourselves, and ourselves part of it; we conform it to our self-images and aspirations" (Lowenthal 1985:348); the past is neither static nor absolute (Lowenthal 1975).

Knowledge of one's past and one's heritage can confirm and enhance one's identity and self-esteem, sustain one's roots, and validate claims to power, prestige, and property (Lowenthal 1985:53). Furthermore, a better understanding of the ways that memory and the past are constructed, maintained, forgotten, and disregarded will allow us to better understand the creation of the American landscape (Shackel 2003).

Historic landscapes are contested sites, where multiple groups and individuals vie for the final say in how and for what they are ultimately commemorated. In the case of battlefields, these antagonisms often take the form of the traditional, patriotic, or heroic portrayals of the past versus those who wish to redefine that past. The National Park Service is tasked with determining how to interpret historic battlefields in a neutral and objective fashion that will appeal to a broad audience with diverse interests. This is a challenging task, particularly because visitors bring their own memories and associations to battlefields.

Furthermore, commemorating painful or disturbing events and memories is particularly challenging. The Best Farm exemplifies Avery Gordon's concept of a haunted landscape (1997). She explains that to be haunted is "to be tied to historical and social effects"; to reckon with this haunting is to "make contact with what is without doubt often painful, difficult, and unsettling" (Gordon 1997:23) The Best Farm is a haunted landscape because events, lives, and experiences have gone unexplored and unrecognized, yet their presence remains through the existence of material evidence, records, and oral history. Some of this history is painful, as it deals with the enslavement and cruel treatment of human beings, or it deals with the conflict, violence, pain, and death of the Civil War. Foote argues that tragedy and violence are always marked on the landscape—sometimes formally commemorated through the sanctification, designation, rectification, or obliteration of sites and landscapes—but even those sites not marked leave an imprint on the landscape, culture, and public memory (1997:7).

The ties between landscape and memory are strong, with the former "often regarded as the materialization" of the latter (Ashmore and Knapp 1999:13). Landscape, memory, and the past are inextricably bound together and implicated in the creation of national identity and socially constituted histories (13). Due to their fixed and static physicality, monuments serve to reify memory and values that are in danger of contestation or obliteration. The establishment of a monument legitimizes the events, values, and ideologies for which it stands (Savage 1999:4).

As Bunch (2007:2) points out, "You can tell a great deal about a country or a people by what they deem important enough to remember; what they build monuments to celebrate; and what graces the walls of their museums." Similarly, Neff (2005:2) notes that monuments teach us as much, if not more, about the people who erected them than about those who they are meant to honor. Therefore, what do these battlefields and military monuments convey? According to Neff (2005:2), these commemorative spaces and structures "seek explicitly to preserve ideals and values in order to communicate them undiminished to the future." Those who build the memorials are attempting to preserve their understanding of the past and convey it unchanged to future generations. Likewise, Gatewood and Cameron (2004:207) argue that "the not-so-hidden agenda of most commemorative sites . . . is to serve as components of a patriotic landscape," and to "exist not just to educate citizenry, but to instill and sustain nationalistic impulses among the viewers." Similarly, Silberman (1999:5) notes that efforts at commemoration "[often serve] to bolster the political power of modern governments or national leaders, making their rule seem both justified and pre-ordained."

Civil War sites are popular tourist destinations today, spurred in part due to the release of books such as *The Killer Angels* and films such as *Gettysburg, Gods and Generals,* and *Lincoln* (Gatewood and Cameron 2004:193). However, an interest in commemorating and visiting battlefield sites has an even longer history, one that began shortly after the end of the Civil War.

The battlefield preservation movement was initially motivated by veterans groups such as the Sons of Confederate Veterans (Martin et al. 1997:172), whose call for the memorialization of battlefields in the 1880s and 1890s reflected the post–Civil War idea that the landscapes were sacred sites because soldiers had sacrificed their lives upon them (Venables 2012:149). The creation of patriotic landscapes was motivated by "the rise of historic preservation, monument building on a grand scale, the institutionalized celebration of the national past, improved transportation, and greater affluence" among white Americans in particular (Zelinsky 1988:95).

Following World War I, there was a great deal of national pride around the United States' status as a world power in military, economic, and social arenas (Smith 2008:xv). Patriotism became "an urgent issue" in the United States, and the government committed more resources to celebrating American victories, power, and success (Kulik 1989:16). Promoting nationalism and maintaining a certain American identity became of utmost importance; it is probably not a coincidence that in the 1920s there was increased support for establishing national battlefields and the passage of the most restrictive and racist immigration bill that the United States had seen (Kulik 1989:16).

Throughout the twentieth century, the role of battlefields evolved from a place to honor military sacrifices to a place to "combine patriotism and pleasure, to enjoy a vacation that would also provide a reassuring sense of social order, a strong feeling of comradeship, and a renewed pride in past accomplishment" (Patterson 1989:136). By the 1950s, national battlefields were firmly established as sites of both education and recreation, becoming popular places for families to stop on a longer road trip. Toward the end of the twentieth century, national programs were established to oversee battle-field preservation. The Civil War Trust, established in 1991, is a nonprofit organization devoted to battlefield preservation and public education; in 1996, Congress established the American Battlefield Protection Program to provide grants and technical assistance for battlefield research, survey and evaluation, planning, advocacy, and interpretation. State and local pro-grams, such as the Maryland Civil War Heritage Commission, were also established in the 1990s.

John Latschar, former superintendent of Gettysburg National Military Park, observed that, traditionally, programs "emphasized 'safe' reconcili-ationist topics. We discussed [the] battle and tactics, the decisions of gen-erals, the moving of regiments and batteries, the engagement of opposing units, and tales of heroism and valor. . . ." (Linenthal 2006:127–128) Thus, as Gatewood and Cameron argue, a battle such as Gettysburg, "came to be recast not as a place of fratricidal struggle or conflict over the racist impera-tive of slavery, but as a battle over heartfelt principles by two determined sides" (Gatewood and Cameron 2004:208). Promoting patriotism, nation-alism, and memorialization of American military history became more im-portant than delving into the messier, more sensitive topics of American cultural history (Smith 2008:xvi) That is, we prefer to focus on the aspects that are pleasing and uncomplicated rather than those that challenge our beliefs about the past and encourage us to consider the legacy of the Civil War in the present (Blight 2000).

As Patterson (1989:136) points out, these national battlefields serve a par-ticular purpose on the American landscape. They provide a place to "com-bine patriotism and pleasure, to enjoy a vacation that would also provide a reassuring sense of social order, a strong feeling of comradeship, and a re-newed pride in past accomplishment" (Patterson 1989:136). Battlefields have come to be seen as holy places and "sacred patriotic space, where memo-ries of the transformative power of war and the sacrificial heroism of the warrior are preserved" (Linenthal 1993:3). The dead are regarded as brave, heroic martyrs who lost their lives on the "altar of the nation" (Neff 2005:2) in the course of a battle over "heartfelt principles" (Gatewood and Cam-eron 2004:207). Gatewood and Cameron characterize battlefields as "holy sites" celebrating the "holy crusade" of war, visited by "pilgrims" (2004:194). The language used in books, brochures, and websites sometimes reinforces the sanctity of battlefields; Gettysburg is repeatedly described as a "hal-lowed ground," "national shrine," and "place of pilgrimage" in promotional literature (2004:194). In contrast to these depictions of sacred battlefields,

Bodnar (1992) regards these landscapes as purely utilitarian sites for professionals to promote national unity, middle-class values, and an official history. Those in positions of power embrace depictions of a timeless past; portrayals of the past as unchanging, abstract, and sacred are important in maintaining the status quo (Bodnar 1992). It is clear that regardless of the interpretation, battlefields serve an important ideological purpose for our public memory. Following Homi Bhabha (1990), I would argue that narrative practices are significant and worth investigating further because they play a key role in the formation of national consciousness.

As a reflection of these national values, battlefield parks tended to focus on battle events and the experiences of soldiers in combat. Promotion of these stories sometimes comes at the expense of a community's local and regional heritage (Martin et al. 1997:157). This issue was addressed at a 1998 conference, *Holding the High Ground,* at which managers of NPS battlefield sites gathered to discuss "principles and strategies for managing and interpreting Civil War battlefield landscapes" (NPS 1998:2). NPS acknowledged that its traditional approach to the interpretation of battlefield sites has stressed "the military tactics and strategy [the veterans] so loved. Like the returning veterans, we focus our interpretation on the experience of soldiers; we view the resource primarily through military eyes" (NPS 1998:2). The participants in *Holding the High Ground* note that the NPS portrays a skewed view of the past at battlefield sites, one that is biased racially and socio-economically and only tells the story of "the literate, the enfranchised, or the landed—those whose thoughts and actions are generally recorded in the historical record" (NPS 1998:2). Though this type of interpretation was "easiest and most convenient" (NPS 1998:9), it ignored significant aspects of American history. Although NPS called for change more than a decade ago in the course of this conference, vestiges of the old ways of interpreting battlefields still remain.

It was within this historical context that Monocacy National Battlefield was established and developed. As with other battlefields in the country, the commemorative process began soon after the Civil War ended. Growing patriotism, nationalism, and a devotion to reconciliation and memorialization of the post–Civil War nation supported the movement to add more markers and monuments and preserve the battlefield (Linenthal 1993). In the 1870s and 1880s, commemorative groups arose and began organizing the creation of monuments honoring those who had fought in the Battle of Monocacy. New Jersey, Pennsylvania, United Daughters of the Confederacy,

Vermont, and Maryland erected monuments at the site in 1907, 1908, 1914, 1915, and 1964, respectively. Glen Worthington, a local farm owner, was one of the first to call for the creation of a national battlefield. His campaign in the 1920s coincided with a government-sponsored systematic study of all battlefields, including Monocacy National Battlefield (Monocacy National Battlefield et al. 2009). Based on the findings of this study, congressional legislation was introduced to commemorate the battle.

On June 1, 1934, Congress authorized the establishment of Monocacy National Military Park (Public Law 73-443 H.R. 7982) but did not appropriate any funds for land acquisition (Reed and Wallace 2004:58). It was not until the centennial of the Civil War approached that people became interested again in the battlefield and wanted to organize for more federal support. Part of the motivation for this movement was the rapid urbanization that occurred in Frederick, especially following the 1950–1952 construction of Interstate 270, which cut through the battlefield. Local community members realized that such development could have a negative impact on Monocacy National Military Park and subsequently organized a grassroots movement to authorize NPS to establish boundaries and begin land acquisition.

In 1973, Monocacy National Battlefield—which consisted of approximately 1,500 acres at the time—was placed on the National Register of Historic Places and designated a National Historic Landmark; three years later, funds were also appropriated for the purchase of land (Public Law 94-578 H.R. 3830). Between 1976 and 2001, NPS acquired six properties (Thomas, Best, Worthington, Baker, and Lewis farms, and the Gambrill Mill property), with most of the funds coming from the federal government (particularly the Clinton administration), though the Civil War Preservation Trust contributed $36,000 for the purchase of the Thomas farm. In 1991, the 1,650-acre battlefield was opened to the public, though there was little interpretive material. Visitation has rapidly increased since then, perhaps due in part to the construction of a new Visitors Center in 2007 (NPS 2015).

Visitors to Monocacy National Battlefield are often surprised to learn that the landscape contains a history beyond the 1864 Civil War battle that inspired the creation of the park. They are even more surprised to learn that a plantation with a large enslaved population existed on the park's landscape in the late eighteenth and early nineteenth centuries; the perception is that slavery was not practiced so far north, less than an hour from the Pennsylvania border. The omission of a substantial discussion about slavery stems in part from the post-war reconciliation movement of the 1890s, when preservationists focused on militaristic honor and glory rather than the racial and social advancements made during the Civil War and Reconstruction (Boge and Boge 1993:21, Smith 2008:xvii). These preservationists portrayed battlefields as sites of military, rather than social or racial, conflict (Blight 2000, Smith 2008:xvii). The cultural conflicts of the nineteenth century were a dividing force, so military parks functioned to "limit controversy over the war and forget what had separated the country in the 1860s" (Smith 2004:129) by avoiding the issue of race and slavery, preferring to focus on what everyone could agree on: the valor, courage, and heroism of the Civil War soldiers (Smith 2008:xv).

Monocacy National Battlefield's interpretive materials—including brochures, web content, exhibits, and waysides—stress the importance of the Civil War battle, and highlight battle monuments and sites of combat. Visitors are encouraged to take a self-guided driving tour around the grounds or solicit the expertise of interpretive staff to learn more about the battle. On the anniversary of the battle, visitors are invited to watch demonstrations of weapons and soldier life. In addition, NPS employees deliver educational lectures to Civil War interest groups, avocational archaeologists, and other interested parties. The Visitors Center, located on a hill overlooking the battlefield, contains exhibits devoted to the Battle of Monocacy and, to a slightly lesser extent, the Civil War in general. The contents of the exhibit are largely devoted to the soldiers' experience. Artifacts in glass cases include weaponry, military pins, saddles, canteens, artillery, and uniforms (Figure 5.1). Around the perimeter of the room is a timeline detailing the political events leading up to the Civil War, and the first panels detail the spread of Civil War battles to the Shenandoah Valley. Most of the exhibit panels are devoted to taking the visitor through each event of the daylong battle and its after-effects.

The Visitors Center is located on a hill overlooking the battlefield. The first floor houses a gift shop, and at one point it contained a small freestanding display case featuring information about and materials from the evaluation study and Phase II testing performed at Best Farm between 2001 and 2003. More specifically, it presents information about the identification of the so-called slave village that would have been associated with L'Hermitage. Included are diagrams of the excavation units, photographs of the Best Farm and the excavation, and artifacts recovered from the investigation. The text supporting these items is focused solely on the excavation and the archaeological process, with little to no interpretation of the data

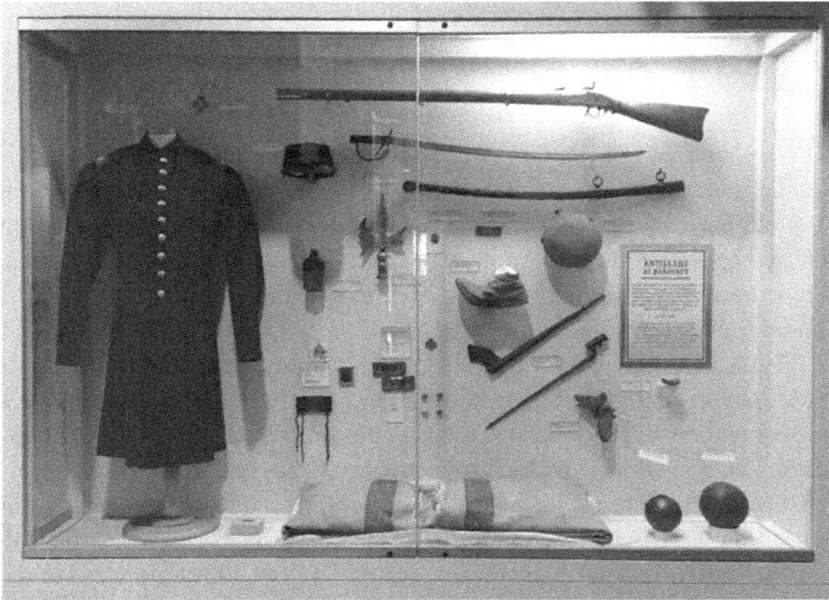

Figure 5.1. Artifact case located on the second floor of the Monocacy National Battlefield Visitor Center, 2018. Photo courtesy of the author.

recovered. The language is quite technical and straightforward, focusing on the facts of the excavation rather than social context. For example, one panel describes the site:

> Fourteen units revealed a linear, trench-like feature that met in a corner. It remains unclear precisely what the feature is; possibly an enclosed area. 479 artifacts of a domestic and architectural nature were found in this area, dating from the late eighteenth to early nineteenth centuries . . . The artifacts displayed here were discovered as part of the archaeological investigation.

A panel titled "Eyewitness leads archaeologists to the slave village" recounts the 1798 journal entry of Polish visitor Julian Niemcewicz, who noted of L'Hermitage, "One can see on the home farm instruments of torture, stocks, wooden horses, whips, etc. Two or three negroes crippled with torture have brought legal action." This exhibit does not focus on the alleged abuse at all; rather, the response to this quote is:

> Although this account exaggerated the amount of acreage and number of slaves, it contained enough verifiable information to help ar-

chaeologists narrow down the whereabouts of the slave village . . . their location relative to the river and "stone house" assisted the archaeologists in determining where to begin their investigation.

NPS shies away from discussing one of the most salient features of this quote, favoring the aspects that contribute to the archaeological excavation. Though the quote provided an excellent opportunity to discuss plantation life, power relations, and oppression, none of these topics are broached. Thus the archaeology of the site is made to seem more important than the actual social events that occurred on site.

The second floor of the Visitors Center is entirely devoted to the Battle of Monocacy and, to a slightly lesser extent, the Civil War in general. There is no mention of the prehistoric occupation of the land, nor do the Vincendières or any other early European families appear on the display panels. Slavery is addressed in a very broad fashion on a few of the panels, but enslaved populations are rarely tied to a specific property on the battlefield. Furthermore, civilians in general are all but ignored, unless portions of the battle were fought on their property. Instead, the focus is clearly on military strategies, combat, and soldiers.

The first panel at the entrance, titled "Monocacy: A Battle for Time," displays large photographs, primarily of white men (in fact, women rarely appear in the exhibit, the only notable example being Mary Quantrell, a Frederick resident who is recognized for having waved a U.S. flag in the presence of Confederate troops). The panel also contains several quotes that glorify the Battle of Monocacy. For example, Glenn Worthington is quoted as having said, "Here was a race between the two great contending forces, the state of which was the capital of the nation, its treasure and its prestige."

The contents of the exhibit are largely devoted to the soldiers' experience. Artifacts in glass cases include weaponry, military pins, saddles, canteens, artillery, and uniforms. Around the perimeter of the room is a timeline detailing the political events leading up to the Civil War, and the first panels detail the spread of Civil War battles to the Shenandoah Valley.

Most of the exhibit panels are devoted to taking the visitor through each event of the daylong battle. Beginning with the Confederates' decision to target Washington, DC, the exhibit text continues through each battle strategy, including Union organization and response, the desperation of the Confederates ("If victorious, we have everything to live for. If defeated, nothing will be left for us to live for." —General Robert E. Lee), morning action at the Worthington Farm, skirmishing at Jug Bridge, taking over Gambrill Mill, retreat over the railroad bridge, the final charge, climax at the Thomas Farm, Washington saved, withdrawal of Confederate troops, etc. If this list is a bit tedious, it is only to convey the exhaustive detail in which the Battle of Monocacy is recounted. Each battle tactic is analyzed for its potential consequences, and the generals leading the Union and Confederate troops—Lew Wallace and Robert E. Lee, respectively—are assessed for their ability to perceive and respond to events.

In addition to describing the battle itself in great detail, the exhibit follows the after-effects of the event. Some are specific to the Battle of Monocacy, such as the number of casualties suffered by each side, while others focus on national events, such as the reelection of Lincoln and the establishment of the Freemen's Bureau.

While the strategic military actions of the battle are clearly the center of attention in this exhibit, other themes are overtly or subtly on display. In very large letters, the words "Honor," "Remembrance," and "Dedication" headline three panels around the exhibit. These words succinctly capture the purpose of creating a national park: to honor those who fought in the Battle of Monocacy, to remember those who died in battle, and to dedicate monuments to the efforts of everyone involved in the battle.

The panel titled "Honor" celebrates the soldiers who participated in the battle for their bravery and devotion to their country and their cause. A photograph of a Medal of Honor awarded to Lt. George E. Davis in 1892 for bravery is on display; the caption notes that though Davis valued this prize, "his greatest reward remained the service he had rendered his country." The glorification of national loyalty is echoed by a statement from the Maryland Senate Joint Resolution of January 1931, which notes that Monocacy National Battlefield park should serve as a "resting place and a shrine where thousands of travelers and tourists could rest and renew their patriotism by a contemplation of 'the lofty deeds which there have been wrought; of the great hearts which spent themselves here.'" According to the exhibit, patriotism and national pride are valued qualities for which soldiers should be honored.

The "Remembrance" panel consists of an enormous photograph of a cemetery, and the text describes the movement of the Union and Confederate dead to their respective burying grounds. It seems that in this exhibit, the Battle of Monocacy, and even the Civil War, is not meant to be remembered as a conflict between "right" and "wrong," or an event for which one side should take the blame. Instead, NPS takes a rather neutral position that enforces the idea that both sides were fighting to protect the causes most important to them, for better or for worse. Lt. General John B. Gordon is quoted as having said:

> It will be a glorious day for our country when all the children within its borders shall learn that the four years of fratricidal war between the North and South was waged by neither with criminal or unworthy intent, but by both to protect what they conceived to be threatened rights and imperiled liberty; that the issues which divided the sections were born when the Republic was born, and were forever buried in an ocean of fraternal blood.

This quote, taken from Gordon's 1903 publication *Reminiscences of the Civil War*, is telling in that it makes reference to the fraternal nature of Union and Confederate forces; they are portrayed as two sides of the same coin, both fighting for opposing, but no less legitimate, causes. Thus the battle is portrayed as a matter of honor, and is therefore justifiable.

The "Dedication" panel, which depicts a large group of men surrounding a monument, notes that, "Monument dedications provided aging veterans an opportunity to honor and remember their fallen comrades." These monuments are also meant to be "an inspiration to future generations." Soldiers are considered worthy of such recognition due to their devotion to their country, and especially because of their willingness to sacrifice themselves for their cause. Sgt. Newton Terrill of the 14th New Jersey Volunteers is quoted as having said, "Every drop of blood shed at Monocacy, every life lost, was sacrificed in a noble cause. Those fallen heroes . . . if they could only know that their lives saved our National Capital from destruction, would willingly exclaim: 'I die content, I gave my life to my country.'"

The prevalence of quotes with thematic elements similar to those of Terrill's gives the impression that the heroic sacrifice on the part of the soldiers is both honorable and appropriate. The heroism of soldiers is celebrated often throughout the exhibit, and even on the informational brochure, which places the following quote front and center on the first page: "From every point of view it was heroism" (attributed to Union Gen. Lew Wallace). In a panel titled "A Soldier's Sacrifice," a "heroic comrade" is celebrated for sacrificing his life so that others might be spared. One quote from an anonymous battle witness insists that, "The enlisted men of the Old 8th are every one a hero—God bless them!" I feel I must add a note of caution here that I do not wish to denigrate truly selfless acts of sacrifice on the part of the soldiers, nor do I want to attack individual actions in any way; rather, I question the way in which these actions are described and honored uncritically. I agree with Irvin Winsboro's (2016) advocacy for a "savage" reading of the Civil War, one that acknowledges the pain and violence instead of presenting a sanitized story of honor and glory.

While the Battle of Monocacy is clearly the central focus of the Visitors Center, it lacks a complex discussion of the slavery issue that gave rise to the war. In addition to the display case about the slave village that I have already described, there are a few panels on the second floor that are devoted to slavery, though the institution is largely discussed from a legal or political, rather than social, perspective. Most of the text relating to slavery is specific to the situation in Maryland: the state constitution, the number of enslaved and free African Americans, and laws that limited the freedom of free and enslaved blacks. Although these panels note that African Americans were severely restricted in their daily lives, even after the passage of the Emancipation Proclamation, the discussion never goes into greater detail about issues of power and control and the way these tensions played out on the plantation landscape. Instead, the focus is more generally on the status of slavery in Maryland, which was a border state and as such subject to greater political maneuverings. One panel notes that antebellum attempts at neutrality were unsuccessful as tidewater counties along the Chesapeake Bay had strong ties to the plantation system and slavery that were central to the economy, while western Maryland was characterized by small farms, mills, and other industries that required fewer enslaved workers. These kinds of facts are characteristic of the exhibit's discussion of slavery, which takes a very detached position and does not go into great detail about the nature of slavery or its role as a motivating force in the Civil War (although it is recognized as one of the causes).

Visitors do have the opportunity to learn about other histories when they visit individual farm sites at the battlefield. The Best Farm features four interpretive waysides adjacent to the parking lot, including one titled "Caught in the Crossfire" that describes the battle fought at the Best Farm on July 9, 1864, and how the Best family reacted to it; another, titled "The Lost Orders," describes how a copy of Confederate military strategy was accidentally left behind on the Best Farm, and later discovered by Union soldiers; a third on the Maryland Civil War Trains' Antietam Campaign, a 90-mile tour that follows the footsteps of Confederate and Union troops beginning on the banks of the Potomac River in Dickerson, Maryland, and continuing northwest to Antietam National Battlefield; and finally one placard for L'Hermitage, which provides a brief overview of the known history of the Vincendières and their enslaved workers and references the 2003 excavation that identified the location of the slave village. There is no signage regarding the 2010–2012 excavations of the slave village, and the site itself gives no indication that any archaeological activity took place there, as all the excavation units were filled in after the completion of each field season, and Johnson grass covers the whole area. However, those curious to learn more about these aspects of Monocacy National Battlefield's history could consult the Monocacy National Battlefield website (https://www.nps .gov/mono/) as there are webpages featuring a history of the L'Hermitage plantation and the Best Farm, a profile of Victoire Vincendière, and information about slavery at L'Hermitage and other farms on Monocacy National Battlefield's property. In general, however, Civil War military history takes center stage.

In some ways, Monocacy National Battlefield is still a nervous landscape today. Monocacy National Battlefield's interpretive focus on the Civil War centers on white soldiers, battle formations, military uniforms, and, to a lesser extent, enslaved individuals and the historical context for the Civil War. This landscape also hosted Indigenous peoples 10,000 years ago, a plantation with a large enslaved workforce in the eighteenth and nineteenth centuries, and migrant workers in the 1950s, but these aspects of Monocacy National Battlefield's history are downplayed or altogether omitted. In doing so, the National Park Service (inadvertently) sends a message about which histories are important and valuable. However, this hegemonic interpretation is not absolute; attempts to incorporate these other stories, such as through the initiation of the L'Hermitage slave village project, have revealed means of resistance on a nervous landscape. Cast in the sense of tension and anxiety, the public study of the history of slavery and African Americans caused some visitors to become uneasy or agitated, as it was a disruption of the conventional interpretation of the battlefield and challenges the notion that slavery wasn't really the cause of the conflict. To incorporate and highlight the history of L'Hermitage would make progress toward inclusivity, heterogeneity, and multiplicity take a step toward the kind of insurgency that Sandercock promotes. Therefore, providing this larger historical context is important not only for educational reasons, but for political and ideological reasons as well.

Of course, making substantial changes to the educational material presented at national park sites is easier said than done. Parks deal with a chronic lack of funding, resources, and staff, which makes it difficult to research and design new interpretive materials. Furthermore, a park's enabling legislation—the law by which a natural, historical, or recreational area becomes a unit of the National Park System—calls out the significant features of the property to which park activities and resources are devoted. A restrictive enabling legislation will limit the degree to which park staff can devote time and money to exploring and interpreting lesser-known histories. In addition, even when there is interest in developing alternatives or companions to the dominant narratives at national parks, NPS staff may fear the political consequences of doing so. As a federal agency, the NPS is under the watchful eye of local, state, and federal government and the public, and it has numerous stakeholders, including advisory groups. A 2011 survey of NPS historians and interpreters found a preference for fixed and final interpretation and an inclination to approach past controversies with caution, which resulted in the creation of interpretive themes that will not rock the boat. One informant noted, "I'm not sure that the NPS, as an agency, is comfortable presenting controversial issues. Perhaps it's the bureaucratic imperative to avoid controversy—better not to be too provocative" (Whisnant et al. 2011:110). The pressure to promote so-called neutral histories and dominant narratives, combined with financial limitations, serve as significant barriers to changing interpretive programming at national park sites.

However, while narratives of memorialization and commemoration have always been politicized, it seems especially timely to reconsider the narrative around Civil War history given the national discussion on Confederate monuments and memorials that is currently ongoing. The movement to remove markers of the Confederacy found renewed momentum in response to the December 2016 shooting of nine people at Emanuel African Methodist Episcopal Church in Charleston, South Carolina, by Dylann Roof, a white supremacist who posed for photos with a Confederate flag before committing the mass murder (Coates 2015). Following this event, South Carolina lowered the Confederate battle flag from the capitol grounds, and Alabama Governor Robert Bentley ordered it removed in Montgomery. Other cities and states followed suit, tearing down or quietly removing Confederate statues, flags, and other memorials (Shapiro 2017). The Southern Poverty Law Center identified more than 1,500 Confederate-related sites in thirty-one states, a number that excludes the "approximately 2,570 Civil War battlefields, markers, plaques, cemeteries and similar symbols that, for the most part, merely reflect historical events" (Graham 2016). Though only a small fraction have been removed at this point, many more are now subject to a debate about the meaning of Confederate monuments, which is a subset of a larger debate about the historical interpretation of the Confederate States of America and the reasons for the Civil War. Stewards of these sites and members of the public are grappling with the significance of leaving the monuments in place vs. removing them vs. providing critical context for the site. The crux of the problem is "the act of honoring the values supposedly symbolized by the Confederacy (and commemorated by a sign such as a flag or a monument) that perpetuates conflict owing to differences in interpreting those values. . . . Were this not the case, it would be a relatively simple proposition to [satisfy] all parties" (Richardson quoted in Winsboro 2016:220). Those opposed to the commemoration of the Confederacy argue that to do so promotes harmful, violent ideologies like white supremacy and anti-Blackness, and upholds a pro-slavery past. Those who wish to protect the monuments view them as symbols of Southern identity, heroic courage, and loyalty as well as the "rise of the South out of the ashes of that war and the persistence through decades of poverty and isolation that have led finally to the region's vindication today as the 'New South'" (Leib and Webster 2015:14). The multiple and complicated meanings that people assign to Confederate monuments indicate that the statues cannot be taken at face value or regarded simplistically; their significance is produced as a cultural text that must be "read" and interpreted (Seger 2022).

These polarizing debates over the significance and value of Confederate monuments have resulted in legal battles to remove or preserve statues, as well as extra-legal activities to deface or destroy monuments. For example, protestors in Richmond, Virginia, spray-painted a statue of Confederate General Robert E. Lee with graffiti reading "No More White Supremacy," "Blood On Your Hands," and "Black Lives Matter," and on June 6, 2020, they toppled a statue of Confederate Gen. Williams Carter Wickham in Monroe Park. Confederate monuments have also been removed via signed orders by city mayors and state governors. The *Washington Post* tracked the removal of Confederate monuments over time and found that five monuments were removed between 1865 and 2014, eight in the two years after the 2015 Charleston church shooting, and 110 in the aftermath of George Floyd's 2020 murder (Berkowitz and Blanco 2021).

Museum professionals, public historians, and community leaders who oversee Confederate monuments are grappling with the issue of whether and how to contextualize, remove, or reinterpret monuments (Allison 2018). The National Park Service, which oversees approximately 233 Confederate memorials, is included in this group. Many of these memorials are listed (or eligible for listing) on the National Register of Historic Places and are therefore given protections under the National Historic Preservation Act. Furthermore, these monuments may have been included in a park's founding mission and enabling legislation, which would increase the difficulty of removing them from the landscape. Oftentimes the NPS does not have the authority to remove Confederate memorials, as it would require an act of Congress to authorize (Comay et al. 2020). Given the difficulty of removing monuments, many parks have sought to reinterpret or contextualize them for the public. In 2017, the National Park Service Washington Office of Interpretation, Education and Volunteers and Stephen T. Mather Training Center published *Confederate Monuments and Memorials Discussion Guide: A Guide for National Park Service Interpreters,* which provides talking points to share with visitors, historical context for the construction of Confederate monuments, and resources for further investigation. For National Park Service staff, reassessing the significance of Confederate monuments, flags, and buildings is key to their mission to "discover American history in all its diversity" and "to tell the complete story of America" (Winsboro 2016:222). More broadly, it demands recognition of the fact that landscapes are dynamic, with ever-changing meanings that are always subject to being challenged. It is with these debates over commemoration that it becomes clear how the interpretation of landscapes is tied to issues of power; "the construction and interpretation of landscapes are constitutive of, reflections of, and points of contention within societal power relations" (Leib and Webster 2015:10). John Winberry, who conducted an extensive survey of Confederate monuments in the South, observed that "Landscapes are subject to change in form and function; but they also change in symbol and meaning. Just as we describe the form of landscape, we must seek also to understand their meanings, both in the past and in the present" (1982:14). The ambiguity of landscapes means that they can always be reevaluated and re-interpreted to serve the needs of a particular time, place, or group.

It is within the context of the national debates described above that Monocacy National Battlefield is challenged to create its public interpretation. Under its relatively liberal enabling legislation, Monocacy National Battlefield's managers may preserve and interpret anything at the park that existed at the time of the Civil War. This opens a broad range of possibilities for expanding the interpretation of the battlefield's history. The L'Hermitage research and excavations provide the opportunity to challenge dominant and hegemonic narratives about American history; this counter-narrative is akin to Byrne's "gaps in the grid," or instances where resistance and contestation are possible on the landscape.

To discuss the history of L'Hermitage with the public is to create a counter-narrative that challenges dominant narratives that ignore, downplay, or romanticize slavery in favor of a whitewashed past (Cook 2016). The shift to counter-narrative is akin to a symbolic excavation, "the unearthing of difficult and long suppressed (and repressed) historical narratives . . . through memory work, the construction and representation of the past" (Alderman and Campbell 2008:388). Archaeology can do this work through actual excavations of historic sites; the results can disrupt the narrative that dominates a particular landscape, as did the discovery of the slave village on the Best Farm. Indeed, newspaper articles that covered the L'Hermitage slave village project often featured headlines that called attention to the project's disruptive nature or its ability to expose new information, for example, "Discovery in Frederick Sheds New Light on eighteenth-Century Md. Slaves" (Hellerman 2010), "Digging Up a Grim Past" (Snyder 2003), "Brutal Slave History Unearthed at Frederick County's L'Hermitage" (Ruane 2010), "Monocacy Battlefield home to historical secrets" (Loos 2013).

In Byrne's analysis of the nervous landscape, these disruptions of hegemonic power are what cause tension to occur. In the case of Monocacy National Battlefield, that tension came about in the course of the Best Farm Slave Village study, when members of the public reacted to the public interpretation of L'Hermitage plantation history. Civil War buffs, families hoping for an educational experience, and others come to Best Farm for its connection to the Battle of Monocacy, and these visitors sometimes made their way out to the archaeological site to observe the excavation process. While many were interested in the excavation and history of the L'Hermitage slave village, some complained (to archaeologists) that there was no point in studying this early period of the Best Farm's history because it detracted from the Civil War history. Similar statements were made after the *Washington Post* published an article on the Best Farm project. Out of nearly 200 online comments, many were by turns curious, supportive, and introspective, while others grumbled that we were wasting time and money on an irrelevant, unnecessary project, preferring that we "move on" and stop focusing on slavery so much.

The supportive comments displayed a fascination with archaeology and an appreciation for the archaeological process and the types of information it can provide about the past. Some examples of these comments:

I am in awe with the article about L'Hermitage. I think it is most important for us to know the roots from which each family in the United States came . . . their struggles and their courageous faith and hope in a better world.
    —Comment in response to "Brutal slave history unearthed at Frederick County's *L'Hermitage*" from www.washingtonpost.com.

All this stuff was found in the soil? Just recently? After repeated plowing, and moving, etc? And it took all this time? They can actually tell what type of lives they led by seeing a bone, food remains?? (after how many years) and foundations? And a couple glasses? Wow, dont [sic] know about everyone else. This is amazing, but creepy.
    —Comment in response to "This is truly extraordinary"
        from www.fredericknewspost.com.

Critical comments tended to question the significance of the project, finding it to be misguided, pointless, or irrelevant:

Well cry me a river. Perhaps the Democrats can get the descendants some repartitions [sic] from the discriminated black farmers' fund set up by DA.

How expert are these Park employees at archaeology? Do they have experience at it? Are they following proper procedures with the extraction and preservation of artifacts that they uncover? Instead of harping on the cruelty of our ancestors maybe the article would have been more useful if we learned more about the discoveries and ultimate finale to this dig? Will there be a museum? Are there living ancestors of the slaves? Help please.

Tell me again:
   What was the White elected President Abraham Lincoln most known for.
   What is carved on his Washington DC Monument.???

I would love to see your evidence of oppression. It is obvious you know nothing of this country's early history thinking a single mother was bru-

tal to her slaves and lived. Your [sic] foolish and responsible for your words.

Seriously, who cares??

So what's the point of this story? The slaves are long dead and so are the people that engaged in that practice.
—Comments in response to "Brutal slave history unearthed at Frederick County's *L'Hermitage*" from www.washingtonpost.com

Other national battlefields have also dealt with this kind of backlash when attempting to highlight other histories, particularly that of slavery. For example, when former Gettysburg National Military Park Superintendent John Latschar mentioned that slavery was one of the causes of the Civil War, the Secretary of the Interior received 1,100 letters from constituents demanding his resignation, a sign that he struck "a raw nerve among many who seek to celebrate the bravery of their ancestors who fought for the Confederacy" (Horton 2001). I interpret this backlash as the result of a situation where absolute power (in the form of dominant narratives that support privileged groups) fails, and a heterogeneity and multiplicity of power and identities are introduced. That is, the disruption of homogeneity and hegemony breeds nervousness in people; this anxiety is "a jolt out of comfort and complacency" (Slater 2013:1).

The new narratives challenge one's understanding of identity and heritage. Heritage is an inheritance that selectively memorializes certain aspects of lived experiences, particularly those elements that a community finds value in retaining and make the past congenial (Lowenthal 1996:148). We are linked to heritage through narrative structures and stories about the past. These stories are central to our well-being as individuals and as members of a group (Chambers 2006). As Lowenthal (1996:143) points out, "Ever refashioned for present needs, heritage . . . [is] possessive, self-serving, and cavalier in [its] use of evidence." The reason for this is that a prime function of heritage is to "sustain traditional perspectives in the face of each generation's autonomy and unlikeness" (Lowenthal 1996:172).

Altering the past allows one to believe what *ought* to have happened *did* happen (Lowenthal 1985:326). One's heritage also informs and shapes one's identity. As Lowenthal points out, "the security of 'I was' is a necessary component of 'I am'" (1985:41). In order to feel grounded in one's identity in the present, one must know one's origins. Knowledge of one's past and one's heritage can confirm and enhance one's identity and self-esteem, sustain one's roots, and validate claims to power, prestige, and property (Lowenthal 1985:53).

I argue that a challenge to one's self-identity or self-understanding breeds nervousness, particularly around the introduction of narratives that cast one in a negative light. "For Americans, a people who see their history as a freedom story and themselves as defenders of freedom, the integration of slavery into their national narrative is embarrassing and can be guilt-producing and disillusioning. It can also provoke defensiveness, anger and confrontation" (Ater 2012:142). White people may feel especially vulnerable, guilty, and/or ashamed, as well as "defensiveness, nervousness, and a variety of fears: fear of being called racist, fear of black anger or judgment, fear of loss of group pride, and even fear of reparations or revenge for a history of slavery and racial oppression" (Gallas and Perry 2014:26). "Black people can experience comparable feelings of vulnerability during discussions about slavery and race. In fact, learning about slavery can be traumatic for any black American and may generate acute feelings, such as shame or distress" (26).

Such individuals find it difficult to assimilate these sites with "heroic notions of the national past" (Foote 1997:35), producing cognitive dissonance, which was first theorized by Frantz Fanon, the psychiatrist and philosopher. Fanon, who was born in Martinique under French colonial rule, argued that "Sometimes people hold a core belief that is very strong. When they are presented with evidence that works against that belief, the new evidence cannot be accepted. It would create a feeling that is extremely uncomfortable, called cognitive dissonance. And because it is so important to protect the core belief, they will rationalize, ignore and even deny anything that doesn't fit in with the core belief" (1952:179). This situation "sets up a sharp clash between old and new narratives, which, because of the role played by historical narratives in identity, can cut to the core of a person's sense of self. It is not hard to see why this process is likely to be difficult and accompanied by resistance; after all, struggles over narratives are struggles over identity" (Gallas and Perry 2014:9). "People and social groups tend to avoid telling stories that reflect poorly on those they identify with, and surely slavery falls into this category for white Americans, and, indeed, for all who identify as American, including those who are African American or otherwise nonwhite. Slavery in the Americas, however, is more than merely a story of exploitation by perpetrators of injustice; it is also a story of violence, cruelty, and trauma virtually unparalleled in human history" (Gallas and Perry 2014:9–10).

A visitor's exposure to a new historical narrative is a messy process. After all, "challenging people's self-concepts and worldviews is threatening because they often feel anxious, fearful, confused, angry, guilty and resentful" (Goodman 2011:38–9). Furthermore, the process is "inherently lengthy and does not always produce immediate, visible results, because rather than assimilating new information, piece by piece, learners are gradually building up an alternative historical narrative, which continues to conflict with the original narrative until the latter can be modified or discarded" (Gallas and Perry 2014:10). In response to this new narrative, visitors may ignore it or reject it, or try to argue against it or rationalize their existing narrative, and they may "engage in expressions of resistance that appear to delay the incorporation of the conflicting information, such as complaining about the unpleasantness or relative unimportance of the new narrative, making jokes or sarcastic remarks, or acting out physically by attending to other matters or leaving altogether" (Gallas and Perry 2014:11). Clearly, this process can be challenging and difficult, but the potential rewards are significant. Though this process may be anxiety-inducing for those who are invested in traditional interpretations of the past, this anxiety can have great power. Slater argues that: "I understand anxiety as productive, both in the sense that it reveals a continuing colonial order and is an articulation of the potential for transformation" (2013:1). A critical engagement with "raw emotions, and an inability to remain self-possessed" and other manifestations of postcolonial anxiety can expose the workings of colonialism and, surprisingly, "models for anticolonial social relations," demonstrating that within anxiety are radical possibilities (Slater 2013:1).

In the late 1990s, the NPS began telling more "stories of shame" (Murray 2014:178). Visitors were exposed to not only the traditional stories of greatness throughout American history, but also stories of tragedy, cruelty, and pain. These stories upend traditional narratives about the past, which can be discomfiting to some visitors. However, Whisnant et al. (2011:34) observe that, in the case of expanding discussions of slavery and the Civil War, "Because of these efforts, millions of visitors to NPS sites, and readers of NPS publications, now encounter a richer and more sophisticated conversation about this wrenching moment in our history."

Historiography is an inherently political act: "representing the past is not neutral, but inherently ideological and selective. It is a social practice that makes certain people, places, and perspectives appear legitimate while rendering others invisible and seemingly unimportant" (Alderman and Modlin 2013:7). Leonie Sandercock points out that these processes of exclusion are intrinsically political, with those in positions of authority molding people's "understanding of the past, causing them to forget those events that do not accord with a righteous image, while keeping alive those memories that do" (1998:2). Those in positions of power are drawn to depictions of a timeless past; portrayals of the past as unchanging, abstract, and sacred are important in maintaining the status quo but have no place in critical interpretations of history (Bodnar 1992). To be uncritical is dangerous, as it allows the unchecked perpetuation of traditional (and often harmful) ideologies. Those who have a stake in maintaining these ideologies will work to preserve their idealized version of the past, even if it does not tell the whole story. The purpose of these ideologies is to produce and reproduce current features of society, particularly exploitative relationships (Althusser 1971). Presentations of the past *are* ideology, and they serve to mask or misrepresent current political or economic realities in favor of reproducing a society characterized by inherent inequality.

Countering official or hegemonic narratives about the past with new, more accurate, and more encompassing narratives creates an "insurgent historiography" (Sandercock 1998). Sandercock suggests that insurgency demystifies that which is controlled by a privileged elite and makes the invisible visible (1998). This is especially relevant to Monocacy National Battlefield because its management by the National Park Service means that its interpretation must be government-sanctioned, which in turn results in an interpretation that fits comfortably with the official narrative of traditional American history. However, to critique and transform these interpretations can be ultimately liberating, as bell hooks points out: "Subversive historiography connects oppositional practices from the past and forms of resistance in the present, thus creating spaces of possibility where the future can be imagined differently—imagined in such a way that we can witness ourselves dreaming, moving forward and beyond the limits of confines of fixed locations" (bell hooks 1994:151).

6

Conclusion

During its existence, L'Hermitage was the site of complex dynamics and experiences. As the previous chapters describe, I interpret this site as a nervous landscape in which the Vincendières imposed a metaphorical grid—in the form of strict spatial and social control—on the plantation landscape, while enslaved laborers found "gaps in the grid" in which to exercise autonomy, resistance, and persistence. Furthermore, applying a more expansive definition of the nervous landscape concept—that of literal nervousness playing out on the landscape—inspired a companion interpretation concerned with ways the landscape of L'Hermitage—and plantation landscapes in general—were sites fraught with nervousness and anxiety. Tensions arose because slaveowners' power was pervasive but not absolute; there was always the chance that enslaved people would resist or otherwise behave in ways that served themselves rather than submitting to the physical and mental control exercised by slaveholders to serve their economic agenda. The ambiguity and precarity of plantation dynamics and interactions stemmed from a mutual mistrust between slaveholders and enslaved people. Slaveowners were concerned that enslaved laborers were deceiving them in some way or planning a revolt; a concern that became an all-consuming question because slaveowners' economic security, status, and perhaps even lives depended on an obedient, docile workforce. On the other hand, no matter how successfully enslaved people gained the trust or affection of slaveowners, they could never be sure whether each day might bring some kind of horror—abuse, assault, death, or sale to another owner thousands of miles away. To be sure, enslaved people were in a significantly more dangerous position. However, regardless of whether their fears and paranoia were founded in reality, slaveowners like the Vincendières had a great deal of power to confront (real or perceived) threats to their security through the manipulation of their environment and the bodies residing in and working on it—and regularly acted on this power. Slaveowners' intense reactions to their fears illustrate that a potent combination of racism, fear, and power has violent, even deadly, consequences.

While these dynamics and activities were major forces shaping the experiences of L'Hermitage's inhabitants, they can feel very distant and even nonexistent when the landscape is viewed today. If one passes by the former plantation while traveling down Georgetown Pike/Route 355, as Julian Niemcewiz did in 1798, one sees a striking contrast to the scene at L'Hermitage, a plantation busy with enslaved laborers and rife with violence and "instruments of torture." Instead, the property is a quiet, bucolic setting for tourism and agriculture—the land is still actively farmed, and a cornfield appears between the road and the historic house complex during the summer months. The only remaining aboveground evidence of the plantation is this cluster of historic structures, the main house, secondary house, and barn. The outbuildings and orchard are gone, and the site of the slave quarters is now an open field covered in Johnson grass.

However, while the landscape might appear different at present, the power dynamics and race-based structural inequality of the colonial and antebellum eras continue to this day, with many of the same features of racism and white supremacy that were established centuries ago. Slavery of the type practiced at L'Hermitage ended in the nineteenth century, but the racial hierarchies, social structures, and ideologies that supported it have persevered. Joe Feagin (2013:x) points out that slavery existed throughout 60% of U.S. history, therefore it is unsurprising that its effects would be felt today. Feagin argues that slavery is the context for the "dominant white racial frame that was generated to rationalize and ensure white privilege and dominance over Americans of color," which continues to be our reality today (2013:x).

I joined the L'Hermitage slave village project about a decade ago, meaning that I have had several years to think about the significance and main takeaways of this project. In my first few years as a participant, I was most fascinated by the uniqueness of the story—French and African people settling in Maryland, by way of Saint Domingue, Catholics among German Protestants, a large plantation surrounded by smaller family farms. As time went on and I continued to conduct research on the history of L'Hermitage, it was not—it *is* not the distinctiveness of this landscape and its people but rather the ordinariness that is striking and compelling to me. The colonial attitude toward people of color, specifically Black people—the fear, fearmongering, and degradation described in seventeenth- and eighteenth-century accounts set in the Americas and Caribbean, the Vincendières' treatment of their enslaved workers—could be equally applied to events, attitudes, and systems from so many other time periods, including the present, because the Vincendières, and more broadly, colonial and slaveholding societies, were not unique, as they all operated from a shared foundation of beliefs, values, and attitudes.

The notion that systems are self-perpetuating and built to last is not particularly notable in and of itself; the links between past and present racial inequality have been expertly drawn by scholars such as Du Bois, who connected chattel slavery and colonization to imperialist schemes of the Jim Crow era, drawing a link between a system founded on "barter in human flesh" to a modern system with an unquestioning belief in whites' "title to the universe" (1935:8, 1920:16). Ella Myers suggests that this sense of ownership described by Du Bois is "best understood as a revision of slavery's chattel"; in the early twentieth century, "white dominion is enacted in ways that are at once familiar and novel" (2019:12).

Michelle Alexander (2010) illustrates how the laws and policies implemented during slavery and Jim Crow never truly disappeared, but reemerged in new formats and continue to discriminate, disempower, and disenfranchise Black people, particularly through mass incarceration which, she notes, "emerged as a stunningly comprehensive and well-disguised system of racialized social control that functions in a manner strikingly similar to Jim Crow" (2). Carol Anderson (2016) catalogs white rage and backlash against instances of Black advancement from Reconstruction to the election of former president Barack Obama. The common thread in these analyses of past and present is the destructive power of white supremacy. Whiteness is defined here as a system that was designed to define who was privileged and who was property or second class, rather than the state of being white (Allen 1997). Whiteness is imbued with inherent superiority while subordinate races (i.e., people of color) are "alien and intrinsically different" (Myers 2019:7). Whiteness confers entitlements, advantages, and proprietary claims. Du Bois "locates in the souls of white people a deep, unquestioned belief that the world—nay, the universe—belongs to those with 'pale white faces'" (7). Du Bois investigates the psychology of white supremacy in "The Souls of White Folk" (1920), exploring how white people come to have a sense of superiority and justify inhumanity toward Black people. He argues that whiteness is the "passionate" belief in one's right to everything and anything—resources, safety, comfort—a total dominion, "the ownership of the earth, forever and ever, Amen!" (1920:16).

Even with this expectation of power and status, white people have historically felt threatened by people of color, who are viewed at threats to white power (Jones and Okun 2001). Chris Hedges argues that "the true credo of the white race is *we have everything, and if you try to take any of it from us we will kill you*" (2018:57). Rebecca Solnit (2020) also engages with this idea, writing that "elites project onto the masses their own ruthlessness and savagery; they fear others on the basis that they may be like themselves. I'm sure you want to kill me so I will kill you first." Consequently, Solnit explains, the logical reaction to fear and paranoia is violence: "the assumption by white supremacy and the police that Black and Brown people are inherently threatening and therefore violence against them, including lethal violence, is inherently justified" (2020).

While racism has been expressed differently in different eras—for example, the chattel slavery practiced by the Vincendières is not present in its precise form today—the racial fears and anxieties of white slaveowners and colonizers, and the paranoid and violent reactions to that anxiety, remain today. The specific details have changed, but the structure—white supremacy—perseveres. Seeing many similarities between my reading of the Vincendières' actions and events of the present reinforces how white power, privilege, and supremacy have contributed to centuries of violence, terror, and oppression. Accounts of the fears and paranoia of colonizers and slaveholders are similar to articles published in newspapers, magazines, and journals in the late 2010s, when I was working on this book. Both types of sources focus on the way that people with structural power respond to economic insecurity with racist paranoia. These fears and paranoias take the form of fears of the Other, loss of status, wealth, and property, loss of the status quo, and loss of being centered in society; fears so great that they affect the behavior of elites and how they organize the environment, and they fuel cruel and racist behavior. These characterizations were also applied to the experiences of colonizers and slaveholders in the eighteenth and nineteenth centuries.

For example, in recent years there has been a great deal of attention paid to white fears of the "minority-majority," that is, being outnumbered by people of color due to immigration and demographic change, and how that might result in a loss of status, power, and privilege for white people. These fears are captured by recent studies, such as "Threats to Racial Status Promote Tea Party Support among White Americans" (Willer et al. 2016), "On the Precipice of a 'Majority-Minority' America: Perceived Status

Threat from the Racial Demographic Shift Affects White Americans' Political Ideology" (Craig and Richeson 2014), "Feeling Threatened about the Future: Whites' Emotional Reactions to Anticipated Ethnic Demographic Changes" (Outten et al. 2012). Charles Blow (2018) argues that "White extinction anxiety, white displacement anxiety, white minority anxiety" and "panic over loss of privilege" are at the core of "draconian" policies that serve to restrict the rights and freedoms of immigrants and, more broadly, people of color.

These demographic changes are often discussed in terms of the negative economic impacts they could have on the white population, stoked by political rhetoric that "routinely link whites' (legitimate) fear of economic insecurity to (illegitimate) antiblack sentiment," but, as Ella Myers writes, "several studies show that perceived symbolic losses to white hegemony (the Obama presidency, a future majority-minority United States), prompt 'whitelash' responses, independent of whites' personal experiences of economic difficulty" (2017).

Political scientist Ashley Jardina describes the loss of status quo and hegemony as such: "For the entire history of the United States, white people have had the majority of social, economic and political power," but "many whites in the United States are starting to feel like their place at the top of the pyramid is no longer guaranteed and that the United States no longer looks like a 'white nation' which is dominated by white Anglo-Saxon Protestant culture" (DeVega 2019).

These recent discussions were largely activated by the political campaign and election of President Donald Trump. Studies following the 2016 election found that many white Americans supported Trump due to a perceived threat to their status. For example, a 2016 study by Major et al. found that "changing racial demographics of America contributes to Trump's success . . . among White Americans whose race/ethnicity is central to their identity. Reminding White Americans high in ethnic identification that non-White racial groups will outnumber Whites in the United States by 2042 caused them to become more concerned about the declining status and influence of White Americans as a group (i.e., experience group status threat), and caused them to report increased support for Trump and anti-immigrant policies." In addition, a study by Diana Mutz found that "traditionally high-status Americans (i.e., whites, Christians, and men)" were fueled by racial anxiety and the fear of loss of dominance to support "the candidate who emphasized reestablishing status hierarchies of the past" (2018:4330). She argues, "The 2016 election . . . was an effort by members of already dominant groups to assure their continued dominance and by those in an already powerful and wealthy country to assure its continued dominance" (Mutz 2018:4338). Trump garnered support of white Americans by stoking racial fears and anxieties, portraying undocumented Mexicans and people from Muslim countries as dangerous and threatening. Adam Weinstein (2020) argues that "the entire appeal of the Trump presidency . . . has been to flatter the id-impulses of excitable whites when they construct non-white people—their existence, their persistent presence, and their agency—as inherent threats to public safety."

This insecurity persists in spite of the fact that white people still hold the majority of power and resources in the United States and globally. Charles Blow (2018) argues that "white Americans, regardless of demographic change, will still control every major social, political, economic and cultural institution in the United States. Population numbers may fluctuate, but this deep institutional control of power in America has historically and will continue to remain in the hands of White America." Touré Neblett (2017) draws attention to this irony, saying "I don't understand how people with such a tight grip on power in America could be so insecure about it."

Regardless of whether these threats are real or perceived, white Americans still react to this racial anxiety and paranoia with discrimination and violence. In a description of current day that could easily have been written about slaveholders and colonizers, Rebecca Solnit says that elites "seem to believe the underclass is only held back from sowing chaos and destruction by the state's threat of violence, and in the absence of that threat all hell will break loose" (2020).

Civil rights activist Michelle Troxclair observed that "there's nothing scarier than scared white people" (Siegler 2020). Evidence of this observation can be seen with devastating frequency in the murder of Black people at the hands of paranoid white people—like Emmett Till in Money, Mississippi, in 1955, Michael Brown in Ferguson, Missouri, and Eric Garner on Staten Island, New York, in 2014. Adrienne Maree Brown writes that "Trayvon Martin and Mike Brown and Renisha McBride and so many others are dead because, in some white imagination, they were dangerous" (2017:14).

It is clear that while racism has been expressed differently in different eras—for example, the chattel slavery practiced by the Vincendières is not present in its exact same form today—the racial fears and anxieties of white slaveowners and colonizers, and the paranoid and violent reactions to that anxiety, remain today. The structures, systems, and dynamics of L'Hermitage did not disappear when the plantation was dissolved, but both pre- and postdated its existence. While L'Hermitage was unique in some ways, it was not truly unique nor isolated, but part of a larger system that rendered it inextricably bound to the world we know today. To create these conceptual links is an important part of breaking the pattern of structural inequality that persists in the United States and globally, and of drawing attention to the ways in which global white supremacy is structural and pervasive (Beliso-De Jesús and Pierre 2020).

Returning from the general to the specific, what do we do with these similarities between past and present, particularly regarding L'Hermitage and Monocacy National Battlefield? I view the identification of these connections across past and present as potential fuel for public interpretation, one that does not appeal to traditional values of battlefield interpretation (patriotism, sacrifice, heroism), or try to remain neutral, or avoid shameful stories, or portray the past as a relic with no relation to the present. Rather, can we imagine an interpretation of history that is expansive, encompassing, complex, even liberatory? For example, developing a more complex discussion of slavery could result in less reliance on facts and figures and more on stories of individual enslaved people. This approach is not without its challenges; the historical and archaeological record contains far less material about the enslaved compared with their enslavers. The plantation system was constructed in such a way as to prevent both the individuality of enslaved people and the preservation of their presence and history. Slaveowners frequently prevented their enslaved workers from learning to read and write, and therefore there are few records of enslaved life aside from oral traditions and records kept by owners, which are biased in that they largely come from a wealthy, white, male perspective. Due to their lack of access to resources and widespread illiteracy, enslaved people could not record their experiences, history, etc. in the same way as white slaveowners. Diaries and documentation from the point of view of the enslavers far outnumber similar records from the enslaved. As Robert Olwell (1998:7–8) points out, "In the written record, often the only source of information about the past, slaves are almost always in the position of the observed rather than the observer. Even in the rare instances when slaves' own words are recorded in the documents, they are filtered through the mediation of a transcriber who is often deeply implicated in the process of domination."

Though slave narratives, biographies, and autobiographies exist, their application to the inhabitants of L'Hermitage are limited; one cannot generalize too much because the experiences of the enslaved varied widely based on the time period, region, slaveowners, size of the plantation, etc. Slaveo-wners often wrote about their enslaved workers as property or objects rather than as human beings with depth and personality and did not record details of their daily lives. Furthermore, because enslaved people were barred from legal citizenship, they could not marry or own property, a fact that severely restricts the number of records available about them (Hait 2016:4).

In her seminal essay "Venus in Two Acts," Saidiya Hartman (2008) grap-ples with the lack of archival information regarding enslaved people, spe-cifically women and girls, asking, "How can narrative embody life in words and at the same time respect what we cannot know? How does one listen for the groans and cries, the undecipherable songs, the crackle of fire in the cane fields, the laments for the dead, and the shouts of victory, and then assign words to all of it? Is it possible to construct a story from 'the locus of impossible speech' or resurrect lives from the ruins?" Noting that enslaved people's existence in the archive is primarily relegated to administrative re-cords such as census records, tax assessments, sale documents, manumis-sion papers, and court records, Hartman expresses her desire to "[redress] the violence that produced numbers, ciphers, and fragments of discourse, which is as close as we come to a biography of the captive and the enslaved." She proposes "critical fabulation" as a methodology to "tell an impossible story and to amplify the impossibility of its telling." This method combines historical and archival research with critical theory and fictional narrative to fill in the gaps of history as well as highlight the existence of those gaps, to describe what could be and what could have been.

In addition, a revised interpretation of the history of slavery must in-clude intentionality around discussions of the realities of slavery. Public interpretation should be honest about how enslaved people suffered and who caused that suffering, rather than sanitizing the details. Archaeologist Paul Farnsworth (2000:155) argues that "violence was an integral part of the context of slavery that shaped the lives, actions, and worldview of enslaved people," so "to talk of symbolic degradation without an accompanying dis-cussion of physical degradation is to omit a major element of control. To talk of planter dominance or planter power without any mention of physi-cal violence is to miss the weapon that was used to enforce that relationship. To speak of resistance, without discussing violence, is to ignore a significant cause of that resistance and only give one side of the story. . . . violence, fear of violence, and avoidance of violence dominated African-Americans' lives on the plantation." On the other hand, focusing exclusively on the misery of slavery risks overlooking the full range of experiences and emotions of enslaved individuals: the fear, sadness, anger, joy, boredom, love, and surprise. How do we tell a story that doesn't focus only on pain and what caused it but also on what comes after, what came before, what has always existed in spite of pain, and will remain?

A public interpretation of L'Hermitage and Monocacy National Battlefield would do well to not just focus on the past, but also connect it to the present. Doing so would demonstrate to visitors that, as William Faulkner (1951:73) wrote, "The past is never dead. It's not even past." I have seen several examples of scholars making these connections for the benefit of public history. *The 1619 Project*, which began as a long-form essay in a 2019 issue of *New York Times Magazine* and expanded to include an educational curriculum, a podcast, and other resources, is a sweeping study of slavery in the United States led by journalist Nikole Hannah-Jones. The initial project included several articles linking familiar elements of present-day life, such as healthcare, infrastructure, medicine, the criminal justice system, music, and sugar, to their roots in slavery. Written in an accessible, engaging manner, these essays effectively argued that current structures and systems were fundamentally shaped by slavery and its legacy of racism and discrimination against Black people.

Another source of inspiration for my imagining of future historical interpretation at Monocacy National Battlefield is Eastern State Penitentiary (ESP), a historic site and designated National Historic Landmark in Philadelphia, Pennsylvania. ESP operated as a prison from 1829 to 1971, and today it takes visitors through the history of prisons and the day-to-day life of prison inmates in the nineteenth and twentieth centuries. In 2016, the site launched the exhibit Prisons Today: Questions in the Age of Mass Incarceration, which explores the current state of the United States criminal justice and prison systems, encourages reflection, and suggests steps that visitors can take to help shape the evolution of the American criminal justice system moving forward. In 2019, Eastern State Penitentiary opened Hidden Lives Illuminated, an exhibit which features twenty animated films created and narrated by prisoners at the Pennsylvania State Correctional Institution at Chester and Philadelphia's Riverside Correctional Facility for Women. These exhibits humanize incarcerated people and critically examine the criminal justice system and how it disproportionately targets people who are poor, of color, and less educated. The museum effectively draws connections between visitors and past and present inmates, as well as systemic issues associated with incarceration throughout history. One visitor to ESP noted that the site is unique because typical prison tourism (e.g., Alcatraz Island) focuses on "[entertaining] an audience that sees crime as a curiosity and not something relevant in their lives" (Ziegler 2016). Focusing on the relevance of the past to the present prevents disconnection and isolation and reminds visitors that nothing in the past or present occurs in a vacuum.

Another effective method of connecting past and present at sites dealing with the history of slavery is to identify descendants and involve them in the process of making meaning of historic sites. Following the initiation of the L'Hermitage slave village project, Monocacy National Battlefield made an ongoing effort to trace and identify the descendants of L'Hermitage's inhabitants. Genealogist Michael Hait conducted substantial research on the lineages of both enslaved and free occupants of the plantation (2011, 2014, 2016). He identified eight generations of the Vincendière family, up through the present day. He also found extensive biographical and descendant information for the Murdock and Ridgely families, both of which had been enslaved at L'Hermitage. In addition, significant research was conducted into the enslaved workers who were sold by Victoire Vincendière to Nicholas Wilson of Iberville Parish, Louisiana. In 2011, Hait identified Cicely Schatzman as a great-great-great-great-granddaughter of John Murdock, and she and her mother, Kym Kennedy, were invited to Monocacy National Battlefield to learn about the L'Hermitage slave village project and tour the site. Kennedy told *Essence* magazine that "research performed by genealogists is important because it gives African Americans a foundation that we don't have as a race, as the result of slavery. Many of us do not have any connection to our history like other races." After handling some of the artifacts recovered during the excavation and touring the L'Hermitage main house, Schatzman stated, "I feel so blessed. All Black people have a history, but so few have the opportunity to see it and touch it."

Not all descendants will want to visit or be involved in the process of making meaning out of history. Identifying and connecting with descendants can be challenging to navigate but is ultimately rewarding as it is an important method of linking the past and present and delivering information and resources to the people who can make use of it. In addition, descendants could potentially play a role in the public interpretation of L'Hermitage and Monocacy National Battlefield, as stakeholders. Something similar has already been implemented at James Madison's Montpelier, a historic site dedicated to the history of America's fourth president. Descendants of the enslaved workers owned by Madison play an active role in guiding priorities and content within the museum's public interpretation. In 2017, a new exhibit opened, called "A Mere Distinction of Color," an in-depth examination of the day-to-day lives of enslaved people who had lived and worked at Montpelier. Giles Morris, then the vice president for marketing and communications, noted that "it was important to the descendants that the displays connect slavery to the persistence of racial inequality and racist violence" (Rosenberg 2017). He described their attitude as, "You have to deal with the humanity of our ancestors" and "You can't leave this story in the past because this is not over for us" (2017). In some of the displays, living descendants of enslaved people read the words of their ancestors. Another installation links slavery to more recent events, such as Dylann Roof's racially motivated mass shooting in Charleston. In 2019, the Montpelier Descendants Community formed an organization to honor and advocate on behalf of their ancestors. Two years later, the MDC became equal co-stewards of the museum and estate of James Madison with The Montpelier Foundation. This power-sharing relationship is a model for historic sites like Monocacy National Battlefield.

Finally, a way to link past and present is through the universality of certain human experiences. In many ways, the L'Hermitage project is a meditation on fear and anxiety, and on their expression in material and intangible ways. Nervousness is attached to the landscape, reflecting a concern with precarity and vulnerability. These findings resulted from more than ten years of archaeological and historical research on L'Hermitage, which did the important work of providing material evidence of the slave quarters. Archaeology serves as a springboard to tell a larger story that connects past and present. My analysis illuminates two key lessons: first, that the Vincendières were not outliers, but were behaving within a structure and, crucially, emotions and personal motivations, none of which were unique to their time. Second, the structures and modes of behaving within which the Vincendières operated have continued into the present and shape our reality today.

Precarity and vulnerability are very human concerns, and that vulnerability is an important aspect of the way we interact and connect with others. At any moment, our existence could be lost or compromised. A fear of loss—and more specifically, loss of something one values, such as our possessions, status, wealth, family, dignity, bodily autonomy, etc.—can motivate us toward self-preservation and protection. In the case of the Vincendères, such inclinations resulted in greater violence, cruelty, and dedication to oppression. It is useful to consider this in order to think about the future, imagining a different mode of being: what are the radical possibilities of viewing our vulnerability as an asset to create something new? The work of digging out and deconstructing the worst parts of our past and present are crucial to constructing a more just future and disrupting oppressive systems.

Bibliography

Abbink, Jon, and Tijo Salverda. 2013. *The Anthropology of Elites Power, Culture, and the Complexities of Distinction*. UK: Palgrave Macmillan.

Agorsah, E. Kofi. 1999. "Ethnoarchaeological Consideration of Social Relationship and Settlement Patterning among Africans in the Caribbean Diaspora." In *African Sites Archaeology in the Caribbean,* edited by Jay B. Haviser, 38–64. Princeton, NJ: Markus Wiener Publishers.

Ahmed, Sara. 2004. *The Cultural Politics of Emotion*. New York: Routledge.

Alderman, Derek H., and Rachel M. Campbell. 2008. "Symbolic excavation and the artifact politics of remembering slavery in the American South: Observations from Walterboro, South Carolina." *Southeastern Geographer* 48(3):338–355.

Alderman, Derek H., and E. Arnold Modlin Jr. 2013. "Southern hospitality and the politics of African American belonging: An analysis of North Carolina tourism brochure photographs." *Journal of Cultural Geography* 30(1): 6–31.

Alexander, Michelle. 2010. *The New Jim Crow: Mass Incarceration in the Age of Colorblindness*. New York: New Press.

Allen, Theodore W. 1997. *The Invention of the White Race*. London: Verso.

Allison David B. 2018. *Controversial Monuments and Memorials: A Guide for Community Leaders*. Lanham, MD: Rowman & Littlefield.

Althusser, Louis. 1971. "Ideology and ideological state apparatuses (Notes towards an investigation)." In *Lenin and Philosophy and Other Essays*, edited by Louis Althusser, trans. Ben Brewster, 142–147, 166–176. New York: Monthly Review Press.

The American Star. 1794, May 1. The Early American Newspapers Database.

Anderson, Carol. 2016. *White Rage: The Unspoken Truth of Our Racial Divide*. New York: Bloomsbury.

Anschuetz, Kurt F., Richard H. Wilshusen, and Cherie L. Scheick. 2001. "An Archaeology of Landscapes: Perspectives and Directions." *Journal of Archaeological Research* 9(2): 157–211.

Archives of Maryland. 2018. "Online Proceedings and Acts of the General Assembly, August 1745–December 1747." Volume 44, page 456. http://msa.maryland.gov/megafile/msa/speccol/sc2900/sc2908/000001/000044/html/index.html

Armstrong, Douglas. 1990. "The Afro-Jamaican House-Yard: An Archaeological and Ethnohistorical Perspective." *Florida Journal of Anthropology* 16: 51–63.

Armstrong, Douglas. 1992. "Spatial transformations in African Jamaican Housing at Seville Plantation." *Archaeology Jamaica* 6: 51–63.

Ashmore, Wendy, and A. Bernard Knapp. 1999. *Archaeologies of Landscape: Contemporary Perspectives*. Malden, MA: Blackwell.

Ater, Renee. 2012. "The Challenge of Memorializing Slavery in North Carolina: The Unsung Founders Memorial and the North Carolina Freedom Monument Project." In *Politics of Memory: Making Slavery Visible in the Public Space*, edited by Ana Lucia Araujo, 141–156. New York: Routledge.

Babb, Winston C. 1954. "French Refugees from Saint Domingue to the Southern United States, 1791–1810." PhD diss., University of Virginia.

Bailey, Megan. 2013. "Beyond the Battle: New Narratives at Monocacy National Battlefield." *Historical Archaeology* 47, no. 3: 97–108.

Bailey, Megan. 2014. "Best Farm Lime Kiln." In *Archeological Investigation of the L'Hermitage Slave Village, Monocacy National Battlefield, Frederick, Maryland*, by Katherine D. Birmingham and Joy Beasley. Regional Archeology Program, National Capital Region, National Park Service, U.S. Department of the Interior, Washington, DC. On file at Monocacy National Battlefield, Frederick, MD.

Baltimore Daily Intelligencer. 1794 April 2. GenealogyBank. http://www.genealogybank.com

Barker, Anthony J. 1996. *Slavery and Antislavery in Mauritius 1810–33: The Conflict between Economic Expansion and Humanitarian Reform under British Rule*. London: Macmillan.

Bates, Lynsey A. 2014. "'The Landscape Cannot Be Said to Be Really Perfect': A Comparative Investigation of Plantation Spatial Organization on Two British Colonial Sugar Estates." In *The Archaeology of Slavery: A Comparative Approach to Captivity and Coercion*, edited by Lydia Wilson Marshall, 116–142. Carbondale: Southern Illinois University Press.

Bates, Lynsey A., John Chenoweth, James A. Delle. 2016. *Archaeologies of Slavery and Freedom in the Caribbean: Exploring the Spaces in Between*. Gainesville: University of Florida Press.

Battle-Baptiste, Whitney. 2011. *Black Feminist Archaeology*. Walnut Creek, CA: Left Coast Press.

Beasley, Joy. 2003. "Current Archaeological Research at Monocacy National Battlefield." *Maryland Archaeology* 39(1–2).

Beasley, Joy, Brandon Bies, Mark Gallagher, Tom Gwaltney, Heather A. E. Hembrey, David Monsees, and Sara Rivers Cofield. 2005. *Archaeological Overview and Assessment and Identification and Evaluation Study of the Best Farm: Monocacy National Battlefield, Frederick, MD*. In National Capital Region, National Park Service Regional Archaeology Program Occasional Report No. 18, U.S. Dept. of the Interior. On file at Monocacy National Battlefield, Frederick, MD.

Beasley, Joy, Mark Gallagher, Tom Gwaltney, and Andrew B. Weil. 2010. *Archeological Overview, Assessment, Identification, and Evaluation Study of the Thomas Farm*. Occasional Report No. 19. Regional Archeology Program, National Capital Region, National Park Service, U.S. Department of the Interior, Washington, DC.

Beasley, Joy, Tom Gwaltney, and Martha Temkin. 2001. "Perspectives on the Past: An Application of GIS at Best Farm." *Maryland Archaeology* 37(2): 22–37.

Beckford, William. 1790. *A Descriptive Account of the Island of Jamaica, Volume 1*. London: T. and J. Egerton.

Beliso-De Jesús, Aisha, and Jemima Pierre. 2020. "Special Section: Anthropology of White Supremacy." *American Anthropologist* 122: 65–75.

Berlin, Ira. 2000. "Slavery in American Life: Past, Present, and Future." In *Rally on the High Ground: The National Park Service Symposium on the Civil War*, edited by Robert K. Sutton. May 8 & 9, Ford's Theatre.

Berlin, Ira. 2003. *Generations of Captivity: A History of African-American Slaves*. Cambridge, MA: Harvard University Press.

Berkowitz, Bonnie, and Adrian Blanco. 2021 March 12. "A record number of Confederate monuments fell in 2020, but hundreds still stand. Here's where." *Washington Post*.

Bhabha, Homi K. 1990. *Nation and Narration*. London: Routledge.

Bhabha, Homi K. 1994. *The Location of Culture*. London: Routledge.

Birmingham, Katherine D., and Joy Beasley. 2014. *Archeological Investigation of the L'Hermitage Slave Village, Monocacy National Battlefield, Frederick, Maryland*. Regional Archeology Program, National Capital Region, National Park Service, U.S. Department of the Interior, Washington, DC. On file at Monocacy National Battlefield.

Blackburn, Robin. 1997. *The Making of New World Slavery: from the Baroque to the Modern, 1492–1800*. London: Verso.

Blakey, Michael L. 2020. "Archaeology under the Blinding Light of Race." *Current Anthropology* 61(S22): 183–197.

Blassingame, John W. 1972. *The Slave Community: Plantation Life in the Antebellum South*. New York: Oxford University Press.

Blight, David. 2000. "Healing and History: Battlefields and the Problem of Civil War Memory." In *Rally on the High Ground: The National Park Service Symposium on the Civil War*, edited by Robert K. Sutton. May 8 & 9, Ford's Theatre.

Blow, Charles M. 2018 June 24. "White Extinction Anxiety." *New York Times*.

Bodnar, John. 1992. *Remaking America: Public Memory, Commemoration, and Patriotism in the Twentieth Century*. Princeton, NJ: Princeton University Press.

Boge, Georgie, and Margie Holder Boge. 1993. *Paving Over the Past: A History and Guide to Civil War Battlefield Preservation*. Washington, DC: Island Press.

Bongie, Chris, ed. 2014. *The Colonial System Unveiled*. Baron de Vastey. Liverpool: Liverpool University Press.

Bourdieu, Pierre. 1984. *Distinction: A Social Critique of the Judgement of Taste*. London, Routledge.

Bourke, Joanna. 2003. "Fear and Anxiety: Writing about Emotion in Modern History." *History Workshop Journal* 55(1): 111–133.

Brackett, Jeffrey Richardson. 1889. *The Negro in Maryland: A Study of the Institution of Slavery, Volume 6*. Baltimore: Johns Hopkins University.

Branton, Nicole. 2009. "Landscape Approaches in Historical Archaeology: The Archaeology of Places." In *International Handbook of Historical Archaeology*, edited by David Gaimster and Teresita Majewski. New York: Springer.

Brown, Adrienne M. 2017. *Emergent Strategy*. Chico, CA: AK Press.

Browne, Simone. 2015. *Dark Matters: On the Surveillance of Blackness*. Durham, NC: Duke University Press.

Brugger, Robert J. 1996. *Maryland, A Middle Temperament, 1634–1980*. Baltimore: Johns Hopkins University Press.

Bunch, Lonnie C. 2007. Statement of Lonnie C. Bunch. Committee on House Administration Hearing on "The Construction of the United States Capitol: Recognizing the Contributions of Slave Labor." National Museum of African American History and Culture, Smithsonian Institution.

Burnard, Trevor. 2004. *Mastery, Tyranny, & Desire: Thomas Thistlewood and His Slaves in the Anglo-Jamaican World*. Chapel Hill: University of North Carolina Press.

Burnard, Trevor, and John Garrigus. 2016. *Plantation Machine: Atlantic Capitalism in French Saint-Domingue and British Jamaica*. Philadelphia: University of Pennsylvania Press.

Burton, Kristin D. 2015. Intoxication and Empire: Distilled Spirits and the Creation of Addiction in the Early Modern British Atlantic. PhD. diss., University of Texas at Arlington.

Butler, Judith. 2005. *Giving an Account of Oneself*. New York: Fordham University Press.

Butler, Judith. 2009. "Performativity, Precarity and Sexual Politics." *Antropólogos Iberoamericanos en Red* 4(3): 1–13.

Byrne, Denis. 2003. "Nervous Landscapes: Race and space in Australia." *Journal of Social Archaeology* 3(2): 69–193.

Camp, Stephanie M. H. 2004. *Closer to Freedom: Enslaved Women and Everyday Resistance in the Plantation South*. Chapel Hill: University of North Carolina Press.

Cannon, Aubrey, and Katherine Cook. 2015. "Infant Death and the Archaeology of Grief." *Cambridge Archaeological Journal* 25(2): 399–416.

Casstevens, Frances H. 2004. *George W. Alexander and Castle Thunder: A Confederate Prison and Its Commandant*. Jefferson, NC: McFarland.

Castells, Manuel. 1983. *The City and the Grassroots: A Cross-cultural Theory of Urban Social Movements*. Berkeley: University of California Press.

Catterall, Helen Turncliff. 1968. *Judicial Cases Concerning American Slavery and the Negro*. New York: Octagon Books.

Césaire, Aimé. 2000 [1955]. *Discourse on Colonialism*. Translated by Joan Pinkham. New York: Monthly Review Press.

Chambers, Erve. 2006. *Heritage Matters: Heritage, Culture, History and Chesapeake Bay*. College Park: Maryland Sea Grant.

Chidester, Robert. 2009. "Critical Landscape Analysis as a Tool for Public Interpretation: Reassessing Slavery at a Western Maryland Plantation." *CRM: Journal of Heritage Stewardship* 6(1).

Childs, Frances Sergeant. 1940. *French Refugee Life in the United States, 1790–1800: An American Chapter of the French Revolution*. Philadelphia: Porcupine Press.

Coates, Ta-Nehisi. 2015. "Take Down the Confederate Flag—Now." *The Atlantic.*

Cobb, Charles R., and Stephanie Sapp. 2014. "Imperial Anxiety and the Dissolution of Colonial Space and Practice at Fort Moore, South Carolina." In *Rethinking Colonial Pasts through Archaeology,* edited by Neal Ferris, Rodney Harrison, and Michael V. Wilcox. Oxford: Oxford University Press.

Cochran, Matthew D. 1999. "Hoodoo's Fire: Interpreting Nineteenth Century African-American Material Culture at Brice House, Annapolis, Maryland." *Maryland Archaeology* 35(1): 25–33.

Collins, David, and Andrew Dial. 2020. "Jesuits and Slavery in North America." The Jesuit Conference, Slavery, History, Memory and Reconciliation Project (SHMR). Washington, DC, 30 July 2020. https://www.xavier.edu/jesuitresource/resources-by -theme/04-jesuits-and-slavery-in-north-america-jan2021.pdf

Collins, Patricia Hill. 1990. *Black Feminist Thought: Knowledge, Consciousness, and the Politics of Empowerment.* New York: Routledge.

Comay, Laura B., Mark K. DeSantis, Scott D. Szymendera, Mainon A. Schwartz, Barbara Salazar Torreon, and Laura A. Hanson. 2020. *Confederate Symbols: Relation to Federal Lands and Programs.* Congressional Research Service Report #R44959. https://crsreports.congress.gov/product/pdf/R/R44959

Cook, Matthew R. 2016. "Counter-narratives of slavery in the Deep South: the politics of empathy along and beyond River Road." *Journal of Heritage Tourism* 11(3): 290–308.

Covey, Herbert C., and Dwight Eisnach. 2009. *What the Slaves Ate: Recollections of African American Foods and Foodways from the Slave Narratives.* Santa Barbara, CA: ABC-CLIO.

Crader, Diana C. 1990. "Slave Diet at Monticello." *American Antiquity* 55(4): 690–717.

Craig, Maureen A., and Jennifer A. Richeson. 2014. "On the Precipice of a 'Majority-Minority' America: Perceived Status Threat from the Racial Demographic Shift Affects White Americans' Political Ideology." *Psychological Science* 25(1): 1189–1197.

Crawford, Osbert Guy Stanhope. 1953. *Archaeology in the Field.* London: Phoenix House.

Croucher, Sara K., and Lindsay Weiss. 2011. *The Archaeology of Capitalism in Colonial Contexts.* London: Springer.

D'Andrade, Roy. 1995. *The Development of Cognitive Anthropology.* Cambridge: Cambridge University Press.

Dalzell, Robert F., Jr. 1993. "Constructing Independence: Monticello, Mount Vernon, and the Men Who Built Them." *Eighteenth-Century Studies* 26(4): 543–580.

Davies, John. 2008. "Class, culture, and color: Black Saint-Dominguan refugees and African-American communities in the early republic." PhD diss., University of Delaware.

DeCorse, Christopher R. 1999. "Oceans Apart: Africanist Perspectives on Diaspora Archaeology." In *"I Too, Am America," Archaeological Studies of African-American Life,* edited by Theresa A. Singleton, 132–158. Charlottesville: University Press of Virginia.

Delle, James A. 1998. *An Archaeology of Social Space: Analyzing Coffee Plantations in Jamaica's Blue Mountains.* New York: Plenum.

Delle, James A. 2000. "Gender, Power, and Space: Negotiating Social Relations under Slavery on Coffee Plantations in Jamaica, 1790–1834." In *Lines that Divide: Histori-*

cal Archaeologies of Race, Class, and Gender, edited by James A. Delle, Stephen A. Mrozowski, and Robert Paynter, 168–201. Knoxville: University of Tennessee Press.

Delle, James A. 2014. *The Colonial Caribbean: Landscapes of Power in the Plantation System.* New York: Cambridge University Press.

Dern, John P., and Grace L. Tracey. 1987. *Pioneers of old Monocacy: the early settlement of Frederick County, Maryland, 1721–1743.* Baltimore: Clearfield.

Dessens, Nathalie. 2003. *Myths of the Plantation Society.* Gainesville: University Press of Florida.

Dessens. Nathalie. 2007. *From Saint-Domingue to New Orleans: Migration and Influence.* Gainesville: University Press of Florida.

DeVega, Chauncey. 2019. "'White Identity Politics' and white backlash: How we wound up with a racist in the White House." *Salon.* https://www.salon.com/2019/07/17/author-of-white-identity-politics-we-really-need-to-start-worrying-as-a-country/

Dominguez, Virginia R., and Jorge I. Dominguez. 1981. "The Caribbean: Its Implications for the US." Headline Series 253, February. New York: Foreign Policy Associates.

Douglas, Mary. 1966. *Purity and Danger: An Analysis of the Concepts of Pollution and Taboo.* London: Routledge.

Douglass, Frederick. 1855. *My Bondage and My Freedom.* New York: Miller, Orton & Mulligan.

Du Bois, W.E.B. 1920. *Darkwater: Voices from Within the Veil.* New York: Harcourt, Brace and Howe.

Du Bois, W.E.B. 1935. *Black Reconstruction: An Essay toward a History of the Part Which Black Folk Played in the Attempt to Reconstruct Democracy in America, 1860–1880.* New York: Harcourt, Brace and Co.

Dubois, Laurent. 2004. *A Colony of Citizens: Revolution and Slave Emancipation in the French Caribbean, 1787–1804.* Chapel Hill: University of North Carolina Press.

Dubois, Laurent, and John D. Garrigus. 2006. *Slave Revolution in the Caribbean 1789–1804: A Brief History with Documents.* Boston: Bedford/St. Martin's.

Earley, Judith, Jeff Everett, and Grace Zhang. 2005. Best Farm, Monocacy National Battlefield Cultural Landscape Report, National Park Service. Washington, DC: Cultural Landscapes Program, National Capital Region, National Park Service.

Egerton, Douglas R. 2000. "The Tricolor in Black and White: The French Revolution in Gabriel's Virginia." In *Slavery in the Caribbean Francophone World: Distant Voices, Forgotten Acts, Forged Identities,* edited by Doris Y. Kadish. Athens: University of Georgia Press.

Egerton, Douglas R., and Robert L. Paquette. 2017. *The Denmark Vesey Affair: A Documentary History.* Gainesville: University Press of Florida.

Ellis, Clifton, and Rebecca Ginsburg, eds. 2010. *Cabin, Quarter, Plantation: Architecture and Landscapes of North American Slavery.* New Haven, CT: Yale University Press.

Epperson, Terrence W. 1990. "Race and the Disciplines of the Plantation." *Historical Archaeology* 24(2): 29–36.

Epperson, Terrence W. 1999. "Constructing Difference: The Social and Spatial Order of the Chesapeake Plantation." In *"I Too, Am America," Archaeological Studies of*

African-American Life, edited by Theresa A. Singleton, 159–172. Charlottesville: University Press of Virginia.

Epperson, Terrence W. 2004. "Critical Race Theory and the Archaeology of the African Diaspora." *Historical Archaeology* 38(1): 101–108.

Equiano, Olaudah. 1789. *The Interesting Narrative of the Life of Olaudah Equiano; or, Gustavus Vassa, the African.* London: Printed for and sold by the Author, No. 10, Union-Street, Middlesex Hospital.

Escott, Paul D. 1979. Slavery Remembered: A Record of Twentieth-Century Slave Narratives. Chapel Hill: University of North Carolina Press.

Fanon, Frantz. 1952. *Black Skin, White Masks.* New York: Grove City Press.

Farmer, John Stephen, ed. 1889. *Americanisms Old & New: A Dictionary of Words, Phrases and Colloquialisms Peculiar to the United States, British America, the West Indies.* London: Thomas Poulter & Sons.

Farmer, Paul. 2004. "An Anthropology of Structural Violence." *Current Anthropology* 45(3): 305–325.

Farnsworth, Paul. 2000. "Brutality or Benevolence in Plantation Archaeology." *International Journal of Historical Archaeology* 4(2): 145–158.

Farnsworth, Paul, ed. 2001. *Island Lives: Historical Archaeologies of the Caribbean.* Tuscaloosa: University of Alabama Press.

Farrell, Zandria K. 2003. "Sacred to the Memory: An Archaeological Investigation into Emotion and Ideology within Two Regional Cemeteries." B.A. thesis, Flinders University.

Faulkner, William. 1951. *Requiem for a Nun.* New York: Random House.

FCCD [Frederick County Court Dockets]. 1797. March term. Maryland State Archives, Annapolis.

FCCD [Frederick County Court Dockets]. 1797. November term. Maryland State Archives, Annapolis.

Feagin, Joe R. 2013. *The White Racial Frame: Centuries of Racial Framing and Counter-Framing.* 2nd ed. New York: Routledge.

Federal Gazette. 1810 December 8. GenealogyBank http://www.genealogybank.com

Federal Gazette. 1811 July 30. GenealogyBank http://www.genealogybank.com

Federal Writers Project. 1941. *Slave Narratives: A Folk History of Slavery in the United States from Interviews with Former Slaves.* Washington, DC: Library of Congress.

Fesler, G., and Maria Franklin. 1999. "The Exploration of Ethnicity and the Historical Archaeological Record." In *Historical Archaeology, Identity Formation, and the Interpretation of Ethnicity,* edited by Maria Franklin and Garrett Fesler, 1–10. Colonial Williamsburg Research Publications. Richmond, VA: Dietz Press.

Fick, Carolyn. 1990. *The Making of Haiti: The Saint Domingue Revolution from Below.* Knoxville: University of Tennessee Press.

Fiedel, Stuart, and Eric Griffitts. 2005. "Phase I Archaeological Identification Survey, MD 85: South of English Muffin Way to 1400 Feet North of Grove Road, Frederick County, Maryland." Report submitted to Maryland Department of Transportation, State Highway Administration, Baltimore. Report on file at the Maryland Historical Trust.

Fields, Barbara Jeanne. 1985. *Slavery and Freedom on the Middle Ground: Maryland during the Nineteenth Century.* New Haven, CT: Yale University Press.

Fischer-Tiné, Harald. 2016. *Anxieties, Fear and Panic in Colonial Settings: Empires on the Verge of a Nervous Breakdown.* London: Palgrave Macmillan.

Fontana-Giusti, Gordana. 2013. *Foucault for Architects.* London: Routledge.

Foote, Kenneth E. 1997. Shadowed Ground: America's Landscapes of Violence and Tragedy. Austin: University of Texas Press.

Forster, Robert. 1990. "Slavery in Virginia and Saint-Domingue in the Late Eighteenth Century." *Proceedings of the Meeting of the French Colonial Historical Society* 13/14: 1–13.

Foucault, Michel. 1980. "Two lectures." In *Power/knowledge: Selected interviews and other writings 1972–1977,* edited by C. Gordon. New York: Harvester Wheatsheaf.

Franklin, Maria. 1997. "'Power to the People': Sociopolitics and the Archaeology of Black Americans." *Historical Archaeology* 31(3).

Franklin, Maria. 2004. An Archaeological Study of the Rich Neck Slave Quarter and Enslaved Domestic Life. Colonial Williamsburg Research Publications. Richmond, VA: Dietz Press.

Franklin, Maria. 2020. "Enslaved Household Variability and Plantation Life and Labor in Colonial Virginia." *International Journal of Historical Archaeology* 24(1): 115–155.

Frederick-Town Herald. 1816. Microfilm, C. Burr Artz Library (Maryland Room), Frederick, MD.

Frey, Sylvia. 1991. *Water from the Rock: Black Resistance in a Revolutionary Age.* Princeton, NJ: Princeton University Press.

Friedman, Lawrence M. 2005. *A History of American Law: Third Edition.* New York: Touchstone.

Galke, Laura. 1992. "You Are Where You Live: A Comparison of 'Africanisms' at Two Sites in Manassas National Battlefield Park, National Capital Region, National Park Service." Paper presented at the 25th Conference on Historical and Underwater Archaeology. Kingston, Jamaica.

Galke, Laura. 2001. "'Free within Ourselves': African American Landscapes at Manassas National Battlefield Park." In *Archaeological Perspectives on the American Civil War,* edited by Clarence R. Geier and Stephen R. Potter. Gainesville: University Press of Florida.

Galke, Laura. 2009. "Colonowhen, Colonowho, Colonowhere, Colonowhy: Exploring the Meaning behind the Use of Colonoware Ceramics in Nineteenth-Century Manassas, Virginia." *International Journal of Historical Archaeology* 13(3): 303–326.

Galke, Laura, et al. 1992. *Cultural Resource Survey and Inventory of a War-Torn Landscape: The Stuart's Hill Tract, Manassas National Battlefield Park, Virginia.* National Capital Region, National Park Service.

Gallas, Kristin L., and James DeWolf Perry. 2014. *Interpreting Slavery at Museums and Historic Sites.* Lanham, MD: Rowman & Littlefield.

Galle, William, and Amy Young. 2004. *Engendering African American Archaeology: A Southern Perspective.* Knoxville: University of Tennessee Press.

Garrigus. John D. 2006. *Before Haiti: Race and Citizenship in French Saint-Domingue.* New York: Palgrave Macmillan.

Gaspar, David Barry, and Darlene Clark Hine. 1996. *More Than Chattel: Black Women and Slavery in the Americas.* Bloomington: Indiana University Press.

Gatewood, John B., and Catherine M. Cameron. 2004. "Battlefield Pilgrims at Gettysburg National Military Park." *Ethnology* 43(3): 193–216.

Geggus, D. 1998. "Indigo and Slavery in Saint-Domingue." *Plantation Society in the Americas* 5(2–3): 189–204.

Geggus, David. 1989. "Sex Ratio, Age, and Ethnicity in the Atlantic Slave Trade: Data from French Shipping and Plantation Records." *Journal of African History* 30(1): 23–44.

Geggus, David. 1993. "Sugar and Coffee Cultivation in Saint Domingue and the Shaping of the Slave Labor Force." In *Cultivation and Culture: Labor and the Shaping of Slave Life in the Americas,* edited by Ira Berlin and Philip D. Morgan, 73–98. Charlottesville: University Press of Virginia.

Geggus, David. 1999. "Slave Society in the Sugar Plantation Zones of Saint Domingue and the Revolution of 1791–93." *Slavery & Abolition* 20(2): 31–46.

Geggus, David. 2001. "The French Slave Trade: An Overview." *William and Mary Quarterly* 58(1): 119–138.

Geggus, David Patrick. 1982. *Slavery, War and Revolution: The British Occupation of Saint Domingue, 1793–1798.* Oxford: Clarendon Press.

Gillikin, Margaret Wilson. 2014. "Saint Dominguan Refugees in Charleston, South Carolina, 1791–1822: Assimilation and Accommodation in a Slave Society." PhD diss., University of South Carolina–Columbia.

Gilroy, Paul. 1993. *The Black Atlantic: Modernity and Double Consciousness.* Cambridge, MA: Harvard University Press.

Go, Julian. 2016. *Postcolonial Thought and Social Theory.* New York: Oxford University Press.

Goodman, Diane. 2011. *Promoting Diversity and Social Justice: Educating People from Privileged Groups.* New York: Routledge.

Gordon, Avery F. 1997. *Ghostly Matters: Haunting and the Sociological Imagination.* Minneapolis: University of Minnesota Press.

Graham, David. 2016. "The Stubborn Persistence of Confederate Monuments." *The Atlantic.*

Green, Garth L. 2002. "Marketing the Nation: Carnival and Tourism in Trinidad and Tobago." *Critique of Anthropology* 22(3): 283–304.

Gregory, Derek, and John Urry, eds. 1985. *Social Relations and Spatial Structures.* London: Macmillan.

Grivno, Max. 2011. *Gleanings of Freedom: Free and Slave Labor along the Mason-Dixon Line, 1790–1860.* Urbana: University of Illinois Press.

Grivno, Max L. 2007. "'There Slavery Cannot Dwell': Agriculture and Labor in Northern Maryland, 1790–1860." PhD diss., University of Maryland, College Park.

Groth, Paul. 1997. "Frameworks for cultural landscape study." In *Understanding Ordinary Landscapes,* edited by Paul Groth and Todd W. Bressi, 1–21. New Haven, CT: Yale University Press.

Grove, William Hugh, Gregory A. Stiverson, and Patrick H. Butler III. 1977. "The Travel Journal of William Hugh Grove." *Virginia Magazine of History and Biography* 85(1): 18–44.

Gusterson, H. 1997. Studying Up Revisited. *PoLAR: Political and Legal Anthropology Review* 20(1): 114–119.

Gutman, Herbert G. 1976. *The Black Family in Slavery and Freedom, 1750–1925.* New York: Pantheon Books.

GWWO, Inc., Architects. 2003. L'Hermitage, The Best House, Historic Structures Report. On file at Monocacy National Battlefield, Frederick, MD.

Hait, Michael. 2011. *The Slaves of L'Hermitage.* On file at Monocacy National Battlefield, Frederick, MD.

Hait, Michael. 2014. "A Summary of Genealogical Research into Descendants of the L'Hermitage Slave Village Community." In *Archeological Investigation of the L'Hermitage Slave Village, Monocacy National Battlefield, Frederick, Maryland.* Regional Archeology Program, National Capital Region, National Park Service, U.S. Department of the Interior, Washington, DC. On file at Monocacy National Battlefield, Frederick, MD.

Hait, Michael. 2016. Cultural Anthropology Report. Final Report of Research, Monocacy National Battlefield, Frederick, Maryland. U.S. Department of the Interior National Park Service National Capital Region Resource Stewardship and Science. Washington, DC. On file at Monocacy National Battlefield, Frederick, MD.

Hallerman, Tamar. 2010 August 20. "Discovery in Frederick Sheds New Light on 18th-Century Md. Slaves" [Radio Broadcast]. WAMU.

Hamilakis, Yannis. 2014. *Archaeology and the Senses: Human Experience, Memory, and Affect.* New York: Cambridge University Press.

Harari, Roberto. 2001. *Lacan's Seminar on Anxiety: An Introduction.* New York: Other Press.

Harrell, David Edwin Jr., Edwin S. Gaustad, John B. Boles, Sally Foreman Griffith, Randall M. Miller, and Randall B. Woods. 2005. *Unto A Good Land: A History of the American People.* Grand Rapids, MI: Wm B. Eerdmans.

Harrigan, Michael, ed. 2021. *Life and Death on the Plantations: Selected Jesuit Letters from the Caribbean.* Cambridge, UK: Modern Humanities Research Association.

Harrington, Jane. 1996. "The Lime-Burning Industry in Victoria: An Occupance Approach." *Australasian Historical Archaeology* 14: 19–24.

Harris, Oliver J. T., and Tim Flohr Sørensen. 2010. "Emotional Aspects of a Fen." *Archaeological Dialogues* 17(2): 145–163.

Harrison, Renee. 2009. *Enslaved Women and the Art of Resistance in Antebellum America.* New York: Palgrave Macmillan.

Hartman, Saidiya. 2008. "Venus in Two Acts." *Small Axe* 12(2): 1–14.

Hartridge, W. C. 1943. "The Refugees from Saint Domingue in Maryland." *Maryland Historical Magazine* 38(2): 103–122.

Heath, Barbara. 1999a. *Hidden Lives: The Archaeology of Slave Life at Thomas Jefferson's Poplar Forest.* Charlottesville: University Press of Virginia.

Heath, Barbara. 1999b. "Buttons, Beads, and Buckles: Contextualizing Adornment Within the Bounds of Slavery." In *Historical Archaeology, Identity Formation, and the Interpretation of Ethnicity*, edited by Maria Franklin and Garrett Fesler, 47–69. Richmond, VA: Colonial Williamsburg Foundation and Dietz Press.

Heath, Barbara Jane. 2016a. "Dynamic Landscapes: The Emergence of Formal Spaces in Colonial Virginia." *Historical Archaeology* 50(1): 27–44.

Heath, Barbara Jane. 2016b. "Cowrie Shells, Global Trade, and Local Exchange: Piecing Together the Evidence for Colonial Virginia." *Historical Archaeology* 50(2): 17–46.

Heath, Barbara Jane, and Amber Bennett. 2000. "'The little spots allow'd them': The archaeological study of African-American yards." *Historical Archaeology* 34(2): 38–55.

Heath, Barbara Jane, and Jack Gary. 2012. *Jefferson's Poplar Forest: Unearthing a Virginia Plantation.* Gainesville: University Press of Florida.

Hedges, Chris. 2018. *America: The Farewell Tour.* New York: Simon & Schuster.

Higman, Barry. 1977. "Slave Population and Economy in Jamaica, 1807–1834." New York: Cambridge University Press.

Higman, Barry. 1986. "Jamaican Coffee Plantations, 1780–1860: A Cartographic Analysis." *Caribbean Geography* 2(2): 73–91.

Higman, Barry. 1988. *Jamaica Surveyed: Plantation Maps and Plans of the Eighteenth and Nineteenth Centuries.* Kingston: Institute of Jamaica Publications.

Hill, Erica. 2013. "Death, Emotion, and the Household among the Late Moche." In *The Oxford Handbook of the Archaeology of Death and Burial. Volume 1*, edited by Sarah Tarlow and Liv Nilsson Stutz, 597–616. Oxford: Oxford University Press.

Hilliard, Sam Bowers. 1972. *Hog Meat and Hoecake: Food Supply in the Old South, 1840–1860.* Carbondale: Southern Illinois University Press.

Hilliard d'Auberteuil, Michel René. 1779. *Essais Historiques et Politiques sur les Anglo-Américains.* Paris: Chez Grangé.

Hofstadter, Richard. 1965. *The Paranoid Style in American Politics.* New York: Knopf.

Holzer, Jenny. 1979–1982. *Inflammatory Essays.* 29 offset lithographs 17 × 17 inches on paper of various colours, published by the artist in an unlimited edition. https://www.tate.org.uk/art/artworks/holzer-inflammatory-essays-65434/26

hooks, bell. 1994. *Teaching to Transgress Education: as the Practice of Freedom.* New York: Routledge.

Horton, James Oliver. 1999. "Slavery and the Coming of the Civil War: A Matter for Interpretation." In *Rally on the High Ground: The National Park Service Symposium on the Civil War*, edited by Robert K. Sutton. May 8 & 9, Ford's Theatre.

Huddart, David. 2005. *Homi K. Bhabha.* London: Routledge.

Hurtado, Aida. 1996. *The Color of Privilege: Three Blasphemies on Race and Feminism.* Ann Arbor: University of Michigan Press.

Jackson, Will. 2016. "The Settler's Demise: Decolonization and Mental Breakdown in 1950s Kenya." In *Anxieties, Fear and Panic in Colonial Settings: Empires on the Verge of a Nervous Breakdown*, edited by Harald Fischer-Tiné. London: Palgrave Macmillan.

James, C.L.R. 1963. *The Black Jacobins: Toussaint L'Ouverture and the San Domingo Revolution.* 2nd ed. New York: Vintage Books.

John, Beverly M. 1999. "The Construction of Racial Meaning by Blacks and Whites in Plantation Society." In *Plantation Society and Race Relations: The Origins of Inequality,* edited by D. Knottnerus and T. J Durant. Westport, CT: Praeger.

John, Beverly M. 2006. "The Construction of Racial Meaning by Blacks and Whites in Plantation Society." In *Creating Black Americans: African-American History and its Meanings, 1619 to the Present,* edited by Nell Irvin Painter. Oxford: Oxford University Press.

Jones, Kenneth, and Tema Okun. 2001. *Dismantling Racism: A Workbook for Social Change Groups.* ChangeWork.

Jordan, Elizabeth. 2006. "'Unrelenting toil': Expanding archaeological interpretations of the female slave experience." *Slavery and Abolition: A Journal of Slave and Post-Slave Studies* 26(2): 217–232.

Joyner, Stefanie. 2003. "Slave Housing Patterns within the Plantation Landscape of Coastal Georgia." Unpublished Master's thesis, University of Florida.

Kelly, Kenneth. 2004. "Historical Archaeology in the French Caribbean: An Introduction to a Special Volume of the Journal of Caribbean Archaeology." *Journal of Caribbean Archaeology* Special Publication #1: 1–10.

Kelly, Kenneth. 2008. "Creole Cultures of the Caribbean: Historical Archaeology in the French West Indies." *International Journal of Historical Archaeology* 12(4): 388–402.

Kelly, Kenneth. 2009. "Where is the Caribbean? French Colonial Archaeology in the English Lake." *International Journal of Historical Archaeology* 13(1): 80–93.

Kelly, Kenneth. 2017. Searching for Slavery at Saint Domingue. Presented at the Society for Historical Archaeology Annual Meeting. Fort Worth, TX.

Kelso, William M. 1984. "Landscape Archaeology: A Key to Virginia's Cultivated Past." In *British and American Gardens in the Eighteenth Century: Eighteen Illustrated Essays on Garden History,* edited by Robert P. Maccubbin and Peter Martin, 159–169. Williamsburg, VA: Colonial Williamsburg Foundation.

Kessel, Elizabeth Augusta. 1981. "Germans on the Maryland Frontier: A Social History of Frederick County, Maryland, 1730–1800." PhD diss., Rice University.

Klingelhofer, Eric. 1987. "Aspects of Early Afro-American Material Culture: Artifacts from the Slave Quarters at Garrison Plantation, Maryland." *Historical Archaeology* 21(2): 112–119.

Knight, Franklin. 1970. *Slave Society in Cuba During the Nineteenth Century.* Madison: University of Wisconsin Press.

Knight, Franklin. 2000. "Imperialism and Slavery." In *Caribbean Slavery in the Atlantic World,* edited by Verene Shepherd and Hilary Beckles. Kingston, Jamaica: Ian Randle.

Knottnerus, J. David, and Thomas J. Durant. 1999. *Plantation Society and Race Relations: The Origins of Inequality.* Westport, CT: Praeger.

Knottnerus, J. David, David L. Monk, and Edward Jones. 1999. "The Slave Plantation System from a Total Institution Perspective." In *Plantation Society and Race Rela-*

tions: The Origins of Inequality, edited by David Knottnerus and Thomas J. Durant. Westport, CT: Praeger.

Kulik, Gary. 1989. "Designing the Past: History Museum Exhibits from Peale to the Present." In *History Museums in the United States: A Critical Assessment*, edited by Warren Leon and Roy Rosenzweig. Urbana: University of Illinois Press.

Laborie, Pierre Joseph. 1798. The coffee planter of Saint Domingo; with an appendix, containing a view of the constitution, government, laws, and state of that Colony, previous to the year 1789. To which are added, some hints on the present state of the Island, under the British Government. London: Printed for T. Cadell & W. Davies, in the Strand.

Lalone, Mary. 2003. "Walking the Line between Alternative Interpretations in Heritage Education Tourism: A Demonstration of the Complexities with an Appalachian Mining Example." In *Signifying Serpents and Mardi Gras Runners: Representing Identity in Selected Souths*, edited by Celeste Ray and Luke Eric Lassiter, 72–86. Athens: University of Georgia Press.

Lanier, Gabrielle M., and Phoebe G. Harding. 2006. *Belle Grove Plantation Overseer's House: Historical Architectural Assessment*. Harrisonburg, VA: James Madison University.

LaRoche, Cheryl. 2007. "Resistance to Slavery in Maryland: Strategies for Freedom, Special History Study for Organization of American Historians." National Park Service, Northeast Region, U.S. Department of Interior.

The Laws of Maryland, 1792. Chapter LVI. An Act Respecting the Slaves of Certain French Subjects, Maryland State Archives, Annapolis. Volume 3181, pp. 686–687.

The Laws of Maryland, Volume I. 1811. Baltimore: Philip H. Nicklin & Company.

Lefebvre, Henri. 1974. *The Production of Space*, Paris: Anthropos.

Leib, Jonathan, and Gerald R. Webster. 2015. "On Remembering John Winberry and the Study of Confederate Monuments on the Southern Landscape." *Southeastern Geographer* 55(1): 9–18.

Leon, Warren, and Roy Rosenzweig. 1989. *History Museums in the United States: A Critical Assessment*. Urbana: University of Illinois Press.

Linenthal, Edward. 1993. *Sacred Ground: Americans and Their Battlefields*. Urbana: University of Illinois Press.

Linenthal, Edward. 2006. "The National Park Service and Civic Engagement." *Public Historian* 28(1): 123–129.

Logan, George C., Thomas W. Bodor, Lynn D. Jones, and Marian Creveling. 1992. *Archaeological Excavations at the Charles Carroll House in Annapolis, Maryland 18AP45*. Copy on file at the Maryland Historical Trust.

Loos, Kelsi. 2013 June 27. "Monocacy Battlefield home to historical secrets." *The Frederick News-Post*.

Lowe, Esther Winder Polk. 1913. Memories. Transcript on file, Enoch Louis Lowe Papers, Maryland Historical Society.

Lyman, R. Lee. 1977. "Analysis of Historic Faunal Remains." *Historical Archaeology* 11: 67–73.

Lowenthal, David. 1975. "Past Time, Present Place: Landscape and Memory." *Geographical Review* 65(1): 1–36.

Lowenthal, David. 1985. *The Past Is a Foreign Country.* Cambridge: Cambridge University Press.

Lowenthal, David. 1996. *Possessed by the Past: The Heritage Crusade and the Spoils of History.* New York: Free Press.

Major, Brenda, Alison Blodorn, and Gregory Major Blascovich. 2018. "The Threat of Increasing Diversity: Why Many White Americans Support Trump in the 2016 Presidential Election." *Group Processes & Intergroup Relations* 21(6): 931–940.

Maryland Gazette. 1795 December 17. GenealogyBank. https://www.genealogybank.com

Maryland-National Capital Park and Planning Commission. 2009. *Antebellum Plantations in Prince George's County, Maryland: A Historic Context and Research Guide.* The Maryland-National Capital Park and Planning Commission, Prince George's County Planning Department, Upper Marlboro, MD.

Martin, Erika, Mia Parsons, and Paul A. Shackel. 1997. "Commemorating a Rural African-American Family at a National Battlefield Park." *International Journal of Historical Archaeology* 1(2): 155–175.

Massey, Doreen. 1994. *Space, Place, and Gender.* Cambridge: Polity Press.

McDonald, William. 1909. *Select Documents Illustrative of the History of the United States, 1776–1861.* New York: Macmillan.

McFaden, Leslie, David Muraca, and Philip Levy. 2003. *The Archaeology of Rich Neck Plantation (44WB52): Description of the Features.* Williamsburg, VA: Department of Archaeological Research, Colonial Williamsburg Foundation.

McKee, Larry. 1992. "The Ideals and Realities Behind the Design and Use of Nineteenth Century Virginia Slave Cabins." In *The Art and Mystery of Historical Archaeology: Essays in Honor of Jim Deetz,* edited by Anne E. Yentsch and Mary C. Beaudry, 195–213. Boca Raton, FL: CRC Press.

McKee, Larry. 1998. "Some Thoughts on the Past, Present, and Future of the Archaeology of the African Diaspora." *African Diaspora Archaeology Newsletter* 5(2): 1–8.

McKee, Larry. 1999. "Food Supply and Plantation Social Order: An Archaeological Perspective." In *"I, Too, Am America": Archaeological Studies of African-American Life,* edited by Theresa A. Singleton, 218–239. Charlottesville: University Press of Virginia.

McKee, Larry. 2000. "The Archaeological Study of Slavery and Plantation Life in Tennessee." *Tennessee Historical Quarterly* 59(3): 188–203.

McKittrick, Katherine. 2006. *Demonic Grounds: Black Women and the Cartographies of Struggle.* Minneapolis: University of Minnesota Press.

Meadows, R. Darrell. 2000. "Engineering Exile: Social Networks and the French Atlantic Community, 1789–1809." *French Historical Studies* 23(1):67–102.

Meniketti, Marco. 2020. The Archaeology of Pivotal Places: The Structuring of Habitual Landscape and the Bush Hill Plantation. Presented at the Society for Historical Archaeology Annual Meeting.

Metcalf, Peter, and Richard Huntington. 1991. *Celebrations of Death: The Anthropology of Mortuary Ritual.* Cambridge: Cambridge University Press.

Midlo Hall, Gwendolyn. 1971. *Social Control in Slave Plantation Societies: A Comparison of St. Domingue and Cuba.* Baltimore: Johns Hopkins Press.

Midlo Hall, Gwendolyn. 1992. *Africans in Colonial Louisiana: The Development of Afro-Creole Culture in the Eighteenth Century.* Baton Rouge: Louisiana State University Press.

Midlo Hall, Gwendolyn. 2005. *Slavery and African Ethnicities in the Americas: Restoring the Links.* Chapel Hill: University of North Carolina Press.

Miller, Richard Roscoe. 1957. *Slavery and Catholicism.* Durham, N.C.: North State Publishers.

Mintz, Steven. 2009. *African American Voices: A Documentary Reader, 1619–1877.* Malden, MA: Wiley-Blackwell.

Moehle, Kurt A., and Eugene E. Levitt. 1991. "The History of the Concepts of Fear and Anxiety." In *Clinical Psychology: Historical and Research Foundations,* edited by Clarence Eugene Walker, 159–182. New York: Plenum.

Moitt, Bernard. 1995. "Women, Work, and Resistance in the French Caribbean during Slavery, 1700–1848." In *Engendering History: Caribbean Women in Historical Perspective,* edited by Verene Shepherd, Bridget Brereton, and Barbara Barley, 155–175. Kingston: Ian Randle.

Monocacy National Battlefield, National Capital Region, Harpers Ferry Interpretive Planning. 2009. *Long-Range Interpretive Plan.* Manuscript, National Park Service, Frederick, MD.

Moore, Sue Mullins. 1985. "Social and Economic Status on the Coastal Plantation: An Archaeological Perspective." In *The Archaeology of Slavery and Plantation Life,* edited by Theresa Singleton, 141–160. San Diego: Academic.

Moreau de Saint-Méry, Médéric Louis Élie. 1784. *Loix et constitutions des colonies françoises de l'Amerique sous le vent, Tome Premier: Comprenant les loix et constitutions depuis 1550 jusqu'en 1703 inclusivement.* Self-published, Paris.

Moreau de Saint-Méry, Médéric Louis Élie. 1785. *Loix et constitutions des colonies françoises de l'Amerique sous le vent, Tome Deuxième: Comprenant les loix et constitutions depuis 1704 jusqu'en 1721 inclusivement.* Self-published, Paris.

Moreau de Saint-Méry, Médéric-Louis-Elie. 1985 [1798]. *A Civilization that Perished: The Last Years of White Colonial Rule in Haiti.* Translated by Ivor D. Spencer. Lanham, MD: University Press of America.

Morgan, Edmund Sears. 1975. *American Slavery, American Freedom: The Ordeal of Colonial Virginia.* New York: Norton.

Morgan, Philip. D. 1979. "Task and Gang Systems: The Organization of Labor on New Plantations." In *Work and Labor in Early America,* edited by Stephen Innes, 189–220. Chapel Hill: University of North Carolina Press.

Morgan, Philip D. 1998. *Slave Counterpoint: Black Culture in the Eighteenth-Century Chesapeake and Lowcountry.* Chapel Hill: University of North Carolina Press.

Morrison, Toni. 1992. *Playing in the Dark: Whiteness and the Literary Imagination.* Cambridge, MA: Harvard University Press.

MSA (Maryland State Archives). 1797. Frederick County Court Minutes. Annapolis, MD.

Mullin, Gerald W. 1972. *Flight and Rebellion: Slave Resistance in Eighteenth Century Virginia.* New York: Oxford University Press.

Murphy, Sarah. 2011. "Slave Power: The Relationship Between Slave and Slave Owner." Transatlantic Teachers Resources, National Archive. Accessed October 2, 2017. https://www.nationalarchives.gov.uk/education/teachers/professional-development/project-resources/transatlantic-teachers-resources-2011/powerful-slaves/

Murphy, Thomas. 2001. *Jesuit Slaveholding in Maryland, 1717–1838.* New York: Routledge.

Murray, Jennifer. 2014. *On a Great Battlefield: The Making, Management, and Memory of Gettysburg National Military Park, 1933–2013.* Knoxville: University of Tennessee Press.

Mutz, Diana C. 2018. "Status threat, not economic hardship, explains the 2016 presidential vote." Proceedings of the National Academy of Sciences 115(19): E4330–E4339.

Myers, Ella. 2017. "Beyond the Wages of Whiteness: Du Bois on the Irrationality of Antiblack Racism." *Items: Insights from the Social Sciences.* Brooklyn, NY: Social Science Research Council. https://items.ssrc.org/reading-racial-conflict/beyond-the-wages-of-whiteness-du-bois-on-the-irrationality-of-antiblack-racism/

Myers, Ella. 2019. "Beyond the Psychological Wage: Du Bois on White Dominion." *Political Theory* 47(1): 6–31.

Nader, Laura. 1969. "Up the Anthropologist: Perspectives Gained From Studying Up." In *Reinventing Anthropology,* edited by Dell H. Hymes. New York: Pantheon.

Nash, Gary B. 1998. "Reverberations of Haiti in the American North: Black Saint Dominguans in Philadelphia." *Pennsylvania History: A Journal of Mid-Atlantic Studies* 65: 44–73.

National Park Service. 2009. *Abbreviated Final General Management Plan / Environmental Impact Statement, Monocacy National Battlefield.* On file at Monocacy National Battlefield, Frederick, MD.

Neblett, Touré. 2017. "Why Do White People Feel Discriminated Against? I Asked Them." *The Daily Beast.*

Neff, John R. 2005. *Honoring the Civil War Dead: Commemoration and the Problem of Reconciliation.* Lawrence: University Press of Kansas.

Niemcewicz, Julian Ursain. 1965. *Under their Vine and Fig Tree: Travels through America in 1797–1799, 1805 with some further account of life in New Jersey.* Elizabeth: Grassman Publishing Co.

Noble, Allen G. 1984. *Wood, Brick, and Stone: The North American Settlement Landscape, Volume 1: Houses.* Amherst: University of Massachusetts Press.

NPS [National Park Service]. 1998. "Holding the High Ground: Principles and Strategies for Managing and Interpreting Civil War Battlefield Landscapes." Proceedings of a Conference of Battlefield Managers, Nashville, August 24–27.

Nugent, Stephen, and Cris Shore. 2003. *Elite Cultures: Anthropological Perspectives.* Psychology Press.

Odewale, Alicia. 2019. "An Archaeology of Struggle: Material Remnants of a Double Consciousness in the American South and Danish Caribbean Communities." *Transforming Anthropology* 27: 114–132.

Olwell, Robert. 1998. *Masters, slaves, & subjects: the culture of power in the South Carolina low country, 1740–1790*. Ithaca, NY: Cornell University Press.

Orser, Charles E., Jr. 1988. "The Archaeological Analysis of Plantation Society: Replacing Status and Caste with Economics and Power." *American Antiquity* 53(4): 735–751.

Orser, Charles E., Jr. 1990. "Archaeological Approaches to New World Plantation Slavery." *Archaeological Method and Theory* 2: 111–154.

Orser, Charles E., Jr. 1991. "The Continued Pattern of Dominance: Landlord and Tenant on the Postbellum Cotton Plantation." In *The Archaeology of Inequality*, edited by Robert Paynter and Randall H. McGuire, 40–54. Oxford: Basil Blackwell.

Orser, Charles E., Jr. 1994. "The Archaeology of African-American Slave Religion in the Antebellum South." *Cambridge Archaeological Journal* 4(1):33–45.

Orser, Charles E., Jr. 1998. "The Challenge of Race to American Historical Archaeology." *American Anthropologist* 100(3): 661–668.

Orser, Charles E., Jr. 2001. "Race and the Archaeology of Identity in the Modern World." In *Race and the Archaeology of Identity*, edited by C. E. Orser Jr., 1–23. Salt Lake City: University of Utah Press.

Orser, Charles E., Jr. 2004. *Historical Archaeology*. Second edition. Upper Saddle River, NJ: Prentice-Hall.

Orser, Charles E., Jr. 2007. *The Archaeology of Race and Racialization in Historic America*. Gainesville: University Press of Florida.

Orser, Charles E., Jr. 2008. "The Anthropology in American Historical Archaeology." *American Anthropologist* 103(3): 621–632.

Orser, Charles E., Jr., and Pedro P. A. Funari. 2001. "Archaeology and Slave Resistance and Rebellion." *World Archaeology* 33(1): 61–72.

Otto, John Solomon. 1984. *Cannon's Point Plantation, 1794–1860: Living Conditions and Status Patterns in the Old South*. (Studies in Historical Archaeology.) Orlando, FL: Academic.

Outten, H. Robert, Michael T. Schmitt, Daniel A. Miller, and Amber L. Garcia. 2012. "Feeling Threatened about the Future: Whites' Emotional Reactions to Anticipated Ethnic Demographic Changes." *Personality and Social Psychology Bulletin* 38(1): 14–25.

Palmer, Jennifer L. 2016. *Intimate Bonds: Family and Slavery in the French Atlantic*. Philadelphia: University of Pennsylvania Press.

Parker, Kathleen A., and Jacqueline L. Hernigle. 1990. *Portici: Portrait of a Middling Plantation in Piedmont Virginia*. Occasional Report No. 3. Regional Archeology Program, National Capital Region, National Park Service, U.S. Department of the Interior, Washington, DC.

Patten, Drake. 1992. "Mankala and Minkisi: Possible Evidence of African American Folk Beliefs and Practices." *African American Archaeology* 6: 5–7.

Patterson, John. 1989. "From battle ground to pleasure ground: Gettysburg as a historic site." In *History Museums in the United States: A Critical Assessment*, edited by Warren Leon and Roy Rosenzweig. Urbana: University of Illinois Press.

Paulus, Carl Lawrence. 2017. *The Slaveholding Crisis: Fear of Insurrection and the Coming of the Civil War*. Baton Rouge: Louisiana State University Press.

Peckham, Robert. 2015. *Empires of Panic: Epidemics and Colonial Anxieties*. Hong Kong: Hong Kong University Press.

Phillips, Ulrich Bonnell. 1966. *American Negro Slavery: A Survey of the Supply, Employment and Control of Negro Labor as Determined by the Plantation Regime*. Baton Rouge: Louisiana State University Press.

Pogue, Dennis J. 2002. "The Domestic Architecture of Slavery at George Washington's Mount Vernon." *Winterthur Portfolio* 37(1): 3–22.

Popkin, Jeremy D. 2003. "Race, Slavery, and the French and Haitian Revolutions." *Eighteenth-Century Studies* 37(1): 113–122.

Popkin, Jeremy D. 2007. *Facing Racial Revolution*. Chicago: University of Chicago Press.

Popkin, Jeremy D. 2008. *Facing Racial Revolution: Eyewitness Accounts of the Haitian Insurrection*. Chicago: University of Chicago Press.

Ranck, Dorothy S. 1985. Settlers of French Origin (Huguenots and Others). In *Monocacy and Catoctin: Some Early French Settlers of Frederick and Carroll Counties, MD and Adams County, PA and Descendants c. 1725–1985*, edited by C. E. Schildknecht, 111–130. Shippensburg, PA: Beidel Printing House.

Reed, Paula S. 2002. "*L'Hermitage*: a French plantation in Frederick County." *Maryland Historical Magazine* 97(1): 60–78.

Reed, Paula S. 2005. "Frederick's French Connection: at *L'Hermitage* on the Monocacy Battlefield: Victoire Vincendière and French Planter Refugees from the Slave Revolt in Haiti in the 1790s." In *Mid-Maryland: Crossroads of History*, edited by Michael A. Powell and Bruce A. Thompson, 135–144. Charleston, SC: History Press.

Reed, Paula S., and Edith B. Wallace. 2004 [1999]. *Cultural resources study, Monocacy National Battlefield*, edited by Paula S. Reed and Associates, Inc., Hagerstown, MD. On file at Monocacy National Battlefield.

Reed, Paula S., and Associates, Inc. 2004. *Thematic Context History [Frederick, MD]— Industry* (unpublished). On file at Monocacy National Battlefield.

Reinhart, Theodore. 1984. *The Archaeology of Shirley Plantation*. Charlottesville: University Press of Virginia.

Rivers Cofield, Sara. 2002. "Contextualizing *L'Hermitage*: a Maryland plantation with French Caribbean ties." On file with the University of Maryland, College Park, and the National Capital Region Office of the National Park Service. On file at Monocacy National Battlefield.

Rivers Cofield, Sara. 2005. "A French Caribbean Plantation in Maryland: Understanding the Regional and Global Context of L'Hermitage." In *Archeological Overview and Assessment and Identification and Evaluation Study of the Best Farm*, Regional Archaeology Program, National Capital Region, National Park Service, Occasional Paper No. 18: 5.1–5.32. U.S. Department of the Interior, Washington, DC. On file at Monocacy National Battlefield.

Rivers Cofield, Sara. 2006. "French-Caribbean Refugees and Slavery in German Protestant Maryland." *International Journal of Historical Archaeology* 10(3): 268–282.

Rivers Cofield, Sara. 2011. "French Refugees and Slave Abuse in Frederick County, Maryland: Jean Payen de Boisneuf and the Vincendière Family at L'Hermitage Plantation."

In *French Colonial Archaeology in the Southeast and Caribbean*, edited by Kenneth G. Kelly and Meredith D. Hardy. Gainesville: University Press of Florida.

Roller, Michael P. 2018. *An Archaeology of Structural Violence: Life in a Twentieth-Century Coal Town*. Gainesville: University Press of Florida.

Rosenberg, Alyssa. 2017 June 20. "At James Madison's home, slaves' lives matter as much as the man who owned them." *Washington Post*. https://www.washingtonpost.com/news/act-four/wp/2017/06/20/at-james-madisons-home-slaves-lives-matter-as-much-as-the-man-who-owned-them/

Ruane, Michael E. 2010 August 26. "Brutal slave history unearthed at Frederick County's L'Hermitage." *Washington Post*.

Russell, George Ely. 2001. Frenchmen in Early Frederick County, Maryland. *The Genealogist* 15(2): 225–255.

Salverda, Tijo. 2010. "In defense: elite power." *Journal of Power* 3(3): 385–404.

Salverda, Tijo, and Iain Hay. 2013. "Introduction: An Anthropological Perspective on Elite Power and the Cultural Politics of Elites." In *The Anthropology of Elites*, edited by Tijo Salverda and Iain Hay. New York: Palgrave Macmillan.

Salverda, Tijo, and Iain Hay. 2014. "Change, anxiety and exclusion in the post-colonial reconfiguration of Franco-Mauritian elite geographies." *Geographical Journal* 180: 236–245.

Samford, Patricia M. 1996. "The Archaeology of African-American Slavery and Material Culture." *William and Mary Quarterly*, Third Series, 53(1): 87–114.

Samford, Patricia M. 2007. *Subfloor Pits and the Archaeology of Slavery in Colonial Virginia*. Tuscaloosa: University of Alabama Press.

Sampeck, Kathryn. 2016. The Spatial Violence of Colonialism. Presented at the Society for Historical Archaeology Annual Meeting. Washington, DC.

Sandercock, Leonie. 1998. "Framing Insurgent Historiographies for Planning." In *Making the Invisible Visible: A Multicultural Planning History*, edited by Leonie Sandercock, 1–53. Berkeley: University of California Press.

Sansay, Leonora ("Mary Hassal"). 2007 [1808]. *Secret History, or, The Horrors of St. Domingo*. Edited by Michael Drexler. Petersborough, ON: Broadview Books.

Schein, Richard H. 2006. *Landscape and Race in the United States*. New York: Routledge.

Savage, Kirk. 1994. "The politics of memory: black emancipation and the Civil War monument." In *Commemorations: The Politics of National Identity*, edited by John Gillis, 127–149. Princeton, NJ: Princeton University Press.

Scharf, Thomas J. 1882 [1969] *History of Western Maryland*. Baltimore: Regional Publishing Company.

Scheinkman, Michele, and Mona DeKoven Fishbane. 2004. "The Vulnerability Cycle: Working with Impasses in Couple Therapy." *Family Process* 43(3): 279–299.

Scheper-Hughes, Nancy, and Philippe Bourgois. 2003. "Introduction: Making Sense of Violence." In *Violence in War and Peace: An Anthology*, edited by Nancy Scheper-Hughes and Philippe Bourgois, 1–31. Oxford: Blackwell.

Seger, Maria, ed. 2022. *Reading Confederate Monuments*. Jackson: University Press of Mississippi.

Shackel, Paul A. 2003. *Memory in Black and White: Race, Commemoration, and the Post-Bellum Landscape.* Walnut Creek, CA: Altamira Press.

Shackel, Paul A. 2005. "Local Identity, National Memory, and Heritage Tourism: Creating a Sense of Place with Archaeology." *SAA Archaeological Record,* 5(3): 33–35.

Shapiro, Gary. 2017 May 15. "The Meaning of Our Confederate 'Monuments.'" *New York Times.*

Shepherd, Verene, and Hilary Beckles. 2000. *Caribbean Slavery in the Atlantic World.* Kingston, Jamaica: Ian Randle.

Siegler, Kirk. 2020. "Nebraska DA Wants Grand Jury to Review Black Man's Death by White Bar Owner." *Morning Edition.* National Public Radio, June 5, 2020.

Sies, Mary Corbin. 2005. "Regenerating Scholarship on Race and the Built Environment." In *Proceedings: Reconceptualizing the History of the Built Environment in North America.* Charles Warren Center for Studies in American History. Cambridge, MA: Harvard University.

Silberman, Neil. 1999. "From Masada to the Little Bighorn: the role of archaeological site interpretation in the shaping of national myths." *Conservation and Management of Archaeological Sites* 3(1–2): 9–15.

Singleton, Theresa. 2001. "Slavery and spatial dialectics on Cuban coffee plantations." *World Archaeology* 33(1): 98–114.

Singleton, Theresa A. 1990. "The Archaeology of the Plantation South: A Review of the Approaches and Goals." *Historical Archaeology* 25(4): 70–77.

Singleton, Theresa A. 1991. "The Archaeology of Slave Life." In *Images of the Recent Past: Readings in Historical Archaeology,* edited by Charles E. Orser Jr., 141–165. Walnut Creek, CA: Altamira Press.

Singleton, Theresa A. 1995. "The Archaeology of Slavery in North America." *Annual Review of Archaeology* 24: 119–140.

Singleton, Theresa A. 1999. "An Introduction to African-American Archaeology." In *"I, Too, Am America": Archaeological Studies of African-American Life,* edited by Theresa A. Singleton. Charlottesville: University Press of Virginia.

Singleton, Theresa A. 2006. "African Diaspora Archaeology in Dialogue." In *Afro-Atlantic Dialogues: Anthropology in the Diaspora,* edited by Kevin Yelvington, 249–287. Santa Fe, NM: School of American Research Press.

Singleton, Theresa A. 2015. *Slavery Behind the Wall: An Archaeology of a Cuban Coffee Plantation.* Gainesville: University Press of Florida.

Slater, Lisa. 2013. "Anxious Settler Belonging: Actualising the Potential for Making Resilient Postcolonial Subjects." *M/C Journal* 16(6).

Smith, Frederick. 2004. "Spirits and Spirituality: Enslaved Persons and Alcohol in West Africa and the British and French Caribbean." *Journal of Caribbean History* 38(2).

Smith, Frederick. 2008. *The Archaeology of Alcohol and Drinking.* Gainesville: University Press of Florida.

Snyder, David. 2003 November 9. "Digging Up a Grim Past." *Washington Post.*

Soja, Edward W. 1985. "The Spatiality of Social Life: Towards a Transformative Retheorisation." In *Social Relations and Spatial Structures,* edited by Derek Gregory and John Urry, 90–127. New York: St. Martin's Press.

Solnit, Rebecca. 2020. "Chrome-Plated Pistols and Pink Polos: The Face of Elite Panic in the USA." 2020. *Literary Hub.* July 1, 2020. https://lithub.com/chrome-plated-pistols-and-pink-polos-the-face-of-elite-panic-in-the-usa/.

Sørensen, Tim Flohr. 2015. "More Than a Feeling: Towards an archaeology of atmosphere." *Emotion, Space and Society* 15: 64–73.

Spencer-Wood, Suzanne M. 2010. "A Feminist Framework for Analyzing Powered Cultural Landscapes in Historical Archaeology." *International Journal of Historical Archaeology* 14(4): 498–526.

Spencer-Wood, Suzanne M. 2016. "Feminist Theorizing of Patriarchal Colonialism, Power Dynamics, and Social Agency Materialized in Colonial Institutions." *International Journal of Historical Archaeology* 20(3): 477–491.

Spikins, Penny, Holly Rutherford, and Andrew Needham. 2010. "From Homininity to Humanity: Compassion from the Earliest Archaics to Modern Humans." *Time and Mind* 3(3): 303–326.

Stein, Robert. 2000. "The French West Indian Sugar Business." In *Caribbean Slavery in the Atlantic World,* edited by Verene Shepherd and Hilary Beckles. Kingston, Jamaica: Ian Randle.

Stine, Linda F., Melanie A. Cabak, and Mark D. Groover. 1996. "Blue Beads as African American Cultural Symbols." *Historical Archaeology* 30(3): 49–75.

Stine, Linda F., Martha Zierden, Lesley M. Drucker, and Christopher Judge. 1997. *Carolina's Historical Landscapes: Archaeological Perspectives.* Knoxville: University of Tennessee Press.

Stutz, Liv Nilsson, and Sarah Tarlow. 2015. *The Oxford Handbook of the Archaeology of Death and Burial.* Oxford: Oxford University Press.

Tarlow, Sarah. 1997. "An archaeology of remembering: death, bereavement and the First World War." *Cambridge Archaeological Journal* 7(1): 105–121.

Tarlow, Sarah. 2000. "Emotion in Archaeology." *Current Anthropology* 41(5): 713–745.

Tarlow, Sarah. 2012. "The Archaeology of Emotion and Affect." *Annual Review of Anthropology* 41: 169–185.

Taylor, Yuval. 1999. *I Was Born a slave. Volume two, 1849–1866: An Anthology of Classic Slave Narratives.* Chicago: Lawrence Hill Books.

Thakur, Gautam Basu. 2012. "Reading Bhabha. Reading Lacan: Preliminary Notes on Colonial Anxiety" In *The Literary Lacan: From Literature to Lituraterre and Beyond,* edited by Santanu Biswas. London: Seagull Books.

Thomas, Brian W. 1998. "Power and Community: The Archaeology of Slavery at the Hermitage." *American Antiquity* 63(4): 531–551.

Thomas, Brian W. 2002. "Struggling With the Past: Some Views on African-American Identity." *International Journal of Historical Archaeology* 6(2): 143–151.

Tilley, Christopher. 1994. *The Phenomenology of Landscape: Places, paths and monuments.* Oxford: Berg.

Tomich, Dale. 1993. "*Une Petite Guinee*: Provision Ground and Plantation in Martinique, 1830–1848." In *Cultivation and Culture: Labor and the Shaping of Slave Life in the Americas,* edited by Ira Berlin and Philip D. Morgan, 221–242. Charlottesville: University Press of Virginia.

Tomich, Dale. 2016. *Slavery in the Circuit of Sugar: the World Economy, 1830–1848, 2nd edition.* Albany: State University of New York Press.

Tracey, Grace L., and John Phillip Dern. 1987. *Pioneers of Old Monocacy The Early Settlement of Frederick County, Maryland 1721–1743.* Baltimore: Genealogical Publishing Co.

Trouillot, Michel-Rolph. 1982. "Motion in the System: Coffee, Color, and Slavery in Eighteenth Century Saint Domingue." *Review* 5(3): 331–388.

Trouillot, Michel-Rolph. 1990. *Haiti: State Against Nation: The origins and legacy of Duvalierism.* New York: Monthly Review Press.

Trouillot, Michel-Rolph. 1995. *Silencing the Past: The Power and the Production of History.* Boston: Beacon Press.

Trouillot, Michel-Rolph. 1998. "Culture on the Edges: Creolization in the Plantation Context." *Plantation Society in the Americas* 5(1): 8–28.

Turner, Frederick J. 1905. "Documents on the Blount Conspiracy, 1795–1797." *American Historical Review* 10(3): 574–606.

Turner, Sam. 2013. "Landscape archaeology." In *The Routledge Companion to Landscape Studies,* edited by Peter Howard et al., 131–142. New York: Routledge.

United States Census Records, C. Burr Artz Library, Maryland Room, Frederick, MD: 1790, 1800, 1810, 1820, 1830.

Upton, Dell. 1988. "White and Black Landscape in Eighteenth-Century Virginia." In *Material Life in America 1600–1860,* edited by Robert Blair St. George, 357–369. Boston: Northeastern University Press.

Venables, Brant. 2012. "A Battle of Remembrance: Memorialization and Heritage at the Newtown Battlefield, New York." *Northeast Historical Archaeology* 41(8).

Vlach, John Michael. 1993. *Back of the Big House: The Architecture of Plantation Slavery.* Chapel Hill: University of North Carolina Press.

Walker, Tracey. 2012. "The Future of Slavery: From Cultural Trauma to Ethical Remembrance." *Graduate Journal of Social Science* 9(2): 153–178.

Wayland, John Walter. 1937. *Historic Homes of Northern Virginia: and the Eastern Panhandle of West Virginia.* Staunton, VA: McClure.

Weik, Terrence. 2012. *The Archaeology of Antislavery Resistance.* Gainesville: University Press of Florida.

Weinstein, Adam. 2020. "Standing Their Ground in Well-Manicured Yards." *New Republic.*

Wetherell, Margaret. 2012. *Affect and Emotion: A New Social Science Understanding.* Thousand Oaks, CA: Sage Publications.

Whisnant, Anne, Marla Miller, Gary Nash, and David Thelen. 2012. "The State of History in the National Park Service: A Conversation and Reflections." *George Wright Society Journal of Parks, Protected Areas & Cultural Sites* 29(2).

White, Ashli. 2012. *Encountering Revolution: Haiti and the Making of the Early Republic.* Baltimore: Johns Hopkins University Press.

Wilkie, Laurie. 1995. "Plantation Archaeology: Where Past and Present Can Collide." *African Diaspora Archaeology Newsletter* 2(1).

Wilkie, Laurie. 2000. *Creating Freedom: Material Culture and African American Identity at Oakley Plantation, Louisiana, 1840–1950.* Baton Rouge: Louisiana State University Press.

Willer, Robb, Matthew Feinberg, and Rachel Wetts. 2016. "Threats to Racial Status Promote Tea Party Support Among White Americans." *Social Science Research Network.*

Williams, Thomas John Chew, and Folger McKinsey. 1967. *History of Frederick County, MD Vol. 1.* Baltimore: Genealogical Publishing Company.

Wilson, Jon E. 2008. *The Domination of Strangers: Modern Governance in Eastern India, 1780–1835.* Basingstoke: Palgrave Macmillan.

Winberry, John. 1982. "Symbols in the landscape: The Confederate memorial." *Pioneer America Society Transactions* 5: 9–15.

Winsboro, D. S. 2016. "The Confederate Monument Movement as a Policy Dilemma for Resource Managers of Parks, Cultural Sites, and Protected Places: Florida as a Case Study." *George Wright Forum* 33(2): 217–229.

Wray, Leonard. 1848. The Practical Sugar Planter: A Complete Account of the Cultivation and Manufacture of the Sugar-cane, According to the Latest and Most Improved Processes. Describing and Comparing the Different Systems Pursued in the East and West Indies and the Straits of Malacca, and the Relative Expenses and Advantages Attendant Upon Each: Being the Result of Sixteen Years' Experience as a Sugar Planter in Those Countries. London: Smith, Elder and Company.

Yates, Donald L. 1999. "Plantation-Style Social Control: Oppressive Social Structures on the Slave Plantation System." In *Plantation Society and Race Relations: The Origins of Inequality,* edited by Thomas J. Durant Jr. and David Knottnerus, 29–40. Westport, CT: Praeger.

Yentsch, Anne. 2008. "Excavating the South's African American food history." *African Diaspora Archaeology Newsletter,* June 1.

Yentsch, Anne E. 1994. *A Chesapeake Family and Their Slaves: A Study in Historical Archaeology.* Cambridge: Cambridge University Press.

Young, Amy L. 1997. "Risk Management Strategies among African-American Slaves at Locust Grove Plantation." *International Journal of Historical Archaeology* 1(1): 5–37.

Young, Amy L. 1999. "Archaeological Investigations of Slave Housing at Saragossa Plantation, Natchez, Mississippi." *Southeastern Archaeology* 18(1): 57.

Young, Amy L. 2000. *Archaeology of Southern Urban Landscapes.* Tuscaloosa: University of Alabama Press.

Zelinsky, Wilbur. 1988. *Nation into State: The Shifting Symbolic Foundations of American Nationalism.* Chapel Hill: University of North Carolina Press.

Ziegler, Treacy. 2016. "Eastern State Penitentiary's 'Prisons Today: Questions in the Age of Mass Incarceration.'" *Broad Street Review,* July 18. https://www.broadstreetreview .com/essays/eastern-state-penitentiarys-prisons-today-questions-in-the-age-of -mass-inca

Zieleniec, Andrzej J. L. 2007. *Space and Social Theory.* London: Sage Publications.

Index

Megan M. Bailey is a research affiliate of the Department of Anthropology at the University of Maryland and has served as an archaeologist for the National Park Service.

Cultural Heritage Studies

Edited by Paul A. Shackel, University of Maryland

Heritage of Value, Archaeology of Renown: Reshaping Archaeological Assessment and Significance, edited by Clay Mathers, Timothy Darvill, and Barbara J. Little (2005)

Archaeology, Cultural Heritage, and the Antiquities Trade, edited by Neil Brodie, Morag M. Kersel, Christina Luke, and Kathryn Walker Tubb (2006)

Archaeological Site Museums in Latin America, edited by Helaine Silverman (2006)

Crossroads and Cosmologies: Diasporas and Ethnogenesis in the New World, by Christopher C. Fennell (2007)

Ethnographies and Archaeologies: Iterations of the Past, edited by Lena Mortensen and Julie Hollowell (2009)

Cultural Heritage Management: A Global Perspective, edited by Phyllis Mauch Messenger and George S. Smith (2010; first paperback edition, 2014)

God's Fields: Landscape, Religion, and Race in Moravian Wachovia, by Leland Ferguson (2011; first paperback edition, 2013)

Ancestors of Worthy Life: Plantation Slavery and Black Heritage at Mount Clare, by Teresa S. Moyer (2015; first paperback edition, 2022)

Slavery behind the Wall: An Archaeology of a Cuban Coffee Plantation, by Theresa A. Singleton (2015; first paperback edition, 2016)

Excavating Memory: Sites of Remembering and Forgetting, edited by Maria Theresia Starzmann and John R. Roby (2016)

Mythic Frontiers: Remembering, Forgetting, and Profiting with Cultural Heritage Tourism, by Daniel R. Maher (2016; first paperback edition, 2019)

Critical Theory and the Anthropology of Heritage Landscapes, by Melissa F. Baird (2017; first paperback edition, 2022)

Heritage at the Interface: Interpretation and Identity, edited by Glenn Hooper (2018)

Cuban Cultural Heritage: A Rebel Past for a Revolutionary Nation, by Pablo Alonso González (2018; first paperback edition, 2023)

The Rosewood Massacre: An Archaeology and History of Intersectional Violence, by Edward González-Tennant (2018; first paperback edition, 2019)

Race, Place, and Memory: Deep Currents in Wilmington, North Carolina, by Margaret M. Mulrooney (2018; first paperback edition, 2022)

An Archaeology of Structural Violence: Life in a Twentieth-Century Coal Town, by Michael P. Roller (2018)

Colonialism, Community, and Heritage in Native New England, by Siobhan M. Hart (2019)

Pedagogy and Practice in Heritage Studies, edited by Susan J. Bender and Phyllis Mauch Messenger (2019)

History and Approaches to Heritage Studies, edited by Phyllis Mauch Messenger and Susan J. Bender (2019)

A Struggle for Heritage: Archaeology and Civil Rights in a Long Island Community, by Christopher N. Matthews (2020; first paperback edition, 2022)

Earth Politics and Intangible Heritage: Three Case Studies in the Americas, by Jessica Joyce Christie (2021)

Negotiating Heritage through Education and Archaeology: Colonialism, National Identity, and Resistance in Belize, by Alicia Ebbitt McGill (2021)

Baseball and Cultural Heritage, edited by Gregory Ramshaw and Sean Gammon (2022)

Conflict Archaeology, Historical Memory, and the Experience of War: Beyond the Battlefield, edited by Mark Axel Tveskov and Ashley Ann Bissonnette (2022)

Heritage and Democracy: Crisis, Critique, and Collaboration, edited by Kathryn Lafrenz Samuels and Jon D. Daehnke (2023)

Memory and Power at L'Hermitage Plantation: Heritage of a Nervous Landscape, by Megan M. Bailey (2024)

www.ingramcontent.com/pod-product-compliance
Lightning Source LLC
Chambersburg PA
CBHW081424110725
29469CB00004B/233

* 9 7 8 0 8 1 3 0 8 0 3 9 0 *